About *A Quarter Inch from My Heart*

Kevin Scott Hall's book is more than a book; it is an intimate letter of a young artist struggling with the peradventure of chance meetings and a relationship that would lead him to grow as an individual psychologically and spiritually. Like all such letters, the reader is drawn into the pathos of the naked emotion of life and love: A growth from *eros* to *phillios* and further to the undeniable *agape*. If you have ever cared for a friend and come to see the holy in the other then this is a work that is a must read.

    Fr Jeffrey L. Hamblin, MD, Christ Church Episcopal, Brooklyn, NY.

In *A Quarter Inch from My Heart,* Kevin Scott Hall explores his amazing love for a dazzling drifter, Maurice, the man who became his "prodigal brother"—and who leaves an indelible mark on Hall's heart and the hearts of all who read this luminous, unforgettable memoir about agape, recovery, and faith.

    Jocelyn Lieu, author of *Potential Weapons* and *What Isn't There.*

Kevin Scott Hall's memoir of an offbeat life and an inexplicable love offers consistently readable ups, downs, and—especially—curves that, in the end, offer life lessons in generosity, persistence and redemption.

Robert Windeler, noted critic and biographer;
author of *Shirley Temple, Julie Andrews:*
A Life on Stage and Screen, and *Sweetheart:*
The Story of Mary Pickford, among others.

See also review on back cover.

A Quarter Inch from My Heart

A Quarter Inch from My Heart

A Memoir

Kevin Scott Hall

Wisdom Moon Publishing
2014

A Quarter Inch from My Heart
A Memoir

Copyright © 2014 Wisdom Moon Publishing, LLC

Copyright permissions are given in the Acknowledgments section, on page ii.

Published by Wisdom Moon Publishing LLC
San Diego, CA, USA

Wisdom Moon™, the Wisdom Moon logo™, *Wisdom Moon Publishing*™, and *WMP*™ are trademarks of Wisdom Moon Publishing LLC.

www.WisdomMoonPublishing.com

ISBN 978-1-938459-24-5 (softcover, alk. paper)
ISBN 978-1-938459-32-0 (eBook)
LCCN 2014936134

ACKNOWLEDGMENTS

This book has been a five-year undertaking, and I could not have completed it, physically and emotionally, without the help of many people.

First and foremost, I must thank the dear friends who are mentioned throughout these pages, who helped in ways both large and small—but always significantly—during the times of crisis that are recounted here. I wish I could acknowledge all of them by first and last name here, but to do so would compromise the privacy of some. And so, although I can't list you by name, you know who you are, and you have my enduring gratitude.

I must specifically mention Rev. Dr. Jacqueline Lewis, Heather Juby, Ph.D., Ericka Mays, and my entire extended family at Middle Collegiate Church; Sandra Whiteknact; the ministry team at Rutgers Presbyterian Church; and the wonderful staff at New York Presbyterian Hospital in New York.

To my immediate family, who has stuck by me through good times and bad, I give thanks. I am blessed to have family, and doubly blessed to have such a decent one.

For help in the early stages of this manuscript, I am indebted to author Jocelyn Lieu and Rev. Dr. Tricia Sheffield. The constructive feedback was needed, and the encouragement to forge on was most welcome.

For much-needed spiritual and psychological boosts, I am most grateful to Jan Fisher, Paula St. Pierre, Dennis Holly, David Henderson, Amy Beth Williams, and John Jamiel.

I am thankful for the hard work and persistent coaching from my own editor, Phyllis Aiyana Stern. She not only whipped the manuscript into professional shape and coached me during my search for a publisher, but she also led me to Wisdom Moon Publishing.

Certainly, I thank Mitchell Ginsberg, Ph.D., the Editor-in-Chief of Wisdom Moon Publishing. He saw and appreciated the human story in the manuscript, and he asked the tough and necessary questions to convince me to go back to the well and reach deeper inside myself to come up with a richer text.

Lastly, may God bless you, my readers. As of this writing, I have a small but very loyal following that embraces all that I do—even the stuff that hasn't been very good—and cheers me on to the next project. You are my lifeblood. Without readers and listeners, the story is lost. Thank you, old fans and new, for being a part of my ongoing journey.

I would like here to acknowledge the permission to quote and to use copyrighted material, from the following sources:

DEDICATION

Her resilient faith, limitless compassion, and remarkable strength of character are often overlooked because of her humble and gentle demeanor. Best of all, she has never let her faith close her heart or her mind.

This book is dedicated to Mom.

FOREWORD

"This is the only real concern of the artist, to recreate out of the disorder of life that order which is art."

James Baldwin

As the writer and storyteller of events that have disordered my life, I am not the one to judge whether or not the events have become art in the telling. For me, the telling brings order and understanding.

This is a memoir. It is not autobiography. It is not investigative journalism. It is the truth as I remember it.

A memoir focuses on a specific time or event in one's life, an event that is a personal watershed and creates some kind of spiritual epiphany or great learning experience.

Such is the case, I believe, with this book. The focus is on the time I knew Maurice, a time of great intensity, promise, missed opportunities, tragedy, and hope. Other events, told in flashback, seek to illuminate that period in my life. True life, despite all our best-laid plans, is a series of unexpected turns in the road, and how we navigate them determines the success of the continuing journey.

I have chosen not to use last names, except in cases of professionals who deserve some recognition for their work. A few names have also been changed, if I felt their names would be recognizable to some and compromise their very personal stories. In other cases, names may have been changed just to avoid confusion with another character similarly named.

"Maurice" is a real name. Although very special to me, I think he symbolizes an Everyman kind of character: the person we might ignore, or turn away from in a huff, or offer a kindness in only the most perfunctory manner. Men like him exist all over our cities and towns. They learn to survive in their own way and sometimes manage quite well without the holiday family meals, the career-minded jobs, and the accumulation of goods that many of us take for granted.

I do not use his last name because his family, wherever they are, did not ask for this story. As much as I may have wanted to, I did not go out of my way to find them or contact them.

In that sense, it is not investigative journalism. There are things about Maurice that I will never know and about which I can only make assumptions.

What I do know about him, and what I've learned about myself, is in these pages. I hope it is of interest to you, the reader. I can only further hope that life lessons will be revealed beyond the actual words on the page.

ABOUT THE AUTHOR

Kevin Scott Hall was born in Maine and grew up in Massachusetts. He attended Gordon College and later received his Master of Fine Arts from The City College of New York. Hall has acted in theater productions, dabbled in stand-up comedy, had a long run as a singer and songwriter, and made three pop music recordings, including the acclaimed *New Light Dawning*. Additionally, he has taught master classes in cabaret performance and directed several nightclub acts. Hall writes a monthly column, "Kevin on Kabaret," and entertainment features for Edge Media Network, and has written reviews and essays for other publications as well. In 2010, he published his first novel, *Off the Charts!* (iUniverse). Hall continues to teach at two City University of New York campuses, and is a member of Toastmasters International. He resides in Brooklyn, New York. For more information, please visit kevinscotthall.com.

Part I

Chapter One

This isn't a story about my friend Neal, the most courageous person I've ever known, but it is where my story begins.

One night in late June of 2005, as I was preparing for a cruise to the Caribbean sailing out of New York the next day, I got a call that turned my blood ice-cold.

"Hi Kevin, this is Joyce." I only knew one Joyce, and she was Neal's older sister. She had certainly never called me before, so there could be only one reason she was calling me that night.

"What is it, Joyce?" I braced myself. I hoped for a moment that Neal was badly injured or seriously ill—anything that would offer some hope of seeing him again.

Joyce explained to me that Neal had been on his annual vacation in Provincetown with his handful of Boston friends—where I had always promised to join him but never did—and that he had felt dizzy after a dinner theater show and collapsed. By the time the ambulance had arrived and transported him to the hospital, he was gone. Like me, he was forty-two years old.

Neal and I had known each other since we were twelve. We were from neighboring towns but when we entered junior high, we attended the same school. Junior High was a pretty scary place if you didn't quite fit in, especially at age twelve, when peer pressure was at its peak.

Neal walked into history class one day in platform shoes, ironed plaid slacks, an Oxford button-down shirt with a blue, button-down sweater tied around his shoulders, hanging neatly down his back. He seemed oblivious to the calls of "queer" and "fairy" that were hissed at him as he walked by.

I was dressed in baggy jeans and a striped cotton shirt and wore thick glasses. I would get the same comments, but I cowered in a back row, trying to blend in with the crowd, praying I wouldn't be noticed.

Neal seemed to want to be noticed, whatever the consequences. I had to get to know him, to learn from his courage. In another era, he'd have been at the front line at the Stonewall Inn, hurling bottles, while I would have been a block away, observing from a safe distance.

Our friendship came to full bloom when we took four years of French in high school together, where we breathlessly shared gossip before, during and after class. In our senior year we took Driver Ed together and when we paired up for our road test, Mr. Linhart said he'd never seen worse drivers in his life; I think we were laughing at each other too much to pay attention.

As much as I loved those times with Neal during school hours, I wasn't about to follow his path completely. I joined a youth group at my local church. In those days, being a churchgoing teenager was at least a rung higher than being a gay teenager. You could still be teased about your goodness, but nobody was about to attack your faith—just in case there was something to it. The youth group I joined was like "the island of misfit toys" from that animated Christmas special. We had been discarded by every possible clique in high school, but Jesus would never turn us away. We became a great group of friends, clinging to each other and holding each other aloft during the stormy seas of the high school years.

There was a time after graduation when Neal and I lost touch. I went off to a Christian college. Neal went off to hairdressing school and the bright lights of Newbury Street in Boston to build a clientele and a career. He was too flamboyant for me and I was still afraid, trying to figure out what I wanted to be and postponing the question of my sexuality.

A few years after that, all of those dutiful years at college hadn't made me the obedient Christian I thought I should be: I wanted to be an actor; I needed to come to terms with yearnings that were not going away. I moved to Boston and got back in touch with Neal, who welcomed me into his world without question or reprisal—as if I were the prodigal son that he knew would return one day.

My path took me to New York, an often difficult climb with stunning views. But I never again abandoned Neal. I would visit him in Boston twice a year for twenty years and considered my weekends in Boston to be my time to "come out" in a way I never could anywhere else. We had very different lives but because we had known each other from the early, painful years, we had a bond that nobody else could ever know or understand.

Speaking haltingly, I told Joyce that I had spoken to Neal just a month before and had planned to visit him in Boston in August, on my way back from my weekend in Ogunquit, where I went with old friends every summer. I told her I was scheduled to leave on a family cruise the next day.

"Absolutely go on the cruise," Joyce said. "Neal would have wanted that. Toast to him on the deck."

I phoned my mother and told her the news, preparing her for my mood the next day. I would be sharing a cabin with her because my father didn't want to go; my sister, Audrey, her husband, Paul, and her daughter, Bethany, would be next door.

Going on the cruise turned out to be the right thing to do. I was in a state of shock the next day and my family wisely let me be, but after that, on the open seas, I was able to reflect on Neal's life while feeling closer to God.

Neal had had a short but magnificent life. He had risen to the top of the world of Boston hairdressing, making good money and many friends along the way. He enjoyed nice things and traveled comfortably, but was also exceedingly generous with his friends and causes that were dear to him.

I grieved Neal's loss because I would miss a future of growing old with him, and because a significant part of my childhood was now gone. But I could not consider Neal's death a tragic loss, although he was much too young. He had lived well, and meaningfully. By all accounts, his funeral, back in our hometown area, was packed, so much so that the locals must have wondered what dignitary had passed away. Rumors had spread through the Internet that he died of AIDS—as if that's the only way gay men die. But no, it was simply a massive stroke; the family history of heart disease did him in, as it had his father and his brother, both of whom had also died in their forties.

The cruise was glorious. I never felt closer to my family and it was just the tonic I needed after the blow of Neal's death. But as that long, hot summer dragged on, I was in a numbing fog; there was a hole in my world without Neal.

My heart had been broken apart. It was now open to new possibilities.

Chapter Two

My life had already had its share of drama by that time. Mine was the unlikely, if not uncommon, story of a small-town boy who had arrived in New York City twenty years before in hopes of making his name and earning his fortune doing what he loved, amidst the sparkling skyscrapers and throbbing traffic of the streets and sidewalks of that frothy city. That September, a new and unexpected chapter in this story would unfold, a compelling narrative that would ultimately cause me to reexamine my life. These events would test me to the limit, and I would be changed forever.

*   *   *

At the end of August 2005, Hurricane Katrina was barreling through the Gulf of Mexico. At just about the same time, I was starting my second year of graduate school at The City College of New York, and it was the first year I had been teaching a speech class, as an adjunct. I had just quit an awful, soul-killing job as a recruiter/account manager at a temp agency and was about to embark on what I hoped was a change of career.

In those lingering days at the end of summer, while meticulously preparing my curriculum, I had little time on my hands but, like millions of others, I was watching The Weather Channel and saw that Katrina was a rare Category 5 hurricane as it churned through the Gulf of Mexico. I gazed, awe-struck, as the hurricane moved in slow motion toward the Gulf Coast. With each hourly update, it seemed to move only a tiny distance on the map. Would it ever make landfall? Would it really be as bad as they were saying it could be?

I had visited New Orleans in May 2004 with three friends from Massachusetts, a blissful long weekend of hazy hot days filled with Hurricane drinks, Mint Juleps, and Jello shots, as we shuffled around the French Quarter. We met a lot of friendly folks during our bar stops that weekend, but only one stood out for me. All the bars were close to each other and I noticed this man in two different bars while I traveled with my friends. It was our last night of the trip and we had to get an early flight out the next day. The other guys said they were going back to the hotel, but I wanted to stay and meet that guy. They laughed and teased me about wanting to get laid. These were the same friends from the Ogunquit weekends in the summer, and for most of the years of our travels, I was single, so more available for such trysts—although the closing of the deal didn't happen nearly as often as the talk that preceded it. It was more about the fun of the talking; I was always shy about approaching men.

In fact, that night, after what seemed like a long time of ordering another beer and watching this guy, he finally came over. "Hi, I'm Maurice," he said confidently. He was a small, energetic black man with a wide, dimpled smile, impressively white teeth (always a thing for me) and a ready laugh. A bartender myself, I noticed that he was drinking Cuervo and ginger ale, but not excessively. I couldn't say the same for myself. I don't recall much of the conversation but we were laughing a lot. At one point, a male go-go dancer tiptoed by and Maurice squeezed his ass. The dancer turned around and said with a wink, "Please don't squeeze the Charmin!"

"Charmin? I thought it was Bounty, the quicker picker upper!" Maurice replied, bringing his voice up a notch and adopting ghetto slang.

Maurice lit up when I said I was from New York. He asked where I was staying, but was a bit cagey about his own story.

"Do you live in New Orleans?" I asked him.

"I've lived all over the place but this is my favorite."

Later, I asked, "Do you have a boyfriend?"

"Yeah, but don't tell my girlfriend!" He was hilarious, but it was hard to get a straight answer from him. He didn't appear to be in a hurry to leave, even as last call was approaching. I thought about inviting him to my hotel, but the thought of getting up in five hours to hurry and catch a plane pretty much nixed that idea. Plus, he seemed both safe and not safe, like a young teenager (although we were about the same age). When I finally decided to call it a night, I gave him my phone number and said my usual remark under such circumstances, "If you're ever in New York . . ." He seemed okay with that, didn't push for anything more, and gave me a tight hug when we said goodbye.

Now, a year and a half later, as the weather drama played out in New Orleans, I wondered how he was, where he was. I hadn't heard from him since that vacation.

On the morning of Monday, August 29, I turned on the television just as Katrina was making landfall to the east of New Orleans. The images were remarkable, but it seemed the city would escape relatively unscathed. There were reporters on the street excitedly telling their stories amid the flying debris and high winds. The hurricane had hit as a Category 3. I watched off and on throughout the day — school would start on Wednesday so I had plenty to do — but it seemed the drama was over.

When I awoke on Tuesday morning, however, an ominous story was unfolding. Not only were there reports of widespread damage on the coast of Mississippi, but New Orleans itself was filling up with water, apparently from a broken levee. The world would soon be transfixed with images of thousands of people, mostly poor and black, stuck on their rooftops or wading through waist-deep water to get to the overcrowded and understaffed Superdome, where they would wait helplessly for days without food or aid. I wondered about Maurice and prayed for his wellbeing. I became addicted to the television coverage for days, anxiously scanning the crowd shots to see if I might glimpse Maurice. Even if I had, what could I do? Would he even remember who I was, even if I had a way of reaching him? Furthermore, recalling that one gauzy evening in New Orleans, would I even recognize him in a crowd?

The combination of the hurricane, the massive flood, and the seeming lack of a government response to the tragedy made for a fascinating and sad story that summer, probably the top news story of the decade after the World

Trade Center terrorist attacks. Little did I know that August how directly I would feel its effects.

Chapter Three

In late September, there were still lingering news stories about Katrina's aftermath and plenty of blame to go around for everyone in government on the local, state, and federal level. The after-effects had produced the largest migration of people since the Dust Bowl, with as many as a half a million people displaced. The population of metropolitan New Orleans had been cut in half, some reports said. Most ended up in nearby Baton Rouge, or Houston, or Atlanta, but without a doubt folks from the Big Easy were popping up all over the country, including in the Big Apple.

School was going well. I seemed to be a natural at teaching and the young college students liked me, despite my initial fear of walking into the classroom. I was fully engaged in writing workshops, and graduate literature classes. I had saved some money from my previous job, but my income was significantly less than what it once was, so I had to be careful with my spending.

One evening in early October, the phone rang. I was watching *Jeopardy*, but I have always had a habit of picking up the phone and then frittering away lots of time talking to friends instead of studying or preparing for the next day's work.

"Hello, Kevin? It's Maurice," he began, and then added, after my shocked pause, "from New Orleans."

"Maurice! Yes, yes, of course! I remember!" I was overly enthusiastic. "How are you? I've been wondering how things have been going for you in New Orleans."

"Well, not so good. I lost everything in the hurricane," he answered. "But I'm in New York now," he continued, sounding as chipper as I had remembered.

"You're kidding! Where?" I felt a New Yorker's sense of unease: What does he want from me?

"This place in the East Village. Just temporarily. How are you doing?"

My life seemed rather mundane compared to what he had probably been through, but I summarized the recent details. At one point, the operator interrupted—Maurice needed to deposit more coins. "Sorry, I'm using a pay phone," he said.

Not wanting to waste more time and his limited resources using the phone, we made hasty arrangements to meet the following night at the Riviera, a restaurant in the West Village.

Twenty-four hours later, we were eating our burgers at the Riviera and he had finished giving me the summary of his journey from New Orleans, which involved him and a neighbor pushing his elderly Aunt Josephine through the floodwaters in an old washtub, a quick stop at the ineffectual Superdome, a long walk and eventual bus ride to Atlanta to deposit Aunt Josephine with one of her relatives, and his further trek to New York, ending up in the Bowery Shelter. Maurice told all of this without self-pity and, by all accounts, he had hit the ground running in New York: He had signed up with Job Partners and was studying to take a test for a job that would involve teaching seniors about new medical insurance options, and he was working part-time at Magnolia Bakery, made famous by the television show *Sex and the City*.

Maurice told me his parents had died in a car accident when he was about twelve years old. He had been raised in upstate New York, somewhere near Syracuse. He had been taken in by a foster family. He mentioned a sister named Tracy. Nothing more was said about family.

Maurice was dressed in black Dickies-type slacks, a Batman tee shirt and gray hooded sweatshirt. He wore sneakers that seemed to still have that wet, soggy smell and he carried a backpack with all his belongings. "I'm not leaving anything at the shelter," he explained.

"Why don't you stay at my place until you get back on your feet," I said. I hadn't even paused. It was like I couldn't control the insanity that was spilling out of my mouth. The truth is, I had heard an unmistakable voice—kind of like Darth Vader—in my head, which said, "Take him in." I'm a pragmatic guy and cannot claim to have ever heard voices before, but I could not deny that that is what I heard. I believe it was the voice of God.

Even so, within a moment of my offer, I thought, *Kevin, you are nuts! You don't even know this guy.*

From a practical standpoint, I had little to give. I lived in a walk-up studio in midtown, the one large room bisected by floor-to-ceiling bookcases. On one side was my bed, a television, desk and a dresser, on the other a small table and a folded up, single-sized futon bed. There was something about his energy and optimism—that child-like quality—along with my desire to *do something*, as perhaps many Americans were longing to do, that firmed up my resolve.

"Really?" His eyes grew wide with disbelief. He hadn't yet seen my small place but, evidently, anything was better than the shelter, where there had recently been a shooting. "It would be so helpful to me while I'm studying for this exam."

"Not a problem," I said, magnanimously. "In fact, I'm going away next week and you could feed and keep my cat company, so that would be a help to me."

It was like I had no filter and my brain was not sending "stop" signals to my mouth. On the one hand, my mind kept trying to short-circuit my behavior, and yet my heart was fearlessly calm.

Maurice asked me if I was absolutely sure, explaining that if he left the shelter there would be a lot of bureaucratic red tape involved to get him back into the system again. We agreed that he would finish out that week, which would prolong some sort of benefit such as food stamps, and then move in with me over the weekend.

It looked as if Maurice was on a fast track to finding his way, working one job and studying for a new career, and with a can-do attitude that was very seductive for someone who wanted to help. I expected him to remain with me for about two weeks.

When Maurice climbed the four flights to my apartment, he seemed neither surprised nor disappointed by the size and rather gritty appearance of the building. It was like many older buildings in New York that landlords are slow to fix, hoping tenants will move out. I also warned him about the cockroaches that were rather plentiful, due to the slovenly man that lived across the hall with his dog, birds, and piles of stuff that come with living alone in a rent-controlled apartment for thirty years.

I gave him the five-second tour and started asking more questions about his ordeal. Sensing my uneasiness, perhaps, he pulled out some identification, a birth certificate and a Virginia license, which he hadn't bothered to renew since having a car when he lived in Richmond a few years before. He was eager to prove his worth to stay in my place, which I considered a dump.

After a time, I ordered Chinese food and we watched *Family Guy*, his choice. I had never seen that irreverent cartoon, but I quickly rediscovered that wicked sense of humor I remembered from our encounter in New Orleans.

While I was up in Massachusetts with my family and trying to enjoy a week of October foliage (there was a convergence of Jewish holidays and Columbus Day that gave me a week off from school), I was growing increasingly wary about the near-stranger who was staying in my apartment. What if he was cleaning me out? Stealing my identity? Why wasn't he answering the phone when I was calling at eleven at night? What had possessed me to do such a thing? Maybe I was crazy and hadn't really heard a directive from above. Was I trying to make a boyfriend out of this unlikely prospect? While there was some attraction to him on my part, that had not been addressed nor pursued by either of us and I was — finally — old enough to know better than to complicate such a situation at that stage of my life. It was pretty clear to me, early on, that that kind of relationship was not how this would or should play out. Maurice never called himself gay but, like the city of New Orleans itself, was open to anything. In fact, he talked more of girlfriends and female crushes than male ones. His shame about his homosexual yearnings was years' deep.

What was in this for me? Was I really so selfless or did I have some need to do the ultimate good, to prove to myself, my family, or the world at large that I was a worthy person?

Furthermore, would I have offered my home to a stranger if he had been white? Did I have white guilt, as James Baldwin had written about, that made me go a little further to help a black man? Did I still need to prove to someone that I was not racist?

And why let him in if I couldn't trust him? I was mentally trying to poke holes in the story of his journey. Why hadn't I asked more questions? How did he leave the Superdome with an elderly woman? Details of his life in New Orleans now seemed too sketchy and with each day of my vacation, I became more convinced that I'd been had. If the truth was different from what he was telling me, maybe I didn't want to know it, because clearly, whatever his true circumstance, Maurice was a man in trouble, with few resources. Small comfort to me, but nevertheless I tried to justify my actions. The voice of God no longer seemed enough.

I returned from Massachusetts and, with trepidation, put the key in the lock and slowly let myself into my apartment. Everything was in place and as it should be and, honestly, there may have been a moment of disappointment on my part—like I couldn't be rid of him that easily. A message had been taped to the TV screen: "I'm working at Magnolia tonight, be home at about midnight." He was calling it *home* already, I immediately noted.

Whatever doubts I may have had about his character and the situation I found myself in, the guy cheered me up. He had an impish humor, big hugs, and a laugh that was infectious to anyone that met him. I had to see him.

As soon as I unpacked my bags and had a bite to eat, I went over to Ninth Avenue to catch a downtown bus. Yes, I wanted to see him . . . and I also wanted to make sure he was telling me the truth about Magnolia Bakery. It was a Saturday night and there was a line of people queuing around the corner from the little bakery. Honestly, I never understood why people waited a half hour for a few cupcakes—there were better ones to be had, without all the fuss.

I stood across the street, hidden from view, and looked in the bright, festive windows. There he was! He was standing behind the counter wearing a white apron and that big, toothy smile, gladly helping those who came in. Customer service was clearly his calling card. In that moment, I was so proud of him for all he had overcome and now he was in my city, making his way back to a better way of life. I was satisfied; I went back home without saying hello.

Before the end of October, we had our first drama. It was the middle of the night, and Maurice had not come home. From the beginning, I had a sense that "I was my brother's keeper" and I took on a parental role that was neither asked for nor refused.

Finally, the phone rang around three in the morning. Maurice was calling me from a downtown precinct. He had gone out after working at Magnolia and, for whatever ridiculous reason, chose to urinate on the street. To his continued bad luck, he was caught. For this little misdemeanor, he would spend the night behind bars. He wasn't nearly as concerned as I was, but I remained calm on the phone. I would save my ammunition for the next day.

I was ready and waiting when he walked in the door early the next morning. "Maurice, I can't have this kind of drama in my life. I'm working every day, I'm trying to get a Master's degree, and we're sharing a small space. If you are going to stay here, I can't have this kind of stupidity going on."

"I know, I'm really sorry. Who knew the cops would be on West 10th Street at that exact time," he said, seeming to find humor in the situation. "I hate the cops!"

"Well, you're just starting to get on your feet again. Don't sabotage it with stupidity."

It didn't occur to me that, by taking him in, I might be stupidly sabotaging my own dreams. I was starting a teaching career, trying to meet writing deadlines, living on a limited income. Where was the logic in what I was doing? How had my judgment become so skewed so quickly? Did I need companionship so badly at that time?

"You're right, you're right," he agreed. Maurice went on to tell me about his night at Magnolia, and how he didn't think Barbara, the owner, was managing the place very well. He had given her suggestions.

I didn't like the sound of that. "Just keep quiet and do your work for a while, until you get more experience and some money."

"Oh, I have plenty of experience," he assured me. He went on to tell me of his days working at the Capitol Club in Washington, DC and another high-profile place in Richmond, before finally settling in New Orleans. He'd had a nice apartment and sped around in a brand new sports car in those days.

"That's great, but you're not there now. You're new to New York and you have to start from scratch again," I said, sounding like my father.

I suddenly remembered the unpleasant exchange I had had with my father decades before, after I had been in New York for about three months. I had called to ask for money. "If you can't make it there on your own, you'd better find another place to live," he told me. He sent nothing and somehow I survived. It would be years before I'd feel comfortable enough to ask him for anything again.

"But you'll be back on top again," I quickly reassured Maurice.

It became clear that there was no way he'd be able to get enough money together to move out by November. I could either let him continue to stay for free, giving him more time to accumulate the necessary funds to move out sooner, or start charging him rent, which would have helped me financially but would have meant more time for him to stay. I decided to let him stay on for free for another month.

In the meantime, I introduced him to my church, figuring he needed to start getting to know some good people and become involved in a community. At that time, Middle Collegiate Church was in a time of transition. Rev. Dr. Jacqueline Lewis had just become the new senior minister that July, replacing the popular Rev. Gordon Dragt, who had presided over the growing church for twenty years.

Rev. Dr. Lewis was a tall, energetic African-American woman committed to continuing the multicultural tradition of the church. The daughter of a military man, Lewis had grown up the oldest of five siblings and lived in many places before the family finally settled in Chicago, which she considered her hometown. She often told the story of how she heard the calling to be a preacher as a young teenager. However, Lewis went on to work in the corporate world for many years before earning her Master's in Divinity from Princeton Theological Seminary. She then served in churches in Trenton and consulted with congregations before being handpicked by Dragt to succeed him at Middle Collegiate Church, becoming the first African-American and woman to hold such a position in the Collegiate churches. In her first year at Middle Church, she completed her Ph.D. in psychology and religion from Drew University. For all of that accomplishment, though, to her parishioners, Rev. Dr. Lewis insisted on being called, simply, Jacqui.

Although Jacqui offered some exciting programs on the horizon, one area that had been somewhat lacking at that time was a strong mission program. I made the church leadership aware of Maurice as a Katrina survivor but the church was a bit limited with resources as to what it could specifically do to help him. Heather Juby, an associate minister who was also a social worker, pointed him to Rutgers Church on the Upper West Side, which had more funds and outreach geared specifically towards Katrina survivors. Although Maurice continued to attend services at Middle, he also attended some events at Rutgers and they took him under their wing as a survivor they wanted to sponsor.

Maurice did not pass his test on new insurance plans. However, according to him, so few people passed and there was such a great need for workers, that Aegis Communications hired him anyway, along with a slew of other applicants. At that time, the laws had changed regarding medical insurance options for senior citizens, and workers were needed to explain the new policies and guide the seniors to their best option.

He was up every morning, starting around mid-November, ironing his shirt and getting out the door early for his commute downtown. However, it didn't take long for him to grow frustrated with the company. Maurice was very smart and, under different circumstances, probably could have run his own company.

"You can't believe the shpil they want us to give over the phone to these elderly folks. They're scared, and Aegis has no humanity, no idea how to talk to people," Maurice told me. "And they treat us like shit," he said as an afterthought. Checks were often late and overtime was "forgotten" to be included.

He had little patience for ineptitude. That impatience, combined with, perhaps, the new company's tendency to mistreat desperate employees (sent to them by a state agency, no less) who needed the work, was not making for a hopeful long-term arrangement. I begged him to stay with it until he found something else, but he was rebellious. "Life is too short. I don't see why I should continue to work for a crappy company."

Nevertheless, he stuck it out through the end of the year and was able to pay me some rent money in December. By then, I was justifying to myself, "It's the holidays, I can't let him go now. He has nobody else."

Things started to go less smoothly at Magnolia Bakery. I'm not sure if it was his inability to work long weekend hours at a low-paying job after working at a stressful office job all week or if he just got fed up with the way Barbara was running things, but she let him go around Thanksgiving. No more free cupcakes.

Still, I felt it incumbent on me to help him get on his feet. What other connections and possible solutions might I be able to find for him?

Our first holiday together, Thanksgiving, was a disappointment. A friend had invited both of us to his place, but we didn't know anybody there (other than our host), and it was an unusual crowd to say the least: a lot of gay men and the occasional female friend, trying to make space to eat in a tiny room. Several of the guys were members of the Diana Ross fan club and we spent hours talking about Diana Ross and passing around souvenir books. The food was fine but, when it came to that, I knew Maurice would have preferred to be in charge. We thanked our host and left a couple of hours after dinner.

We walked through the empty city, looking at holiday windows in Macy's and Lord & Taylor, and by the time we got back to the apartment, Maurice said, "They were really nice and everything, but I feel like I missed a real Thanksgiving." For Maurice, besides the food, it wasn't about the number of people but about the quality of conversation.

It was about nine o'clock on Thanksgiving night and it seemed nothing was open, but I made a few calls around the neighborhood and, sure enough, the Film Center Café was serving turkey and trimmings for about $15 per person. Good enough.

We went over to the restaurant on Ninth Avenue and pretty much had the whole dining room to ourselves. After we ordered what was to be our second turkey meal of the day, we looked up at the television monitor, high in the corner of the room.

We both burst out laughing as we realized that the television was playing — of all things — *The Wiz* . . . starring Diana Ross.

That 2005 holiday would forever go down in our history as the year of the Diana Ross Thanksgiving.

Chapter Four

Besides school and Middle Church, I had a community at Rose's Turn, a historic piano bar in the West Village where I had worked since 1994. Active in both a church and a bar, it would appear that I was living a double life. I worked as a bartender during the Sunday happy hour and Dan would play Broadway and pop tunes and folks would sing along. Every hour or so, I would come out from behind the bar and sing a couple numbers.

I was still good at compartmentalizing, although I had explored that pattern in my life during therapy back in the '90s. I had my bar life and my church life and my teaching life and my office life, my performing life and my solitary writing life, my friend life and my sex life. I put up a good front, but there didn't seem to be a unified whole.

I was at Rose's only once a week most weeks, but with the music and the regular, good-natured clientele, it was a lot like TV's *Cheers*: everybody knew your name. Maurice blended in quite well there also; kind of the secular version of Middle Church, you saw all types there and nobody judged anybody else.

I began to reach out to my communities to get Maurice some seed money for Christmas. I wanted to present him with a stocking full of well wishes. People were happy to give because they knew the person and his need; it wasn't just some faceless charity organization.

Because Thanksgiving had not been what he'd hoped for, I wanted to do something special for Christmas. Of course, he thought in terms of food. He wanted a turducken—a chicken stuffed inside a duck, stuffed inside a turkey! It had to be special-ordered from The Cajun Grocer in Louisiana—to the tune of about $100. That would be my gift to him.

My long-time friend Sandra, who lived near Middle Church, agreed to host the turducken Christmas dinner about a week before the holiday. We invited a fourth person, a nice guy from my choir who was about eighteen years old. That's who Maurice wanted to invite, which I thought odd. It wasn't romantic on Maurice's part; I just think he could easily relate to the youthfulness of a teenager because, in many ways, he was still a teenager. It reminded me a bit of what I'd read about Michael Jackson—he'd never really had a childhood, so continued to live a child-like existence, hanging out with kids at his Neverland Ranch.

Sandra was herself a transplant from the south, by way of Jackson, Mississippi and Baton Rouge, and she still carried the accent, although she'd made the East Village her home for many years. She did not suffer fools gladly and was quick to speak her mind on an issue, especially if it involved social justice. You had to tread lightly around her when it came to political discussion because she was avidly left-wing, and God help you if you disagreed. However, Sandra had a soft heart and could cry easily over the misfortune of others. She had an Irish heritage and it showed in her dark hair, pale complexion and short but sturdy frame. Although she was probably only a few years older than Maurice and I (she wasn't one to reveal her age), her chiding way with mischievous Maurice made a good combination and before long he began referring to her as "Mama."

While I went to church, Maurice joined Sandra at her homey but tiny apartment to prepare the meal. When I arrived, she said with a wry smile, "This is the first time I've been ordered around in my own kitchen."

"I'm not surprised," I said.

"But it's gonna be so good!" Maurice squealed with anticipation.

Sandra had plenty of Dixie-style jazz music playing in the background; conversation was upbeat and festive, never forced. The four of us ate so much that day, and yet we had bags and bags of leftovers to take home.

Maurice and I took the bus uptown after the meal and extensive clean-up. We got off the bus at Bryant Park and looked at the Christmas tree, the shops and skaters. It had been a great day.

"I love you," I said to him for the first time, as we waited for traffic on Sixth Avenue.

He brightened up like a Christmas tree. "Wow, that's so nice," he said. Perhaps he didn't trust himself or me to say it back, but that was fine with me. He needed to hear it.

Yet, as the Christmas season unfolded, it seemed that Maurice's demons were getting the better of him. This could probably be expected from someone who had lost everything and was forced to spend the holidays in a strange city, sleeping on a couch in a new friend's cramped apartment. I was still thinking it was post-traumatic stress syndrome, something he would come out of eventually.

However, the problems were deeper than that. He would disappear for long periods of time without calling, sometimes overnight. I suspected drugs and asked him about it. Like a little boy with his hand caught in the cookie jar, he denied, denied, denied, with wide-eyed sweetness, going so far as to roll up his sleeves and show me that there were no needle marks on his arms.

"Well, you don't have to be shooting up," I countered. "I'm trying to give you a new start here, Maurice. Don't screw it up. You have so much potential."

My weakness has always been that I would fall for "potential," somebody I could fix, rather than someone who was reasonably well-adjusted from the get-go. My tendency to want to fix extended to both lovers and friends. Friends have often found that characteristic charming, up to a point.

"I just get depressed," Maurice said. "I need to be by myself. I sneak into the movies and just stay there all day." Sure enough, he seemed to have seen everything that was current.

"But why can't you call? I'm not going to judge you, but just give me a call and say 'This is Maurice, I won't be home tonight, but I'm fine.' That's all. Just a little consideration so I can sleep at night."

"Okay," he said. Maurice was dirt-poor, but he was also fiercely independent, having fended for himself his entire life. It would be a battle royal trying to get him to stick to some rules.

Looking back on that time, I wonder how I would have reacted if a roommate was trying to set down ground rules for me. I'd probably say, "I'm an adult and pay my rent, I don't have to play by any rules."

But, without our ever discussing it, Maurice seemed to like having someone around with a parental voice and, quite frankly—having never been a parent—I took to it quite naturally myself.

When Maurice was at his best, there was nobody better: charming, funny, thoughtful, smart, engaging, and with a simple faith that was often moving. But his other side could rear its head at any time.

"If I ever see so much as a grain of cocaine or anything else or there is any fishy person calling here or coming up to this apartment, you will be out on your ass in a New York minute," I lectured. I still assumed he had drug issues, although he was not admitting it.

"That will never happen," he promised. "This is my sacred space." I think he really believed that and it was a promise he kept: Whatever destructive habits he had, he kept them out of the apartment.

Still, the remnants of his dark side could mean long hours with him lying on the bed watching TV, gripped by inertia. In a small space, and as someone who needed time to write and study, it was extremely frustrating for me. He would always offer to leave—"Just tell me, I can go"—but I would rarely ask that, only because I feared the alternative. His finding trouble out on the streets was worse than having him hanging around the apartment.

Oddly, my cat, Liberty, sensed Maurice's demons. There was a while that winter when I thought Maurice would have to go because Liberty would often snarl when Maurice would walk by the bed, hiding underneath and ready to pounce. What did she know that I didn't know?

Because I was so busy on Christmas Eve and was planning on leaving on Christmas morning, I presented Maurice with his stocking on the morning of the 24th. He really couldn't believe people were giving him all this stuff: gift cards from Saks, Macy's, Old Navy, Best Buy, and more, along with checks and over $600 in cash. He read cards from people he didn't even know by name.

Handing cash to someone who had none, and little self-discipline, was probably not the smartest charitable investment I could have made. I can vouch for the gift cards being spent on clothes and it seems a good chunk of the cash was spent on CDs. "Save it for something you really need," I lectured again.

"Music is my therapy," he answered. Where the rest of the money went, I couldn't vouch for and I hated to guess.

On Christmas Eve, I was singing with Middle Church's gospel choir at their annual midnight concert. Maurice was to meet me there and then we'd go out to breakfast at an all-night diner and I'd say goodbye. I'd be taking a bus up to Massachusetts to spend the holiday with my family; Maurice would stay in the apartment, tending the cat that hated him.

As much as I hated leaving him alone on the holiday, I didn't yet quite trust him enough to introduce him to my family. Would he brood all through the three days at my parents' house? Would my family have misgivings about him just as I sometimes did?

On the night of the concert, the church was standing room only. The entire time we were singing, I was scanning the pews looking for Maurice. I was proud of my church and our music and, more than that, I wanted to spend Christmas Eve with him, if not the entire holiday. He wasn't there.

During the post-concert hugs and offers of best wishes to each other, I was sad and angry that Maurice had never shown up. I realized that this was probably an emotionally difficult time for someone in his circumstances, but I expected some consideration and to not have to go off to Massachusetts without word from him, wondering what the hell happened to him.

Needless to say, the couple of days in Massachusetts were spent preoccupied by what was going on with Maurice in New York. I hadn't heard from him and, if he was at the apartment, he wasn't picking up the phone while I was leaving long, pleading messages on the machine. I can't remember much else about that Christmas, other than it was a typical family Christmas. No memory stands out except for my slow burn. Who knew if Liberty was even getting fed?

I returned a day or two after Christmas, arriving in New York at midday. When I unlocked the door and walked in, the TV was on and Maurice was lying there watching it, in some kind of funk. I said nothing. I quickly unpacked my bags and grabbed some gym clothes out of the dresser and went into the bathroom to change. I did not want to say anything to him but wanted to convey my sheer disgust for his behavior. So I quickly changed and left the apartment, slamming the door behind me. It was difficult to do, because he clearly had a look of sorrow and disappointment on his face. Completely ignoring him was probably the hardest thing for him to bear, and for me to do.

I worked out my aggressions on the weight machines and treadmill for as long as humanly possible before returning home. He was still there, in the same position as when I left him.

Finally, I spoke. "Why the hell didn't you call me? And where the hell were you on Christmas Eve?"

He looked pathetic, lying there hugging the pillow. "It was Christmas, I was depressed."

"So what's your cure for depression? A three-day bender?"

Maurice did not answer.

"I need to be able to rely on you," I continued. "My life is already difficult. I don't need extra drama." I was in a constant state of stress about him, my teaching and schoolwork, and the ever-precarious finances.

"I know."

It's like he knew the right thing to do, but didn't have the willpower and self-confidence to do it. I knew he was incredibly grateful to have me in his life—there was no one else to speak of, to my knowledge—and yet he seemed to find ways to sabotage that connection. Except that the connection wasn't sabotaged. I was still there.

What he didn't count on was that I was possibly more stubborn than he was. I was convinced there was a divine hand that had guided me to take him in, and until I heard a divine voice telling me that time was up, I was going to keep on keeping on.

Damn it, I was going to demonstrate that love could overcome his troubles, however formidable they were—if it killed me.

From an early age, I had faced long odds, as had he. I was determined to win this battle.

I was the ultimate survivor. I had proven it time and time again.

Chapter Five

October 6, 1994

I had just left 88's, a piano bar and club on West 10th Street in the Village. I was there to drop off a photo and copy for a graphic artist who had agreed to design a flyer for me for an upcoming show.

It was close to midnight and I took the subway up to 42nd Street. I had just moved into a fourth floor walkup in Hell's Kitchen six months before. In 1994, that area by Tenth Avenue truly was still hellish.

That night, cops had blocked off my street at Ninth Avenue because they were rounding up prostitutes, a common sight around there in those days. I passed the cop cars, eyeing them with curiosity as I made my way west.

When I was almost at Tenth Avenue, a black man on a bicycle rode up next to me on the sidewalk and stopped, straddling the bike.

"Do you know what's going on back there?" He seemed friendly and intelligent and it was an honest question.

I shrugged. "I'm not sure, but I think – "

Suddenly, I felt a heavy punch in the middle of my chest that literally took my breath away. I let out a god-awful scream, nothing I could ever duplicate for an acting class. My arms instinctively went up and then I saw his fist coming at me again, a glint of silver in his grip.

A second scream.

I watched him remount the bike and pedal away, rather relaxed, and turn right on Tenth Avenue.

What the fuck just happened?

One hand was over my chest, one hand was still gripping the paper bag holding Haagen Dazs Brownie a la Mode, a pint I had just picked up on the corner of Ninth.

I stood there wondering what to do next. Should I continue home and see how badly I was hurt? I was shaken but not in any pain. Or, should I turn around and get the attention of those cops back there?

I chose the latter option, a decision that turned out to be very lucky.

I walked slowly, steadily, back to the first squad car I saw, parked diagonally across the middle of the street. A cop was standing outside the front door of the car, watching me approach with an up-and-down study of me that seemed to be saying, "What the hell is this?"

I came up to the hood of the car. "I think someone just tried to stab me," I said.

"Sir," he said, coming over to me, "I think he got you."

I looked down and saw a sea of blood from my chest to my knees. At the sight of it, I came out of my adrenaline-induced shock and felt myself falling onto the hood of the car. I heard the officer yelling for his partner and then I blacked out.

I awoke just a few minutes later, it turned out, as they were helping me out of the back seat of the squad car and carrying me into St. Clare's Hospital, which was just a few blocks north.

I was rushed into the emergency room and placed on a table. The bag containing the ice cream was still in my grip and had to be pried loose. I was afraid but there was also something comic about it, like what you'd see on TV: I was looking up at a circle of faces ringed around my table.

The only thing about the next few minutes I remember is that I would feel faint and blackness would crowd around my eyes as I felt myself going under. "Don't let me die!" I heard myself screaming and then an oxygen mask would be placed over my face and I'd return to the living. That process repeated itself, it seems, more than a few times over several minutes.

A doctor, who happened to be African-American, wheeled over an X-ray machine to place over my chest. I sensed he knew the perpetrator had been black. He seemed to look at me defiantly and I regarded him suspiciously. Even there, in my state of emergency, race was playing its ugly part.

Meanwhile, a handsome white cop with a mustache and smelling of aftershave kept whispering in my ear. "What did this guy look like? Can you give me a description?" And then, more ominously, "Is there anyone nearby we can call? Any next of kin in town?"

I never did get my ice cream.

Chapter Six

One night in early January 2006, I tossed and turned for hours. Maurice was not home. Finally, the phone rang. A sigh of relief. It was him.

"I'm at St. Vincent's hospital with Rosa. She had chest pains so I brought her here," he told me.

Rosa was his friend for the moment from his job at Aegis. Maurice's alibi turned out to be true, because about a week later she called asking for him and I slyly asked her how she was doing after her hospital ordeal. She told me everything turned out fine but that she couldn't have gotten through it without Maurice.

So that became the pattern: if Maurice had been doing something noble or work-related or with a friend, he would call to let me know. If he had been doing something he was ashamed of, I'd never hear from him and would just go about my business until he showed up at the apartment—sometimes the next morning, sometimes two days later.

By mid-January, the Aegis job had ended. I can't say I blame Maurice for that job loss. By all accounts, it was a new business and they were getting most of their entry-level employees from Job Partners or some other city agency—desperate people who needed a job and had no recourse if paychecks were late or they weren't getting paid what they were promised.

All was not yet lost. Maurice found a job bartending for private parties for a start-up film company. However, immediate cash was always a danger. I had also recommended him as a host at a couple of private affairs for a wealthy friend of a friend. Through January, I was still getting my share of the rent.

As we got to know each other, I was enjoying the funny, smart, engaging side of Maurice as well as the home-cooked meals. By then, he had also crammed the closet full with clothes he had bought at the nearby Salvation Army store. He knew how to find a bargain and he could put together a smashing outfit from secondhand clothes.

That winter, we watched the Olympics on television. One night, we were enjoying the female figure skaters. One of them missed her triple lutz and the snotty commentators were saying that the judges would have to deduct. A moment later, the skater glided in front of the seated judges and serenely lifted one leg over her head as she passed.

Without missing a beat, Maurice, in a girlish voice, said, "Smell this!"

It was on-target, crude . . . and hilarious. I rolled off the bed laughing and Maurice, never skimpy with the laughter, joined me. It was like that for the rest of the night, as we injected comments that we supposed the athletes were thinking.

I have never looked at a figure skater the same way since.

*   *   *

The truth is, when Maurice had returned from the Magnolia Café that night back in October after I'd returned from Massachusetts, and saw me sitting up in bed watching television, he pounced on me like an eager puppy, knocking me back and straddling me while tickling me and kissing my neck. For a moment, this was both my hope and my terror and the two unresolved parts of my psyche fought—erotic temptation versus being sensible. We had a couple of fevered kisses and explored each other's bodies with our hands, fully clothed. I'd like to report that "being sensible" won out but, more accurately, I discovered that he wasn't aroused. I've never been one to hang around if someone isn't excited by my presence. I'm insulted, and the emotional door closes.

Besides, I couldn't reconcile the fact that if I had indeed heard a directive from God to take Maurice in, then how could that mean sexual pleasure for myself? On a more practical level, I knew my own limitations. Despite a lifetime of religion and seven years of psychotherapy—individual and group work—for some reason, I had trouble fitting friendship and sex into the same equation. It was one or the other. I had a feeling this was something shared by many American men, both gay and straight. I'd heard that, for many, the sex petered out after about two years but that committed couples stuck it out after that, allowing the initial heat to transform into something else, more of a comforting candlelight. My experience had shown me that most gay male couples, without the hold of a marriage vow, moved on to someone else after that chemistry had faded.

In any case, this was too much, too soon, and fraught with peril, in my mind. "Being sensible" had been a pretty good guide for me, I think, but my lack of spontaneity and inability to let go and take a risk has also had consequences. I had lost out on opportunities, both in love and in work.

I pretended I hadn't noticed his condition, and didn't want to embarrass him. I rolled over on top of Maurice and looked down into his espresso eyes. "We can't do this, Maurice. I know myself. If we do this, it will end up being a one night stand and you'll be back on the street." I pushed myself off of him and sat on the edge of the bed.

He went into joke mode, ghetto voice. Had I crushed his ego? "You turnin' this down, suckah? 'Cause I know plenty who want it!"

"I'm sure they do!" I laughed. "But if you want a place to stay, I don't think that's the way to stay here."

I think he was relieved. Perhaps I was one who was not going to take sex as payment for "services rendered." That may sound as if I were saintlier than some others, but I was not. Just damaged in my own way.

Some friends later voiced disbelief that there was no hanky-panky going on. Believe it or not, once I came to the decision, it was not that difficult to remain living with him, and the sexual temptation disappeared almost overnight. Once I close a door, I am very stubborn about opening it again. Although he pursued me first, it didn't seem genuine, and I was never one to keep going after someone who didn't want me in the same way. I also sensed that if a romance was to blossom out of this, going the sexual route was not going to be the best way to get there with him (or me — my own history with that kind of start was also not a winning hand).

As time went on, Maurice found no trouble meeting men, and I had no doubt he was getting plenty of sex on those nights he wasn't around — certainly more than I was. I've always found it extremely difficult to date or bring somebody home while having a roommate. Even if the other person was accommodating to a situation that might arise, for me to say, "I might be bringing somebody home tonight" — even if it was a steady date, never mind a hookup — was too shaming for me.

* * *

I was, after all, the son of my parents. I carried their conflicting natures within me.

My mother had somehow maintained a public show of piety throughout her long marriage and social life, despite the fact that she had married a "bad boy." Very late in their marriage, when they were well into their sixties, I interviewed them for a videotaped project. We were becoming more communicative as I got older and I realized I knew so little about their early life. Paul, my sister Audrey's husband, taped as I asked the questions while my parents sat on the couch.

"When did you know Dad was the one?" I asked.

Without hesitation, my mother's eyes grew wide and she exclaimed, "When he kissed me!"

"Jesus!" Audrey laughed, and Paul joined in, trying not to shake the camera.

Her brief answer told me volumes about her. After that kiss, she became the pursuer and she ultimately won her quest — although not without a lot of self-sacrifice over the years.

Dad was, to his friends, the life of the party. He could throw back drinks and entertain long into the night with his musical skill or storytelling talent. His cursing was nearly Shakespearean in its creativity. His occasional no-shows at dinnertime, when my mother faithfully kept the six of us coming to the table evening after evening, year after year, provoked the angriest outbursts from her. His was a midlife crisis that seemed to stretch for a long, long time.

As of this writing, after fifty-plus years of marriage, I think my mother takes pride in the fact that she held on to that commitment, whatever considerable bumps in the road there may have been. She eventually tamed his nature somewhat, and their twilight years have demonstrated the soft light of that comforting candle. But what a journey to get there! I don't think I could do it.

* * *

So was Maurice my "bad boy"? Was I playing the part of my mother? Was I trying to fix Maurice in the way I had seen my mother wrestle with fixing my father all those years? What was that definition of insanity?

The first time I turned on my computer and saw that Maurice had been viewing pornography was shocking to me, I'm not sure why. Perhaps something about his using my appliance for his personal pleasure while I was away. (I had given him permission to use the computer, figuring he needed it for job-hunting and email and such.) I also noticed that the kinds of things he was looking at were not what I imagined his tastes to be. From what I could tell, he had been dating — yes dating, no problem for him — men, both white and black, but mostly white. The porn was all straight and the common fetish of all of it seemed to be big-bootied black women. That made me wonder two things: first, if that's what he liked, why wasn't he pursuing them; and second, it seemed clear that he could not have found me attractive at all. I'm a gay man who loves his big black diva women — but it's a look I can't quite pull off.

Porn is easy fantasy-making and solace for one who wants some pleasure without the trouble of going out for the hunt, but I recognize its dehumanizing nature, even if I've partaken like millions of others. It's not the most profitable industry on the Web for nothing. It's just another step down a dangerous road in our visually-oriented culture: we pick our entertainers, our presidents, and our mates increasingly through a visual lens. The look becomes the first requirement rather than one part of a whole picture that we don't have time to explore if the first requirement isn't met.

So here we were in our shared apartment. In separate beds, ten feet apart, we kept our sexual secrets and sought it out in our own way. Sex with each other became a taboo subject for discussion. Friendship was the pathway, and that was a revelatory thing — for both of us, I suspect.

"Take him in" was the directive from on high. I assumed God was giving me a job to do. But what if God gave Maurice to me because He wanted me to have a gift?

All my life, I've thought that I wasn't quite good enough, that I had more work to do. So, with Maurice, I moved into work mode, and there was plenty of it. Being a savior and a martyr is a high calling indeed . . . but what does such a person deny himself in the process?

Furthermore, was I the savior . . . or the victim?

Chapter Seven

By February, Maurice was out of money and the bartending gigs had stopped. He was able to get back on food stamps temporarily, which was a small help — he could stretch $90 for almost an entire month and feed both of us.

I had to sit down with him and have the difficult talk about finding a way for him to move out of the apartment. He seemed content to stay there forever, but the place was impossibly small for two people and we were not partners, so I was not about to go on supporting him indefinitely. I thought if there were a target goal in mind, it would give him the necessary kick in the butt to find steady employment and keep it.

My guilt at kicking out a needy person was somewhat eased when, one night while watching television, I was doing my bills and looked down at one of my credit card statements.

"Someone stole my credit card!" I shouted. "Someone used this for a whole week!" Immediately, I called the bank that had issued the card and had it cancelled.

I examined the statement more closely. In early February, someone had used the card on a number of small purchases at places like diners, drug stores, and delis. The person obviously did not want me to notice the charges.

Although Maurice was silent during my panicked outbursts, it honestly never occurred to me that he stole the card until I went to the local police precinct the next day to file a complaint.

"Is there anyone close to you who could have used the card?" the officer asked me.

Bingo! I don't know if I successfully hid my shock from the officer, but after a moment I said, "No." I filled out the complaint and raced back to the apartment.

When I came in, Maurice was, as usual, watching television. I started crying.

"What's the matter?" he asked, genuinely concerned.

Finally, I managed to say, "Maurice, I have to ask you to leave."

"What happened?"

"I think you stole my credit card." He remained silent so I struggled on. "After all I've done for you, how could you do that to me? I don't have much, but I give you everything you need."

"If that's what you think, there's nothing I can say."

"Nobody else could have taken it. I keep them well hidden and I don't use them much." I was wracked with pain; I still didn't want to put him out on the streets. He looked pathetic. "Did you take it?"

"I don't have it," he answered evasively.

"Well, we may find out. I filed charges and maybe the Duane Reade has a camera they can check."

The threat didn't make him any more forthcoming.

The discussion of his moving out quickly took on more urgency.

We agreed, without too much arguing, that Maurice would move out by April 1. By then, he had a good relationship with Rutgers Church—he had even been paraded in front of the congregation to speak about Katrina and its aftermath—so he was able to tell them of the goal and get them to work with him on meeting it.

The rest of the winter leading up to his departure date was uneventful for both of us, except that he'd made a new friend named Patricio, a hairdresser. I didn't like him from the moment I heard his oily voice over the phone.

"Who is this Patricio?" I asked Maurice.

"Oh, just someone I met," he answered, rolling his eyes as if he, too, didn't think much of him.

"I don't like him."

Again, one might expect Maurice to assert his independence and tell me to go to hell, but he seemed to agree with my assessment. "I know, I need to find some better people to hang out with."

"What about the people at Middle?" I asked.

"They are friendly enough on Sunday morning but nobody wants to do anything during the week." It's true, he had called a couple of people from the church but they were too busy to meet, which was hurtful to him and to me, as it was my home base.

All through that winter, I was astonished at how Maurice, without a nickel to his name, had no shortage of dates—men, at that point—while I was having trouble meeting anyone. I began to hate going to a bar with him because he could easily talk to anyone, or people would gravitate to his smile and energy, leaving me skulking against a wall. Where did he get the confidence? Of course, he was a man of extremes: he could shine with confidence . . . or grovel in the pit of despair.

It reminded me of an episode of *Sex and the City*. Smart, hardworking Miranda had broken up with Steve but was letting him stay on her couch until he could afford to move out on his own. In the meantime, he had begun dating. "He's living on my couch and doesn't have a job," she marveled to her friends. "And he's dating, no problem!"

I had a sense that Maurice gravitated towards men because he lacked the confidence—and money—to date women. He could more easily get things out of men.

Patricio continued to call.

Towards the end of March, Maurice had found an apartment on Craigslist, his own bedroom in a huge Crown Heights apartment for $600 a month. It seemed too good to be true—I wanted it myself. He called the person who had advertised the room, set up an appointment, and went to speak with the people at Rutgers about the apartment.

The next day, a Tuesday, Maurice called me at work and said he had gotten $600 from Rutgers and was going out to see the apartment and put down the first month's rent if all went well.

*   *   *

I had a bad feeling. Three days later, Maurice had not returned — everything of his, as far as I could see, was still in the apartment, including his toothbrush — I reluctantly called Rutgers.

Rev. Pyrch got on the phone. Yes, she had seen Maurice and given him the $600. Then, she explained, he had come back the next day saying he needed another $600 as a security deposit. She had been a little uneasy, but handed it over, getting a promise from him to return with a receipt and to let her know if he needed help moving.

Now we were both frantic with concern. I figured Maurice had done something really stupid. I immediately called Patricio.

"Hi, my name is Kevin and I'm Maurice's roommate. He hasn't come home for a few days and I was wondering if you had seen him lately."

"Yeah, he was over here a few nights ago but there were a few friends just hanging out and he left around midnight." Patricio didn't seem alarmed.

"Look, I don't know what fun is for you, but Maurice has had substance abuse problems in the past and I'd appreciate it if you didn't do that stuff with him."

"Look, honey, get a hold of yourself," he said. "Maurice is a big boy and I'm sure he can take care of himself."

"You'd better hope so," I replied, and slammed the receiver down.

I then went to the local precinct to see if I could file a missing person's report. No such luck. "He's over 25 and sane. There's nothing we can do about it. He's probably just taking a break," the jaded officer explained.

That Sunday, I agreed to meet with the ministers, deacons, and elders of Rutgers after their worship service.

Middle Church is an intentionally multi-cultural, multi-ethnic congregation. Rutgers, from what I saw during that visit, was mostly white. I couldn't help but think that perhaps white guilt had played a part, that they had been moved and taken in by the plight of a poor black man. The mixed-race Middle Church leadership, on the other hand, had been sympathetic and had even offered some help to Maurice, but many, including Jacqui, had observed his slickness and called him on it. Middle Church hadn't given away the house and the keys to Maurice.

The Rutgers people and I gathered around a table and a light lunch was offered. I explained how I met Maurice and gave a rundown of our life together since then.

I have never met more gracious, kind people in my life. They were out $1200 and their charity case had disappeared with it, and yet one gentleman said, "Well, I hope he uses the money well, perhaps to go back to New Orleans or find family."

"He's just a troubled soul," another woman said tearfully.

By then, I too was in tears. It was a sad, unexpected end to what we had hoped was a road to recovery and responsibility.

On Tuesday, a full week since his disappearance, I started gathering up his clothes and video games and CDs—he had been forever plugged into a Walkman during his jaunts around the city—and boxing them up to give to goodwill. I figured he had taken the money and moved on to another city, hurt that I didn't want to continue living with him.

Still a little suspicious of what he was up to, and his recent associations, I also had the locks changed on the apartment door, to the tune of $400.

He had more stuff than I had imagined, three or four trash bags full, and at last I carted it around the corner to the Salvation Army.

I went into a deep period of mourning for the loss of this sad, unreliable person, and for the uncertainty.

Chapter Eight

The passing weeks did not make things any easier. I tried googling Maurice, looking at my old phone bills for long distance phone numbers he had called, everything. I continued to collect his mail. One day, something came from a hospital. I opened it up. He had been admitted overnight to Columbia Presbyterian in Harlem around the first week of April. I could not read at all what the diagnosis or the problem had been, but it looked serious and the bill was for several thousand dollars. Around the third week of April, there was another odd envelope. I felt no qualms about opening his mail since I hadn't heard from him and wanted to find clues of his whereabouts. It was some kind of check stub for a one-day bartending gig the week before. So he was in town.

Finally, on a Saturday morning in early May, the phone rang and I picked it up.

"Hi Kevin, it's Maurice." He had that same hopeful, lost puppy yearning in his voice that I remembered.

"Maurice! Where the hell are you?" I said, not in an accusatory way, but with joy and relief. "I was so worried about you."

"I'm back in New York. I'm staying at St. Paul's House." He explained that it was a men's shelter in nearby midtown. After a little more small talk, he asked if he could see me.

I offered to treat him to breakfast, so we arranged to meet at a diner on Eighth Avenue.

When I saw Maurice walking toward me, he had that big grin on his face and he was almost bouncing on the sidewalk. We gave each other a big hug. I had never seen him look better. I later figured out that the reason for that was probably because St. Paul's House had a curfew and a strict no-drug policy—so he was clean. His skin looked clearer, softer.

Over bacon and eggs, he explained that the Craigslist ad was a sham and that he was unable to get his money back from, or even find, the person who had taken the initial $600. He had been deeply ashamed and didn't know what to do.

"I was walking across the Brooklyn Bridge and I stood there for a long time wondering if I could crawl across those steel beams so I could jump."

"Why didn't you just call me?" I asked.

"I couldn't. But finally, about a week later, I came back but when I saw you had changed the locks, I figured I was dead to you."

"You could have left a note. I changed the locks because I didn't know where you were and one of the last guys you were hanging out with was that asshole Patricio."

"Yeah," he said, bowing his head to his plate. "He was an asshole and he's out of my life." I suspected a drug deal gone bad. I'm not sure I ever believed the Craigslist scam story—if that had really happened, any reasonable person would have gone back to Rutgers and explained the situation and legal action would have ensued. On the other hand, Maurice was smart but not always reasonable. And he definitely would not want to involve cops in his predicament.

"So, I took the rest of the money and went back to New Orleans," he said. "There was nothing there for me."

That, I knew, was an outright lie. I can't say why I didn't confront him on it or present evidence of the hospital stay or the bartending job—probably I was ashamed of my own behavior in opening his mail. I let it slide. I was crossing that fine line between helping and enabling with ease by now.

In any case, he was at St. Paul's House and, as I said, seemed healthy and in a disciplined lifestyle.

He explained to me how things were at St. Paul's. The men staying there each had their own locker. Breakfast was at eight and after that, the men had to leave for the day. They were to return by nine o'clock at night or lose their bed and not be allowed back to St. Paul's.

Maurice had proven himself quite valuable in the few weeks he had been there. He said he was the most disciplined among that group of men, many of them chronically homeless for long periods of time. He got up early and helped prepare the set-up for breakfast. It was hard for me to imagine that Maurice, at such a low point, could be the king somewhere else.

"I could never live the rest of my life like this," he said, noting the sadness of those men competing to hold onto their beds at St. Paul's. Even there, there was a hierarchy of power and seniority.

St. Paul's gave him a job cleaning and painting a vacant studio apartment on West 51st Street, preparing it for its next tenant. He invited me to that apartment, where he would be working by himself the following Monday, for a picnic lunch.

Before we left each other, he asked one favor. "Chicago is playing at Radio City Music Hall next week. I would love to go. Do you think this could be an early birthday present for me?" His birthday was not until late June.

The nerve of him! What he had put me through with six weeks of worry, changing the locks, screwing over Rutgers, bagging and getting rid of his stuff . . .

"I'll think about it," I said.

"Is it okay if I come by and pick up some of my stuff?"

Oh boy. "Maurice, I gave your stuff to goodwill. After a couple of weeks, I had no idea I'd ever see you again."

His face fell. "Everything?"

I nodded. "I'm so sorry. Why didn't you call?"

"Like I said, after the locks were changed, I felt the lowest of low."

Now I felt guilty. Of course, I would take him to the Chicago concert. His inexplicable hold over me was complete. He really was like my child in so many ways, and I'm not sure I was passing the parenting test.

On Monday afternoon, I went over to the apartment he had been working on for a picnic. He had provided the food and had laid out a dropcloth across the hardwood floor, where we would eat.

It almost felt like a first date and, indeed, Maurice seemed to be a new person. I asked if he had any "ins" to get me the apartment, and he talked about his future. All the pain of the previous six weeks and the loss of all his clothes had been forgotten.

Things seemed to be on the upswing again and I was happy to have him back in my life. I could have done the right thing and called the people at Rutgers to tell them he was back, but I was afraid and ashamed: afraid they'd demand the money back from him, which he clearly didn't have, and ashamed that I was embarking on this friendship again, without holding him accountable to his actions.

The following Tuesday night, we met and walked over to Radio City Music Hall for the Chicago concert. He had to get special permission from St. Paul's House to stay out late so that he could be allowed to come back to the shelter after "lights out."

Because I had gotten the tickets late and had to go with what I could afford, we ended up in the rear mezzanine—the nosebleed section. It didn't matter; he was very grateful and the acoustics were terrific.

As soon the strains of "Does Anybody Really Know What Time It Is" were heard, Maurice was on his feet. Chicago, most popular during the '70s, had a mostly older, white audience, it seemed, so nearly everyone around us politely stayed seated. This drove Maurice nuts.

He couldn't stop himself: his head would bop back and forth, the fingers would play imaginary chords or play notes on a trumpet. He loved that Chicago horn section! After a few songs, he couldn't take it anymore. "Come on, white people!" he urged with that big game show host grin on his face, "Get on your feet!"

This seemed to be all the encouragement they needed, and many happily got to their feet. He was no longer dancing alone.

Strangely, I had spent years trying to make a career out of music, but he clearly loved just listening to music more than I did and never had the opportunity to put any of that love to practical use.

That was a lesson for me. Music always remained elusive and magical for him, and it had become a chore for me.

We left on a high from the concert. We stopped at a Duane Reade so he could pick up a few things. He didn't want to go back to St. Paul's House but he knew he had to. He gave me a long hug and thanked me for the birthday gift.

It was only early May; no doubt, there would be another gift for his real birthday.

Chapter Nine

October 7, 1994

Within an hour of being brought to the emergency room, I was told that the suspect who had stabbed me had been caught. They wanted to bring him in for me to identify. Subtext: In case I didn't make it, they wanted a positive ID.

Two cops ushered him into the room as I lay there, exhausted. The guy stood there between the two cops. He said nothing, but offered a meek, puppy dog smile. He wore a white windbreaker – why hadn't I noticed that before? It didn't matter.

"That's him," I said in a monotone.

They took him away. That was it.

It wasn't nearly as dramatic as what you'd see on a television show.

Soon after that, my friend Kura showed up. Kura always had a show-stopping smile and a short bob of sunny blonde hair. That look made her perfectly suitable to play the angel that night. She lived nearby and had been the one to pick up the phone from that odd, late night call from the police. In such cases, I later learned, the police won't leave a message on a machine. They had found her number in the day planner in my backpack. Kura had the unenviable task of calling my parents and she basically became the center of operations for the next several days.

My condition stabilized, but that first night I was kept near the emergency room, awaiting a regular room. I didn't sleep much, hearing the agonizing screams of a gunshot victim brought in in the middle of the night and otherwise contemplating what I had just survived.

The night nurse kept coming in to check on me. She had such a soothing voice and caring manner, one of those everyday heroes we never hear about on the news.

"Isn't it something?" She asked me. "In one minute, your whole life can change."

I was still in shock. How had this happened? Was I really here, or would I wake up in my bed at home?

How would my life change?

Chapter Ten

St. Paul's House was being a good parent. With the strict curfew, the odd jobs offered with a small stipend, and the days free with the expectation that the men would look for employment, Maurice's behavior was kept in check. He could not get into trouble or he would lose his bed.

However, it could not have been an easy life and during our visits, his complaints grew louder and more frequent.

"One of the guys was sick last night, short of breath, and the rest of us were begging the authorities to get him to a doctor. They basically just said, 'He'll be all right; this happens all the time.' They are so jaded to the suffering in there!"

Or this: "Those priests don't care about any of our problems. To them, it has just become a job of filling the beds and making sure everything is run efficiently. They don't care about the circumstances that got us there."

He told me there were men who had been at St. Paul's House for *years*. "I would rather die than spend the rest of my life in there." To him, after a couple of months, it became like a prison — and he wanted out.

One night I was sitting in my apartment and boredom got the best of me. I sat at my computer and googled Maurice once again. The only thing that came up was what I had found before, his graduation from a high school in Syracuse, New York.

I decided to investigate further, to sate my curiosity once and for all. I pulled out my credit card and charged $39 to one of those sites that specializes in criminal background checks. Within hours, I got the results.

The offenses weren't terrible, certainly not violent behavior. However, my eyes widened in panicked disbelief: breaking and entering and grand theft when he was about twenty, reckless driving, writing a bad check, forgery, passing counterfeit bills, cocaine possession, parole violation. These latter charges all occurred in the '90s; the last offense was another bad check in 2002. There had been a few stints in prison, six months here, a year there. He had lived his early adult years in Dade County, Florida, and most of the '90s and beyond in Richmond, Virginia. That much he had told me, but he left out those other pesky details.

I let Maurice stay in my apartment during the days on the weekends when there wasn't much job-hunting to be done. Otherwise, he'd have to stay on the streets until St. Paul's House opened again at eight o'clock. He repaid my kindness by whipping up a gourmet meal on a Sunday afternoon. He could create an astonishing meal out of scraps. As one who hates to cook, this became a valued service and a way in which he could give back to me.

After one such meal, I was ready to confront him. I looked him straight in the eyes. "You stole that credit card from me last winter, didn't you?"

This time, he came clean. "Yes. After I saw how much I had hurt you, I vowed I would never do anything like that again."

"Why didn't you tell me?"

"Well, it seemed to be over and I knew I wasn't going to go there again." He paused before continuing. "But after I left in March, when I came back a week later to pick up my clothes and you had changed the locks, I knew I had lost your trust and that almost killed me." That, and my subsequent removal of all his clothes and CDs, had been a big blow to him even after we'd reconciled.

"Without trust, there is nothing," I told him. I walked over to my desk and retrieved the National Criminal Records Report, a few pages long. "I did a little research last night and came up with your criminal background."

His head fell, defeated. But then the completely unexpected: he looked up and smiled, his dark eyes twinkling. "That must have freaked the hell out of you."

"It did," I said evenly, but looking at him grinning at me, I couldn't remain the stern parent for long. I started laughing and then he joined in. "You should have seen my eyes as I was scanning down the pages," I howled. "They were completely bugging out!" I was now crying with laughter and he was right there with me. With Maurice and me, when things were really bad—as they often were—we found solace in laughter. What else was there to do? Enough tears had already been shed in our lives.

After the laughter subsided, I continued. "But seriously, Maurice. You no longer have to hide shit from me. Your past is your past and you can't change that. But you can change the future. But if you can't trust your best friend, what help can you possibly get for yourself?"

"And what about you?" he countered. "What made you do a criminal background check on me?"

I was speechless; embarrassed. In that moment, I actually thought his point about my lack of trust had equal weight to my own. He knew how to make me feel guilty, and then sorry. And how to make me remain committed to him.

Nevertheless, I'm a firm believer in a master plan. Many would surely say to me, "What the hell were you thinking?" A valid question. But the fact is that if I had done a criminal background check on him back in October, I would have never invited him to stay with me.

And that would have robbed both of us of a life-changing experience, which would have been a greater crime. The master plan was bigger than my fears.

Chapter Eleven

I made the mistake of second guessing the long-term caretaking skills that St. Paul's House had developed over the years, however ghastly living there must have been. As much as he complained about it, staying there was keeping him on a tight leash. My decision to let him stay at my place on Saturdays and Sundays, even while I was not there, loosened that leash.

One night I had a dinner date with someone and afterwards I invited him over for a nightcap. When we walked in, Maurice jumped up from the bed in surprise.

It was around midnight. "What are you doing here?" I asked him, perturbed, while at the same time introducing him to my date, who certainly had a look of surprise on his face.

"I'm sorry, I'm going, I'm going!" Maurice said, grabbing his stuff and heading out the door. I no longer had no worries about where he might be headed; he seemed to have an endless supply of overnight options.

It was an odd moment trying to explain to my date that this guy that had fallen asleep on my bed was *not* my lover. After a quick drink, my date was gone, never to be seen again.

Naturally, Maurice did not come back the next morning and I had no way of getting hold of him.

At last, he called on Sunday afternoon. "I lost my room at St. Paul's," he explained, sounding sad and pathetic.

"You knew you had to be back by nine o'clock." I was getting good at remonstration.

"I know. I fell asleep. What's worse is they wouldn't let me back in to get my stuff. They cut the lock on my locker and threw out my stuff." There wasn't a lot of stuff at that point, but now he was down to the clothes on his back. Again.

To make matters worse, he had an upcoming interview on Tuesday at R.R. Donnelley, a prestigious printing firm. I had secured him a contact for that. I had been proofreading there and met a customer service representative, who was responsible for getting food and ordering cars for the clients—making the client comfortable, basically. Anyway, that guy gave me the information to contact his boss, and said we could use his name. Customer service would be a perfect job for Maurice. He needed that job.

There was no time for reprisals at the moment. "Come home," I told him, unaware I had used the word 'home' to refer to my place. "We'll go to the Salvation Army and get you some clothes for your interview."

He came back to West 45th Street. He made a nice Sunday dinner from whatever meager ingredients I had in my cupboard. We made a date to hit the nearby Salvation Army the next day after I got home from work.

The trip to the Salvation Army and nearby thrift shops that Monday was one of my favorite times with Maurice. For about thirty dollars—all I could spare—we bargained and cajoled our way to two big bags full of clothes: shirts, ties, socks, and slacks. It was an unbelievable bounty for which we were both rightly proud. We were laughing as we got back to the apartment and unpacked our loot and Maurice modeled some of the shirts and ties. He would be all set for the interview.

Tuesday night, he returned home and I was eagerly waiting. "How did the interview go?" I asked him.

His eyes grew wide. "That place is unbelievable," he said to me in awed, hushed tones. He was acting as if he didn't deserve a place like that.

"Well, let's say our prayers," I said.

"Right now," he agreed. With that, we held hands and he offered up a sincere childlike prayer for help. It was moments like that that completely disarmed me.

A few days later, R.R. Donnelley called. They wanted to see him for a second interview. We jumped up and down around the room.

Although the interview went well, David, the manager there, told him they didn't have anything open at the moment, but that Patty, with whom he'd had a second interview, liked him very much. "We need to find him something," she had apparently told David. R.R. Donnelley had, like so many, fallen for the charms of Maurice at his best.

Nothing happened immediately at R.R. Donnelley, but I think the interviews gave Maurice much-needed confidence. Before the end of the summer, he secured a job at a place called Focus Pointe on Madison Avenue. The work was similar: providing customer service to clients and people who came in to do market research interviews for the day. It was a steady three or four days a week in a corporate atmosphere, an amazing job for him.

Maurice had told me he had a degree in broadcasting from the University of Rochester and had, at various times during his life, worked at CNN in Atlanta and for Disney in Florida. He also boasted of working more recently at the prestigious Capitol Club in Richmond and Signatures Restaurant in Washington, DC, as well as the Bon Temps Café in New Orleans in the summer of 2005. All of those restaurants were included on his resume. The problem was that all of those restaurants had since closed, so there was no way to check. However, he was a big fan of the Food Channel (he once said Paula Deen was "the only black woman" on that channel and that they needed more) and during one of the *Iron Chef* contests, he blurted out, "That's so and so! He was my boss at Signatures!" I don't remember the name now, but it sounded authentic enough to me.

What was clear to anyone who met Maurice was that he was highly intelligent and it would not have been out of the question for him to have worked at any of those places. He not only had ease with food and drink, presentation as well as preparation, but he was addicted to NPR and CNN and could talk current issues — local, national and international — with anyone.

He was a case study in contradictions. His favorite show was *Law and Order*, especially the original and *SVU* versions. Also, at church, he could immediately turn to a passage in the Bible without pause and follow along with the reading. In addition to Chicago and the Commodores, his favorite artist was Keith Green, a Christian artist of our college years, the early '80s, who had died in a plane crash at a tragically young age. Maurice could still sing Green's songs and one of my best gifts to him was finding and ordering one of Green's CDs from Amazon.

His favorite fictional character was Batman and he collected a lot of Batman memorabilia. Not only did he lose his parents at a young age as Batman had, but he had a dual nature: first, at heart, a good, helpful disposition; and second, that dark, solitary side. I think his life's challenge was to find a way to reconcile those parts.

My challenge was perhaps the same—for myself, not him.

I chose to focus on the best side of his contradictory nature. Some immediately saw the bad side and could not be convinced otherwise, forever suspicious of him and not wanting to get to know him. It was their loss; it was his loss.

My willful blindness to his faults was certainly one of my shortcomings. On the other hand, he needed a person he could trust and who could have faith in him. My willful blindness kept the relationship going, for better or for worse.

Chapter Twelve

The interview with R.R. Donnelley and job at Focus Pointe were turning points in my relationship with Maurice, as well as a boost in his self-confidence. He was definitely becoming a great friend with whom I spent a lot of my time.

In the middle of that summer, my friend Wayne called me and told me the apartment upstairs in his building had become available. It was basically a two-family tenement building in the Bay Ridge section of Brooklyn. The landlord lived out of state, so that meant Wayne and his partner Hector lived on the second floor, a deli occupied the first floor, and I—or we—would have the third floor. It was five rooms compared to the two rooms I had in Manhattan, and for the same price. The catch was, for anyone who has been a Manhattanite, that it was Brooklyn. Goodbye to the convenience of walking all over town or quick subway rides or reasonable cab fares.

Nevertheless, I told Wayne I would come out to see it and I would bring along Maurice. With the uptick in his luck, I was willing to commit to the roommate arrangement.

It was a Saturday in mid-July when we took the long ride out there on the R train. We rang the doorbell to Wayne's apartment and he brought us up to his place and we had a few minutes of chitchat before he showed us the empty apartment.

The apartment was long and narrow, stretching from the front to the back of the building. The layout was slightly different than theirs. We didn't have the extra walk-in closet that Hector was able to fashion into an office, and we had a built-in wall that gave it a more closed-off feeling. Still, there was more than ample closet and storage space, a nice bathroom, a large bedroom, a living room and dining area, as well as a kitchen. The second bedroom, adjacent to the large one facing the street, was impractical: double doors on one side and two closets against one wall prevented putting a double bed in there.

All in all, though, we were pretty impressed. Maurice was not as bothered by the commute as I was, with all my activities in the city. Wayne took us on a tour of the neighborhood and we walked all the way down to the bay where we could see the Verrazano Bridge and Statue of Liberty in the distance. I thought all the millionaires in New York lived in Manhattan but that was clearly not the case, as we saw street after street of great stone houses and elaborate gardens. It was old-money Italian, we were told, although Wayne noted that there were a lot of Middle Eastern and Asian people in the neighborhood as well.

"Not a lot of black people," Maurice commented to me privately. I agreed.

Returning from the waterfront, we met Hector, who had arrived home, and the four of us went to a nearby restaurant for dinner. It was dark by the time they walked us south on 3rd Avenue to show us all the shops and restaurants before pointing us to the Bay Ridge Avenue subway stop.

I was considering one other apartment, an L-shaped one bedroom on West 152nd Street in Manhattan, within walking distance of City College. Soon after our trip to Bay Ridge, I took Maurice up there one evening to check it out. I thought for sure he would prefer Harlem, being more comfortable in a predominantly black neighborhood.

As soon as we turned onto West 152nd, the street was lively with folks playing music on their stoops and we got a waft of marijuana smoke as we passed a huddle of young people.

"Don't take this apartment," he said with conviction, before we had even reached the building.

"What are you talking about?" I asked. "These people are just hanging out. This doesn't scare me."

"You don't need this. Bay Ridge is more peaceful. I don't want you walking through this every night."

He was so certain, that we turned around and headed back before even looking at the apartment. As I thought about it, I believe he was more speaking about his own fears rather than mine; although he didn't like the racial make-up of Bay Ridge, he'd rather have taken his chances there than to be amidst whatever temptations lurked for him on the streets of Harlem.

The summer went on rather uneventfully.

I made a trip to Montreal over the Fourth of July weekend and an annual trip with my old friends to Ogunquit, Maine, in August. I still did not consider Maurice a "partner" and I felt I was doing enough for him that I felt resentful about the possibility of inviting him on those trips and picking up payment for most of his weekend expenses. Still, while I was away, I felt a pang of loneliness with my old friends and found myself calling Maurice to "see how things were going" for him in New York. The truth was, I missed him.

In mid-August, I called a man-with-a-van service and the three of us packed as much stuff as possible in it to make a trip out to Bay Ridge. Although I lived in a Manhattan studio, I had learned how to use space well, so I was shocked by how much I had accumulated over twelve years of living there. Even with all the stuff we carted in the van that day, it still looked as if nothing had changed in my Manhattan studio.

That day in Bay Ridge, we decided to take a walk around the neighborhood, our main destination being Jennifer Convertibles and PC Richards, where I would buy a sofa, chair, and TV. For whatever reason—not something I even gave a thought to—I was wearing a pink polo shirt that day.

"Did you have to wear pink?" Maurice asked, as we stepped out onto the sidewalk along 3rd Avenue.

"Are you ashamed to be seen with me?" I laughed and tried to put my arm around his shoulders.

"Get away from me," he warned with a smile, putting up his fists in a stance of mock toughness. "You know I could care less what anybody is, but maybe you could ease your way into the neighborhood before you brought out the flaming colors."

"Oh, for God's sake, you are ridiculous!"

"Uh huh," he said, his voice turning to exaggerated ghetto slang. "It's bad enough I'm a brother out here, but I don't need the double whammy of being strange fruit!" We laughed uneasily at his gallows-humor reference.

Trying to decide on furniture at Jennifer Convertibles was a lot of fun. We sat on different sofas, argued about colors, and engaged the handsome, friendly Hispanic salesperson with many questions. We finally decided on a tan sofa and matching chair and arranged for delivery on the Tuesday after the move.

Maurice made sure to get the salesperson's card as we left. "Ooh, I gotta make sure to come back here again and ask Jonathan some more questions," he said. He had been embarrassed by my pink shirt, but he was far more flirtatious than I was when there was an actual contact to be made, and in this case with someone who probably wasn't even gay, and about half our age.

Moving day was scheduled for Monday, August 29, 2006 — the one-year anniversary of Hurricane Katrina. I had decided that the living room at the back of the apartment would be more suitable for his bedroom and I would use the small room next to mine as an office. Maurice agreed; he would sleep on the convertible sofa. I could still not give a firm commitment to a living arrangement. The idea was for Maurice to live with me "until he got back on his feet." When he left, all of that new living room furniture would still be mine.

Maurice and I planned to spend the weekend before the movers arrived boxing up more stuff and throwing away bags and bags of trash.

That Thursday night, Maurice and I had an intimate moment over dinner. I grasped his hand across the table. "I need you, Maurice. I'm realizing now how much you have given to me."

"I need you too," he said. "This is going to be a new beginning for us."

It was true: A big change was coming and, although I would not miss the cramped, roach-filled studio with sloping floors, it was a neighborhood I had called home for twelve years. And although he didn't say so, I wondered if Maurice was feeling the uncertainty of losing another home or the possibility that I would abandon him once I got to Brooklyn.

Spontaneously, we each said a simple prayer, thanking God for our friendship and what we had, and asking for His guidance during this time of transition.

We talked long into the night. I had never felt so close to him.

Chapter Thirteen

October 1994

I had a steady stream of visitors coming to see me in the hospital the day after the stabbing. To my surprise, the story had been on the news that morning. My attacker was a wannabe serial killer who had randomly attacked two other guys earlier that same week. Surprisingly, we had all survived.

I heard from friends I hadn't spoken to in years. There would be no sleep for me that day. Also, those were the days before patient privacy laws had been passed, so I was visited by reporters from all the major dailies. The next day, a photo of me in the hospital bed took up nearly an entire page in the Post. Slow news day, I guess.

My father called early in the afternoon. He told me he would man the phones at home but that my mother and sister were on their way. My guess is that, having lost his mother at age twelve, he was never good at dealing with hospitals and illness. Even so, it would be a long time before I could forgive him for not coming and, instead, sending his wife and daughter. I realized that day that women are stronger than men when it comes to a real crisis, matters of life and death.

When Audrey, a nurse, came into my room, I saw a side of her I had never seen before. She was immediately grilling the nurses about what I was being given and how often. They definitely stepped it up a notch after they met her.

My mother, a quiet, pious woman by nature, also rose to the occasion. A woman who could easily cry over an episode of **Lassie***, she knew how to be a subdued, strong lion when needed the most.*

Those days after the stabbing were rather easy for me. I was getting lots of attention and being waited on hand and foot.

But after the news died down and my friends went back to their lives and my mother and sister went back to Massachusetts, the worst days of the ordeal were about to set in.

Some friends had told me how lucky I was to be alive, and the doctor told me the same thing: "The knife slid in between your heart and lung, about a quarter inch of space on each side. If it had moved either way, you probably wouldn't be here today."

I wasn't ready to feel lucky. The way I saw it, there were seven million people in New York City and only a small handful had been violently assaulted the same night I was. That was luck? If I had not stopped at the corner deli to get ice cream, I would have been home in my apartment and never seen or heard of my attacker, Elie Granger.

With those odds, how come I couldn't win the lottery?

I was angry that I had worked so hard for so long for little reward, and that this asshole stabbed me in the heart, so to speak, when I took a moment to let my guard down and talk to a stranger.

I had been living paycheck to paycheck as it was. I didn't feel like going through a lengthy recovery and starting over yet again. Why couldn't the miserable bastard have finished the job he started so I wouldn't have to keep working so hard?

*   *   *

A little over a week after the near-deadly assault, I was back at my job as a proofreader at the downtown law firm of Haight, Garder, Poor & Havens. Believe me, I didn't want to go back, but I was only part-time and I couldn't survive on disability pay even if I'd wanted to.

"You're making the rest of us look bad," Margaret, my supervisor, told me.

I also went back to my psychotherapist. Rafe was the most intelligent, understanding therapist in the world — I was even in a weekly group that he facilitated — but this latest ordeal seemed like something out of even his realm of experience. I didn't want to talk to him, didn't want to talk to the group. This was my own pity party and if you hadn't been the victim of a violent crime, there was nothing you could say to me.

Despite the numbing rage inside of me, I was as determined as I ever was. I had a show scheduled in November and nothing was going to stop me from doing it. I remember my friend Charlie, when he visited me in the hospital, was the only person who made me laugh when he came up to my bedside and whispered conspiratorially, "Dahling, think of the publicity!"

Why shouldn't I try to squeeze some lemonade out of this lemon?

I started sending out press kits to everyone I could think of. I had a friend who was working for New York Newsday *and that contact helped me get an interview with one of the staff writers.*

The reporter called me one night and we had a long conversation. I was in a chipper mood — I wasn't about to show her that the stabbing had knocked me down — and joked with her about my bad-luck career up to that point. At the end of the interview, I invited her to the show.

A couple of days later, on the eve of the first show, the feature appeared in Newsday, *complete with a big close-up headshot. It so happened that it was the same morning as my therapy appointment when I picked up the paper.*

The tacky headline was "Singer Takes Another Stab at Success." What followed was a snarky piece — the writer had turned my tragedy into an attempt at humor. She told of my sending out flashy tabloid cut-outs about my stabbing ordeal. She revealed my bitchy comments about the cheesy cabaret music scene. Worst of all, she compared me to Kato Kaelin, the notorious houseboy in the O.J. Simpson murder case — an opportunist capitalizing on a tragedy.

Of course, the difference was that I was not covering up someone else's murder. I was the victim here. I had worked hard all my life. She didn't see the inspiration in my story — which is what I tried to convey to her — but only the humor of some no-talent guy going for broke. I had been stabbed in the front a few weeks before; now she had stabbed me in the back. I honestly don't know which felt worse. For some journalists, the cleverness of the story wins out over truth. It wouldn't be the last time I'd be assaulted by the press.

I cried in Rafe's office as I showed him the article of my betrayal at the hands of the media. He tried to tell me the old cliché that any publicity was good publicity. It's the only time he was ever completely wrong about something and it was then I knew that I was on my own with the crime victim ordeal. Nobody could understand.

Nobody ever could understand. It's the way I survived high school. It's the way I survived dating discomforts. It's the way I carved out a performing career. It's what made me a good teacher, being a creative leader in front of a classroom, not having to collaborate with colleagues. In my world, "I" always trumped "we." I was more my father than my mother.

I was finding a way to shut down Rafe and go back to the only way I knew — going solo.

Naturally, the Newsday *reporter never came to my show to see if I had any talent. For her, it was on to the next story, never mind the carnage she left behind. It was probably for the best anyway. I put on a brave face and got through the songs and probably did a defiant speech about "moving on and being strong" but the truth is, the ordeal was still too recent. I was too raw. I had a decent-sized audience of friends who came out to support me, but they were polite at best as I tried to rally myself to the occasion. In fact, I was in such a state of numbness that to this day I can't tell you what I sang or spoke of during that show.*

People smiling at you, then stabbing you. Is this what life was about? I didn't know if I would ever trust anyone again.

Chapter Fourteen

Here I was, finishing a master's degree, heavily involved with my church, enjoying lots of friends after living in New York City for twenty years, and for the most part taking care of this person I had invited in. Yet, for all that I had, I did not have one special person in my life who cared about me on a day-to-day basis and loved me unconditionally, no matter what I was doing or how much money I was making. In my mid-forties, I still wondered where I had gone wrong and if it was too late for some good things that most took for granted.

I went to work on Friday and when I returned home in the evening, Maurice was not home. No big problem, we still had all of Saturday and Sunday to get the work done.

However, when Maurice stayed out all night on Friday, my anger came to a boil. I didn't need him in bed all day recovering from "whatever" as I tried to clean while going up and down four flights of stairs with bags of trash. On Saturday, I slowly and reluctantly began the process without him. As usual for him on these weekend benders, he hadn't called.

On Sunday, he still wasn't home. I was livid. This was too much work for one person and it was too late for me to recruit any of my other friends. And, furthermore, what would they think, coming over to help me pack while Maurice was out partying somewhere.

By Monday, Maurice still hadn't shown up and the movers were due at about noon. I looked around the apartment and there was still much work to be done. What could I do? I just had to soldier on.

I don't know how I did what I did that day. Up and down, up and down those stairs until I was out of breath and my calves and thighs ached. My neighbors surely hated me because the sidewalk out front had been transformed into a mountain of garbage bags. By the time the four movers arrived, I was on a mission. I knew if I stopped to rest, I would never get up again, so I became a demanding boss, urging them to keep going and I myself — twice the age of most of the guys — was right there with them, hauling boxes down the stairs. The last thing to go was the mattress and box spring; I wasn't taking it because the new apartment, previously occupied by the owners, already had a fairly new queen-sized bed.

In my sweat-soaked t-shirt, after the last item had been loaded onto the truck, I made my way to the subway for the long commute to Bay Ridge, unsure if I would beat the movers who were winding their way through the traffic with the truck.

As it turned out, I beat them by a long shot. The movers got lost — couldn't figure out how to get to Bay Ridge even with a map. I was exhausted and furious. I called the company and told the dispatcher I didn't want to pay for the extra hour they were on the road.

When, at last, they arrived, I was right there to pitch in with moving the things upstairs — this time, thankfully, only two flights. The guys kept stopping intermittently to have a beer or bottle of water, but I kept going—and I don't think they were too happy with my dogged determination.

When all was said and done, I had to go to a nearby ATM to get more money and, with tip, the move had cost me close to a thousand bucks. I was completely broke as I was about to start my new life in Brooklyn.

But for the moment, all I could think about was my sheer exhaustion. My body had never experienced such physical exertion—six hours of hauling heavy boxes and bags up and down, all told, six flights of stairs. I may as well have run a marathon or participated in a decathlon. I could see why movers, doing this daily, would need a little break now and then.

Wayne and Hector popped by when they got home from work that night and, naturally, asked where Maurice was.

"He never showed up today. I don't know where he is, but I'm through with him. I've never worked so hard in my life. He can go back to living on the fucking streets for all I care."

It took that kind of exhaustion and fury for me to abandon the pretense that all was well with Maurice. I could have said, out of my own shame, "Oh, he had to work today." Then I would have figured out how to deal with him on my own, leaving others out of the private shame of my relationship. I finally told the truth to an outsider.

They concurred and I absolutely meant what I said. I was miles beyond angry. He had become dead to me. Exactly what Maurice had been afraid of months before when I switched the locks—he was dead to me. He had pushed me to my absolute limit. Who else would put up with this shit? I was too drained to even contemplate forgiveness for whatever lame excuse he might have had, if he even dared to show up at my door.

*   *   *

Maurice dared to show up at my door.

Hector called me on my cellphone a little after eight on Tuesday morning. I stumbled out of bed and pushed my way through boxes to get to it and stop that annoying ring.

"Kevin, I'm sorry to tell you this, but I let Maurice into the building a little while ago. He buzzed our apartment, maybe you couldn't hear him. I went down and opened the door and he came in. I didn't know what to do." Hector had been obviously too scared to stop him.

"It's okay," I said. "So where is he?"

"Well, I assumed you let him in and everything was fine. But I just left for work and I looked up and saw him sleeping on the floor outside your door."

"Oh, for Christ's sake!"

"I'm still out on the sidewalk. Do you want to me to stick around for a few minutes in case you need me? Should we call the police?"

"No, it's okay. He's not dangerous, just pathetic," I told him.

"Are you going to let him in?"

"Yes, I'll talk to him." I had a feeling that was not the answer Hector wanted to hear.

"Okay," he said hesitantly.

"Really, Hector, I'll be fine. Go to work."

I took a deep breath and braced for the coming confrontation. The thing is, I was still bone-tired. I'd hit the pillow the night before and fell into an instant deep sleep, and was still partially submerged. I didn't have the energy for fireworks.

I opened the door to the hallway. Maurice, in his post-bender fetal position of shame, peeked up.

"Come on in."

Wordlessly, he came in and sat down on a folding chair in the living room and I did the same a few feet away.

"I'm sorry," was all he could say.

"And?"

"I have to work this afternoon." He was still at Focus Pointe; only three days a week, but it was something.

"Well, your clothes are here somewhere," I said, gesturing to the mountain of boxes and suitcases.

"I need a place to live."

"Really? What a shocker," I said. "Maybe you should have thought of that before going on your weekend party spree."

"I was depressed. It was the anniversary of Katrina."

"And unlike last year, this year you had a place to go, a place to live. And someone who cared about you." I was intentionally using the past tense verbs, for effect. I was just warming up. "Do you have any idea what I've been through for the past few days? By myself, cleaning out that entire apartment. Thirty bags of trash brought down to the street, countless boxes up and down stairs, six hours of moving at a cost of a thousand dollars. And you recently helped me pick out living room furniture and a TV set, all of which I paid for. You paid for nothing and you did nothing to help. I am exhausted beyond belief and I have to start teaching tomorrow. I have nothing to say to you."

"I'm sorry," he repeated.

"Sorry doesn't begin to cover it."

"I need a place to live." He didn't seem to have any other line of defense.

"I need to think about that," I said, glad that I hadn't given him a set of keys. "You may take a shower and clean yourself up. Then take a bag of clothes, whatever you need. Come back next weekend and we'll talk again."

"I don't know where to go. I can't go to work without a place to live." He wasn't crying—probably just as tired as I was—but he was begging. I really didn't want him to lose that job, but I couldn't just let him back in without punishment. No friend had ever done anything so hurtful to me.

"Five days. You've done it before, you can do it again. Now go clean yourself up and get out of here."

He slowly found his things and went into the bathroom. I thought I heard him sobbing while he was in the shower, but I walked away and dried my own tears. I couldn't back down.

That night, Wayne and Hector came up to get the scoop. "I kicked him out, but told him I'd talk to him next week."

They regarded me with a doubtful look.

"Look, he does have a job and he's a really nice guy. He's just troubled, possibly manic-depressive. He was depressed because it was the anniversary of Katrina and here he was being upended again." I know they were thinking I was out of my mind, and there may have been some truth to that. Interestingly, too, in the spur of the moment and in need of an excuse, I, for the first time, suggested Maurice might have a mental illness. To me, that was less shameful and easier to deal with than his being simply an asshole.

"Well, even if he's a good guy, if he has mental problems, is it really a good idea for us to have him in the building?" Hector asked. It seemed to me it was all about Hector's comfort level—and why not? He lived downstairs. The situation wasn't exactly getting me off on the right foot as a new tenant, or as a longtime friend to both of them.

"I haven't made a decision," I said, although I knew I'd take him back. "But rest assured, if he lives here, he will be helping me with rent and I can definitely handle him."

Having been through times both good and bad with Maurice over the previous year, I was able to forgive even this worst offense. Nothing he did was out of malice, I thought. He had self-destructive habits, often masked in bravado. But was it due to a mental disorder or immaturity? Probably both. Making guesses without fully knowing, I wanted to keep trying with him. His heart was good, and I felt thatwas enough.

Without that same emotional investment, however, Wayne and Hector were never able to forgive Maurice. For them, he became the stranger upstairs who lived with Kevin. I can't blame them for behaving that way, but it was a shame because he needed all the friends he could get. I was blaming them for not taking him on as a friend. Still, why would they befriend someone who, in their minds, showed a lack of judgment as well as a lack of respect for me?

I had chosen the difficult path to love the unlovable. Why was I surprised that so few others would take up my cause?

Chapter Fifteen

When Maurice returned the following Sunday, I let him back in, but with a strict set of rules: pay the rent, no drugs, no more lost weekends without a call. I also asked him where he had spent the previous week.

All he said was, "You don't want to know."

Surprisingly, Maurice had held onto his job at Focus Pointe, although he warned me that a new manager had been hired who didn't seem to like him, and he feared his hours would keep getting cut back. I feared it was back to Maurice's pattern of not trusting a boss.

I told him that now that he was settling into a new home, he could begin to look around for other work.

And a real home it was. The Bay Ridge apartment was a luxury for both of us: a floor-through with five rooms and recently remodeled bathroom. The second bedroom was tiny and you had to walk through it to get to mine, so I made that into an office and set up all my computer equipment and bookshelves there. Maurice's bedroom would actually be the living room, with the sleep sofa as his bed. I often told him he got the better deal because it usually gave him first dibs on the remote control and what would be watched on television. Best of all, the living room had a double-width window. There was a tree nearby and also, during the summer months, ivy crept up the back of the building and over much of that window, so when lying on the couch, one could look out through the sheer green curtains into a sea of plant life. Maurice told me he found a lot of peace staring out into that greenery, as lush as any he'd seen in the South.

Maurice loved the couch, but giving him the couch instead of a real bed was, I realized, a way for me to lessen my own commitment, in case the problems continued. It is easier to kick out someone who lives on your couch than someone who has a real bedroom. Sadly, it was enough of a commitment for him—as much as he was used to, anyway.

The fall of 2006 was probably the best time in my friendship with Maurice. He was working, albeit part-time, and felt as if he had a real home since God-knows-when. We went to the local Salvation Army store and picked up kitchen gadgets so he could pursue his passion for cooking. It didn't take long for me to get used to having home-cooked meals when I returned from a long day at work, school, or church activities. Most of them were high-cal—fried chicken, shrimp jambalaya, ribs—so, even though I made time to hit the gym three times a week, the weight began to pile on my midsection.

I also think Bay Ridge was far enough off the beaten path that he was less tempted to make the trip to Manhattan to find troublesome friends. Bay Ridge residents had a low tolerance for crime and were perhaps more suspicious of people of color than other urban neighborhoods, so he had to remain on his best behavior there. That brought some stability to his life and, therefore, mine.

Columbus Day in October was an Indian summer kind of day and, oddly, I hadn't made time to do anything with my day off. We decided to take the train to Coney Island, walk on the boardwalk, and maybe have a picnic.

Despite the warm weather, there weren't a lot of people there that day. We strolled along the boardwalk while engaging in simple observations about our surroundings, looking out at the blue horizon where sky met sea. I was in a rare state of relaxed "being"—not thinking of the past, not thinking of what I had to do in the future. When I allowed it, Maurice could bring that out in me: a sense of not worrying, living in the moment, enjoying another person's company for the sake of it.

We walked up to Brighton Beach and out to the streets to try to find food for lunch among the Russian bakeries and delicatessens. It wasn't easy because there weren't any familiar fast food places or lunch spots, but we finally found some local treats and went back to the boardwalk.

We sat on a bench looking out at the ocean and didn't say much. I had to keep turning away: even wearing sunglasses, tears kept falling from my eyes and I'd surreptitiously wipe them away. I was happy, *happy*! I couldn't explain it: I had nothing that I thought I needed for happiness—money, career, love in the way I thought it should be—but as I sat there on the bench with this man who had unexpectedly come into my life, I felt peace. His many issues may have kept him from stepping up to the plate and becoming a financially solvent roommate, friend, partner, whatever—but that day, I could not put a price on what he was giving me. In his eyes, I was okay. No, great.

When the day was over and it was time to get back to my day-to-day life, I went back to thinking that I needed more.

Maurice grew more impatient with Focus Pointe, which was cutting him down to two, maybe three days a week. "Should I find something else?" he asked me.

"Well, look around, but don't quit until you have something else," I advised. His share of the rent and bills was on a sliding scale to his income but I was afraid of his going months without any job and then I'd have to support him and I'd never get him to move out on his own. Despite the feelings in my heart during quiet moments like the day at Coney Island, that was always the game plan: to get him to move out on his own. Because we weren't sleeping together as a couple, I couldn't wrap my head around the idea of him living forever as a tenant in my living room. The thought of us sharing a bedroom was too scary for either of us to contemplate. So we kept that short but vital distance from each other's heart—perhaps a quarter inch.

Anyway, having a best friend sharing my apartment wasn't quite doing it for me. I ignored what my heart was telling me, insisting to myself that I could do better.

A congregant from Rutgers had heard that Maurice was in New York and sent me an email asking if I knew how to get a hold of him. "Easy," I replied. "He's my roommate."

She had a job lead at a place called TomKats Catering, which did food service for film sets, most notably the new Silvercup Studios in Queens. I was skeptical of the operation, but a lead was all the excuse Maurice needed to abandon Focus Pointe. (He never gave a two-week notice for a job, just stopped showing up for work.)

The pay was decent, but it required Maurice's getting to work by six o'clock in the morning, which meant getting up at about 4:00 a.m. in Bay Ridge in order to take the slow trains out to Queens. Catering also involved long hours, so he would put in twelve-hour days regularly.

I should have insisted he stay at Focus Pointe, even on a part-time basis. That gave him just enough money to pay me a little for the rent and to have what he needed to get by week to week. Besides that, Focus Pointe was a reputable company and offered a comfortable office and connections to career-minded folk.

When he started getting the checks from TomKats, he would sometimes cash the check on a Friday and then disappear for a night or two on one of his benders—just what I feared. Having a lot of money in hand was a dangerous thing for Maurice. Naturally, he was unable to put any aside for savings. I wondered if his lack of a savings plan was his way of insuring that I did *not* evict him from the apartment: if he never had money, how could I put him out on the street? But why couldn't I have put him out on the street for breaking my new, strict rules? Again?

As it turned out, TomKats was a fairly shady operation. Checks were often late, hours were uncertain (sometimes he'd get a call at midnight saying they needed him at six the next morning or, conversely, that his shift had been cancelled the next day), and, once again, Maurice didn't like the way his boss was running the operation. TomKats wasn't going to last long.

I was able to introduce him to Henry, the manager of Rose's Turn. Although Maurice was not a professional singer (required for bartenders in the piano bar downstairs), he had good customer service skills, and Henry said he would like to have Maurice as the door person at the club.

It wasn't much—just sixty dollars in cash plus tips for six hours on a Friday or Saturday night—but, again, it was just enough spending money to get him through the week until the next real job came along.

The night of his first shift, some time in November, I happened to be bartending in the showroom upstairs and at nine o'clock, when he was to start, he wasn't around. Henry asked me where he was. I gave an excuse that the trains took a long time coming from Bay Ridge and that Maurice may have underestimated the time. My reputation was on the line and just as I was about to slink away, embarrassed, Maurice burst into the bar with a smile, breathless, at 9:20. "It took an hour to get here with those trains," he told Henry. His job and my reputation were saved. For the moment.

For Thanksgiving, I was able to talk Wayne into having an upstairs-downstairs dinner using both apartments. Hector would be away for the long weekend. Trying to get the right balance of a crowd was going to be a chore.

Maurice definitely wanted to make a turkey and stuffing; I would do pies; Wayne would do side dishes; and the guests would bring wine and other items as needed. That morning, the building was filled with the fragrance of the foods being cooked. As I went up and down running errands for last-minute things at the store, I couldn't understand why Wayne's door was closed the whole time.

At last, I knocked. I heard some shuffling about and then the door was opened. I stood in open-mouthed shock as I looked at my friend Mark-Alan smiling on the other side of the threshold. Mark-Alan was a longtime friend of ours, who had moved to Florida in early 2005. Wayne had flown him up for the weekend as a surprise guest for the dinner. At last, I screamed with recognition and delight and we embraced. Mark-Alan was one of the funniest, brightest lights in my life and he would indeed add to the festivities of day. The dinner would include Maurice, Wayne, Mark-Alan, and our friends Victor and Cal, and me. All guys—not always my favorite combination—but it seemed like a good group.

Maurice was in his element and he and Mark-Alan immediately took to one another. Early on, Mark-Alan pulled me aside. "Are you two a couple?"

"No," I said.

"Why not? He's great!"

"It's best that we're just friends for now. A lot of issues," I said by way of explanation. I appreciated that Mark-Alan saw the magic that was Maurice, when many did not.

We had the main course at Wayne's dining room table. There was so much food, and Maurice's turkey, moistened with orange and lemon slices, was the star attraction. In terms of the food, it was perhaps the best Thanksgiving meal I'd ever had. And the company, a combination of people that would likely never meet again, was also memorable.

After a while, the small talk threatened to devolve into something resembling the Diana Ross Thanksgiving of the year before, so I took a risk and spoke up as we were making progress on our plates. "Let's go around the table and just take a moment to say what we're thankful for."

This suggestion was met with rousing optimism by everyone except Victor, who was well on his way to becoming a cranky drunk. Most were thankful for the friends and the chance to have dinner together. Mark-Alan was thankful to Wayne for making the trip possible and to Maurice for the dinner and new friendship.

Maurice typically rose to the moment on such occasions. "I am thankful that I have a home to live in," he began, rendering the petty concerns of the rest of us moot for the moment. "And thankful for Kevin, who has been so good and patient with me. Without him, I'd probably be dead in a gutter somewhere. And thankful to God, who is giving me great moments like this, which I don't deserve." I swallowed a lump in my throat. He found such joy in the moment; he didn't need more.

What could we do but say "cheers" to that and clink our wine glasses together?

After dinner, we moved upstairs to our apartment for dessert and coffee. Some tensions were developing at that point because Victor was nursing an old grudge against Wayne and me, and Mark-Alan had to talk to him alone outside because he was becoming belligerent. I, however, was used to these kinds of scenes at the holidays — all part of family life.

I had made a deal with Maurice when he moved in that if he did the cooking, I'd do the cleaning. That day was one day that I regretted that deal; I felt as if I were washing dishes for days. Still, we had plenty of leftovers, which kept us happy, and that Thanksgiving goes down in history as one of great memories of my life, and probably Maurice's too.

Chapter Sixteen

After the attack, my physical recovery time was rather brief, considering the near-miss location of the chest wound, but emotionally, I was sliding. On the phone one day, I griped to a friend, wondering where the silver lining was. "The silver lining is you lived," he stated.

There could be no greater truth, but I was too bitter to hear it. I was still wishing Granger had finished me off. I had always been able to bounce back from anything, large or small: I had patiently waited out years of being slammed into lockers in high school, hardly ever missing a day of school; I had endured an angry father who drank too much and a mother who had just enough strength to maintain a working household, let alone take on my psychological issues; in New York, I had survived awful jobs and no jobs, shaky tenures with questionable roommates, endless rounds of futile auditioning, the heartbreaks of foolish young love, and even a mugging at gunpoint.

From all of it, I had bounced back. I was like the Weeble, a toy that had been advertised for several years when I was a kid: "Weebles wobble but they don't fall down."

This recovery was proving to be more difficult because it seemed to take on the weight of all of those other issues, some of which had never been resolved.

As for that defiant, the-show-must-go-on stance I had adopted for that performance in November, there had been no reviewers there to commend my performance and no reporters to follow up on my progress. I was yesterday's news, papery dry and blowing aimlessly in the momentary breezes.

The Christmas season has always my favorite time of year, but when it rolled around in 1994, I was in no mood for it. My mind was in a state of shock and nothing, neither joyful nor tragic, could seem to pull me out of my cement-like, day-to-day existence.

If anyone had tried to talk to me about Christmas miracles, I'd have met him with, at best, a stone face, if not a scowl. After that first week of survivor's glee back in October, I was sinking down, down into the depths of something that was beyond the reach of even Rafe. I didn't think it was possible, but the grind of my office job was worse than it had ever been, my eyes glazing over legal documents as I counted down the hours until the end of the day, only to go home and stare at the television screen.

The trip back to Massachusetts for the holidays was my first out-of-town getaway since the stabbing. And while my parents' house in the woods on a dirt road was certainly getting out of the city, it promised to be anything but relaxing. My anger at my father hung over me like a shroud: Why hadn't he come to New York during my hour of greatest need? My siblings' bickering over trivial matters threatened to make me come undone, a tightly-wrapped Christmas package collapsing to reveal nothing inside.

My fears were not unfounded. As I walked into the living room and plopped my things down, the pettiness was already starting. I looked to the sliding glass door on the far side of the room. Outside the door, on the deck, sat a plump, five-foot-high Christmas tree, sparkling with tinsel and multi-colored lights. The wrapped gifts were piled on the other side of the door, inside. My sister, Wendy, said with a snort, "Ma decided she didn't want to bother with putting on ornaments and vacuuming up pine needles this year. Doesn't that look dumb?" I shrugged, smiled wanly, and took my luggage to my room.

In November, I had met with the district attorney. My medical bills — over $10,000 — were coming in and I had no idea what to do. I asked the DA if I could sue Granger. He shrugged. "You could only sue if someone like Donald Trump stabbed you. Someone with deep pockets."

There wasn't much to learn about Granger beyond what was in the newspaper accounts. I seem to remember that he was an aspiring screenwriter. He worked for a delivery service like FedEx. He had assaulted a city councilman the year before. He liked to ride his bike. But nothing about his family or where he came from. What could have been his motive?

To make matters worse, one of the two police officers who tackled Granger an hour or so after he stabbed me — a heroic deed for which he was roundly praised in the press — committed suicide a few days before Christmas. I had met the officer in November when I gave my testimony to the grand jury; he had been so young, polite, and compassionate. In addition to the tragedy of his loss, how would it affect my case?

I don't remember much about the time leading up to Christmas day. I spent a couple of long days curled up on the couch looking at the tree lights and smelling the baking pies. We must have gone to the Christmas Eve service at the church we'd attended since I was a small child, but I don't remember being moved. We certainly carried on our tradition of singing Christmas carols late into the night back home after the church service.

That had always been a highlight at our house. My father would pull out the dog-eared Christmas book and we'd go through it from beginning to end. He'd play piano and we'd sing along to most of the hundred songs in the book. Immediate family and a few close friends would participate. My best friend, Paula, from my growing-up years, and her mother, Gig, who were like family, joined us every year. The evening would always start out reverently, but after a couple of hours and a fair amount of eggnog, the musicality would go right out the window. Paula and I would try to out-belt each other and Gig, a heavy smoker, would cough and rasp her way through the latter part of the evening. We'd all try to add jazz riffs and fancy endings to the simplest songs like "Silent Night." Often we'd fall to our knees gasping for breath from laughing so hard at a particularly creative and ridiculous rendition of a classic. My father and I were more alike than not: When the going got tough, we knew how to perform.

I have no particular memory of the Christmas Eve sing-along of 1994. Surely it happened and surely I carried on as usual, but my mind was elsewhere.

I did not sleep much that night, and it wasn't because I was anxiously anticipating the arrival of Santa Claus. I got up early, at the first light of day, before anyone else in the house had stirred. I felt the need to gaze at the tree lights again.

I tiptoed out of my room and walked into the living room. I was stunned by what I saw. A light snow was falling and about an inch of fine powder had already fallen. The snow had softly blanketed the tree on the deck and the glistening lights were now muted reds, blues, yellows, and greens.

I stood alone staring at the tree, my hands hanging limply at my sides, tears creeping out of the sides of my eyes. Soon the tears were cascading down my cheeks and I covered my face with my hands so that my gut-wrenching sobs would not wake up the household. In that moment, the feeble little tree that had been exiled to the cold porch became the most beautiful Christmas tree I had ever seen.

No stocking stuffer, brightly wrapped gift, scrumptious pumpkin pie, or heartfelt song would come close to matching the gift of that tree in 1994. In the early hours of Christmas morning, a simple tree covered with colored snow became a symbol of peace and hope for me. My struggle to overcome the psychological damage of the October event would go on for at least another year, but that morning, in letting go of my grief, I was at last able to embrace life.

I wanted to live.

Chapter Seventeen

As 2006 was winding down, I managed to get Maurice into Rose's Turn to help me tend bar on nights when I was working upstairs in the cabaret room. Management at Rose's Turn was pretty easygoing, so, although letting Maurice help me out was against policy, they went along with the arrangement. Sometimes I could have run the shows myself, so I was giving up some of my own income in order for him to make money, but he needed to keep busy and feel as if he were contributing.

That year, things were much more stable and I felt ready to invite him up to Massachusetts for Christmas with my family. Just before that, though, I suggested Maurice call David at R.R. Donnelley and check in about any job openings. "You never know," I said. "You made a good impression and maybe something has come up."

He did so and about a week later, David called back and told Maurice that there was a customer service spot open on the midnight shift, Sunday through Thursday. Here was the break we had both been looking for! We were both so overjoyed and I was so proud of Maurice's persistence and interviewing skills. He was to start right after Christmas, so he would be able to come up to Massachusetts for a couple of days and then begin his new job.

I had previously taken friends home for the holidays, or as a stop-off for the band if I was doing gigs in New England during the late '90s. I was always worried about whether or not my family was going to like my friends; almost always, they did.

*   *   *

It may seem odd to young people these days, but I didn't officially come out to my parents until I was well into my thirties. I felt there was no reason to until I was in a relationship. What I didn't consider until much later is that by not coming out openly and unashamedly early on, my insecure, self-loathing might have prevented good relationships.

Nevertheless, when I met Ken in a neighborhood bar in 1998, I fell for his smile immediately. His personality was also a good match for mine. It is the only time I fell into a relationship that felt natural and inevitable. About six months into it, I asked him to move into my studio apartment and he accepted.

One thing Ken was adamant about, however, was that I tell my family I was gay. "If we're going to live together, don't you think it's time to tell them who you are? And I'd like to meet them someday, and not as your roommate." Ken himself had previously been married to a woman and had a teenaged daughter. Likewise, coming out could not have been easy in his community.

Did I mention that Ken was black?

My friends have often good-naturedly teased me about my exotic taste in men—or, as one put it, "You are the United Nations of dating." I can't really explain it myself, other than to say that I grew up in a small community that was almost exclusively white and during my formative years when I should have been dating, the white boys were bullying me relentlessly and the white girls were turning me down for dates and proms left and right. A core of inner resolve and determined dreaming kept me from killing myself (or pulling a Columbine-type attack on somebody else), and I finally found some sense of community in my church youth group. What an assemblage of misfits we were—in our own ways, we were not fitting into the desired cliques at school but, through loving and steady leadership, we forged a bond with each other that was life-long. That group saved my life, but didn't help my dating prospects much.

From there, I went to a Christian college. I found acceptance and my own leadership qualities began to take shape and emerge. However, it was also an odd place to navigate dating, even as a straight person. There were dating couples, but, I wondered, were they fornicating? How did one date and not "go all the way"? That school also had an overwhelmingly white population. There was one interracial couple (black male, blonde white girl) that dated for a long time. Back then, I thought they were incredibly brave. And incredibly hot. I always wondered if they got married.

For a person who was struggling with homosexual yearnings within that environment (and I was later to learn there were many of us), to whom should we confide? And "coming out" and dating was certainly out of the question. These days, I imagine homosexuality and faith is an endlessly debated hot topic on that campus.

Needless to say, I left college as a virgin at twenty-one. I had fallen in love with a couple of girls by then, but the feeling was not returned. Perhaps they knew something I hadn't yet acknowledged.

After that, I moved to Boston and lived on my own and went to work making up for lost time. I found the gay bars and I went to them, taking advantage of short-term encounters as well as long-term attempts at dating. I was finding myself as straight kids do when they are teenagers. I no longer felt that I was sinning. After years of prayer and self-torture (and there would be many more such years), I was coming to some sense that, for whatever reason, God made me the way I was and, now an adult, there seemed no use to try and change it. If there were ever to be such a change, I guess it would be revealed to me. (And, by the way, I was still open to that revelation—there had been some experimentation with women in my twenties as well but . . . the plumbing just wasn't compatible, shall we say.)

In any case, by the time I broke free from small-town America, I couldn't wait to explore. I wanted little part of the culture I grew up in and made an intentional effort to seek diversity. It was a mission of self-education, in some sense, to be around people I had never mixed with before. To this day, I am part of one of the most diverse congregations in America at Middle Church, and teach at the City University of New York, one of the most diverse student bodies in the world, and have been part of the music business my entire adult life — the best music has always been about uniting people. It is in those places where I am most comfortable, most at home.

As for dating, I was never one of those gay men who looks for his mirror image. Having grown up in an all-white community that often did not treat me well, I have to work harder to overcome my own prejudice of white men. That doesn't mean I do not harbor some prejudice toward people of other ethnicities or classes or sexes or orientations. I believe it is the human condition and, particularly, the American condition, to divide and judge based on such demographic factors. But I believe it is our ever-present duty as human beings to work to bridge those gaps, to work toward understanding and love, always.

So, that is the background I brought to my situation when I partnered with Ken. He was absolutely right about my need to "come out" to my family.

However, easier said than done. After fifteen years in New York, I still saw my parents as a smarter version of Archie and Edith Bunker — not exactly open to my being gay or in an interracial relationship.

Nevertheless, I went home by myself for a weekend the summer after Ken and I started dating to tell them the inevitable.

My parents were seldom in the house together, let alone the same room (secret to a long marriage, perhaps?), and so I found that Sunday afternoon was upon me and I still hadn't had the conversation. My mother was in the living room, however, and I thought, *It's now or never*. I told her I needed to tell her something.

In my family, that phrase alone is about as rare and unwelcome as "I have cancer," but, without a word, my mother sensed the importance and moved to her chair. "What is it?"

I stuttered and stammered and shed tears (I always tell myself not to cry, but I share that tendency to cry easily, like my mother) and finally came out with the necessary two words, "I'm gay."

By then, also teary-eyed, she said, "Well, I had already thought you might be." Like they say, mothers always know. She came over and hugged me.

"I thought you and Dad would hate me and not want me to come home anymore," I bawled. Imagine being a man in your thirties and still thinking that.

"Oh no! We love you no matter what!"

In that moment, I realized that parents, like children, do not always remain stagnant in time. A child may be remembered by his family the way he was when he was sixteen, but he will likely (and one hopes) change. The same is true of good parents. We may remember them as they were when we moved off to college, but they are still watching and learning from their children, they are still watching television and reading books and meeting new people. They are growing too.

We talked a little bit more. She admitted that it was an issue she was struggling with, in regards to her faith, but she did not preach to me and did not waver in her love for me.

Realizing my bus was leaving in a couple of hours, Mom made an offer I couldn't refuse. "Do you want me to tell your father?"

"Would you mind?" No matter what she said, he was still Archie in my mind.

About a week later, my mother called and I asked, "So did you tell him?"

I'll never forget what she said, and vowed to one day put it in a book. Here it is: "Well, your father was in the military, so I think he understands these things better than I do."

How about that: *because* he had been in the military, he could understand gay issues! Not only was he completely fine with my being gay, but his military service was his point of reference! So much for "Don't ask, don't tell." They may not have been telling, but our servicemen were doing it . . . back in the 1950s!

Now, I did not tell them Ken was black. One obstacle at a time. I've always found it difficult to say things like, "I'm dating David and he's Asian" or "Oh, and my pastor is a black woman" or "She's my best friend and she's of Puerto Rican descent." It sounds ridiculous coming out of my mouth, and yet I've learned that some white people want to hear it to mentally prepare for the sight they might see one day. I suppose the same happens in families of all ethnicities; I can't say.

I did bring Ken to Wendy's home for Thanksgiving. She and her family were living in Connecticut at the time. I didn't "prepare" her with the race factor and, by all accounts, they did not seem surprised or bothered by it. However, Wendy did tell my mother later. By then, the plan was to bring Ken home for Christmas and she felt, probably correctly, that they should be prepared for this surprise.

On the drive up to Massachusetts on Christmas Eve, Ken—who had courageously asked for this—kept saying, "Turn around, we don't need to do this."

I laughed. "Oh no, we're going to do this once and for all."

When we arrived at Audrey's house, there already was a houseful of people and we were both greeted warmly. A notable exception was the absence of my father. I kept thinking, "He's up at his house getting drunk because he can't handle this and he's going to make a scene."

About a half hour after our arrival, my father came in, completely sober, and threw his arms around Ken, saying, "Great to meet you, Ken. I've heard great things about you!" I was gobsmacked. The same man hadn't hugged me until I was about twenty-five.

But the best surprise was yet to come. After the meal and festivities, Ken and I went up to my parents' house where we'd be staying. My mother brought us to the guest room. "You two can stay in here."

Ken and I looked at each other. Was this my parents, allowing an interracial gay couple to sleep together under their roof? This was an honor that even Ken's mother did not allow us when we visited her in Atlanta earlier that year.

Lesson learned: Never sell your parents short.

*   *   *

So, in 2006, Maurice and I took a bus up to Worcester early on Christmas Eve after we had gone to church services at Middle. We wanted to make sure to get there early enough for Maurice to make dinner for my parents, something he insisted on doing as his gift for them. My father picked us up at the bus station and we had a half-hour of small talk during the drive to the house. My father was surprisingly shy around people he didn't know; Maurice was actually quite ebullient with strangers. Although there was nothing unusual or memorable about the conversation, I was tense. I'd like to think that race was not an issue—in previous years, I had brought home friends of different ethnicities on different holidays, including Ken. It may have been a contributing factor. A general discomfort, perhaps.

Soon after arriving, Maurice got busy in the kitchen. Despite that gesture, I got the impression that my father didn't much care for Maurice and my mother probably didn't either, although she was more polite. But that's nothing against my parents; everybody reacted that way to Maurice—either with immediate affection or mistrust. I think sometimes he tried too hard and it came off as slick. Audrey and Paul, and their daughter, Bethany, liked him very much, although they had met him a couple times on visits to New York—his territory.

We had our usual sing-along later that evening. My mother put out desserts and finger foods. Audrey, Paul, and Bethany came up, as did my brother and his two daughters (his wife was entertaining her family at their house). Paula, her husband, Ron, and son, Luke, came as well. Jerry, a longtime friend who had vacationed with me in New Orleans and met Maurice for a quick second back then, also came and they reintroduced themselves.

At one point, my eight-year-old niece, Erika, her big blue eyes wise beyond her years, asked Maurice, "Do you like white people?"

Maurice, barely pausing, smiled and said, "Some of them."

My father, over seventy but still as energetic as ever, started firing up at the piano a little after nine. While Paula and I did our usual theatrics and a few others sang along, Maurice was unusually subdued and shy, except for a funky dance he performed in the kitchen, much to the delight of three-year-old Luke. Perhaps Maurice didn't know what to make of all this family togetherness at the holidays. In the end, it seemed that everyone had a good time, even though it wasn't one of our rowdiest Christmas Eves.

On Christmas morning, my parents, Maurice and I exchanged gifts while sipping coffee. Maurice had brought Café Du Monde, a favorite New Orleans coffee. My mother was kind enough to have bought Maurice a couple of things so he would have something to open—a pair of gloves, a Paula Deen cookbook, and a book on Cary Grant, one of Maurice's favorite actors, oddly enough.

Soon after, we headed down to Audrey's house. This had become an adult tradition, Audrey and Paul serving our family and his. Paul's mother immediately took to Maurice, and they spent all afternoon engaged in conversation about Katrina and politics. Paul and Audrey were creating a feast fit for royals, but I sensed that Maurice was eager to be allowed to do something in such a large kitchen.

After dinner, there wasn't much to do but take naps. For Maurice, who was a warm-weather person, a house in the woods in the middle of winter left few options, so there was a lot of sitting on the couch and watching television—an activity frowned upon by my father since we were kids. Even as an adult, every time he walked into the living room, I felt his judgment about how lazy we were. It didn't matter that it was a holiday, we should have been chopping wood or cleaning the barn!

Usually, after all the hubbub of the holiday passed, my family played cards or, if the mood was quieter, Scrabble or Boggle. Yet there was no such activity on Christmas night that year, just watching reruns on Paul and Audrey's big screen TV and making light conversation.

The next day, Audrey and Paul had to work and yet all the leftovers from Christmas dinner were in their refrigerator. We were a bit annoyed by that and didn't quite dare break into their house and raid the refrigerator, but it didn't seem right to be eating hot dogs and macaroni and cheese on December 26th. For Maurice, half the fun of holiday food was eating leftovers for days afterward. I took him to nearby Gardner so he could get a sense of the area, having never visited New England before. Not exactly scenic, but it got us out of the too-quiet house for a couple of hours.

That night, I drove Maurice to Worcester. He would take the bus back to New York so he could start at R.R. Donnelley the next night; I would stay in Massachusetts for a few more days.

As we neared the station, Maurice said, "Your parents are really nice but they don't talk too much."

At times, he had said the same thing about me, that I wouldn't often go deep into conversation. "I told you," I said. "We're New Englanders. We just eat and grunt."

"How could you stand it growing up?"

I laughed. "I couldn't! Why do you think I got out so fast?" Of course, I had since come to appreciate the relative quiet of home, in small doses, although surely there were roiling currents beneath the calm surface.

We hugged and Maurice thanked me for bringing him up to Massachusetts. "It was nice to have somewhere to go for a change."

I had thought the two days were kind of a flop—not the usual crowd on Christmas Eve, no white Christmas, and a polite reception for Maurice.

Apparently, it was enough for him. Once again, Maurice was giving me a lesson in gratitude about the precious small things in life.

It was a lesson I seemed to need to have repeated again and again.

Chapter Eighteen

It was 1995. I wanted to live, all right. I was about to embark on a year of eat-drink-and-be-merry-for-tomorrow-you-may-die, apparently the giddy next phase of recovering from a near-fatal assault.

I took a leave of absence from my job in late January. I felt I would absolutely kill myself if I had to be around that cesspool of negativity in the office for another day. I learned later that one of the supervisors was angry that I was granted the leave because she had been denied a similar leave a couple years before. So much for well-wishing co-workers.

I rented a car and drove south, stopping in Columbia, Maryland, where my sister, Wendy, lived at the time. She and her husband, Jim, had just welcomed their first child, now six months old. There was something healing about being around a baby, a reminder that the cycle of life goes on.

I stayed there for a couple of days, and then continued south. There has always been a great sense of relief to me to get into a car by myself and drive for miles and miles, seeing new country and new people. When I tired, I stopped at a Motel 6 somewhere outside of Raleigh-Durham and ate fast food, read a book, and continued on my way again the next day.

The goal was Atlanta, I'm not sure why—it was just a place where I'd never been and wanted to see. I checked into a small Victorian hotel on Peachtree Street and immediately set out on foot to explore the town. I was killing time until I could hit the nightclubs—such a guilty pleasure going out to clubs in a town where nobody knows who you are. I could be free of any kind of saintly image I had cultivated. I didn't have to be the over-achieving overcomer of bad luck and mishaps, setting an example for all those who knew me. I could party until dawn if I wanted to, and if I stumbled back to my hotel, by myself or otherwise, who was to know? It is so much the American way, indulging in our dark sides in private while pretending to everybody we know that there is no dark side.

That weekend was to set the tone for the coming months. I was too broke to actually buy drugs, but if someone had grass or coke to enhance the party, I was game. I still had a medical bill for several thousand dollars that would remain untouched for several months, creating havoc with my credit rating, but I couldn't deal with all the bureaucratic red tape and phone calls. I chose to ignore it for as long as possible. My own poverty probably kept me from harmful addictions.

As soon as I returned to New York, I went into my therapy session and announced to Rafe that I was through with treatment after seven years between him and a previous therapist. I needed to navigate my recovery on my own, thank you very much. I was surprised he didn't offer much of a fight, as he had in the past. He probably saw my rebellion and figured fighting me was only going to increase my animosity. I stayed a little longer in the group, but got a lot more fight from them when I announced I would be leaving. That only hardened my resolve, as if to say, "Fuck you, losers. Time for you to get up and get rid of the crutches." It was highly debatable who the real loser was.

I decided to quit my office job, but not before taking a 40-hour course at International Bartenders School. Life was too short, I wanted fun.

I was lucky enough to land at Rose's Turn, a historic piano bar in the Village. I got only one steady shift per week to start, the Saturday happy hour, but it allowed me to do my own thing, and I partnered with Clare, who would play piano for my shift for nine years. She became a lifelong friend.

I had started teaching cabaret classes the year before, having been hired by another pianist to do the directing. Now I wanted to run the show: I left him and went into business for myself, hiring my own pianist to work for me.

I didn't have money to do any shows, which meant hiring expensive musicians, but I got back on stage as a stand-up comic. This was a world that was truly sad: the best at it are among the most talented people in the entire industry, but stand-up, for the most part, as I saw it, tended to be the garbage dump where those who have failed in all of their other performing choices ended up. I guess they figured, "Maybe I can't sing or dance or act, but I can talk to people and my grandmother thinks I'm funny." It was truly an education to sit through hours of stupefying comedy waiting to have my five minutes on the stage. I don't know how funny I was in relation to everyone else, but I'm fairly certain I at least had intelligence and an awareness, which, I'm guessing, at least put me somewhere in the top half of the heap.

That summer, I managed to redo my show from the previous November. For the new flyer, I posed in leather and chains at a microphone, sporting a beard and a scowl. I called it "Unleashed." It was obviously meant to be tongue-in-cheek, making fun of my good guy image. This time, my comedy routines about the stabbing were more refreshing. Time had passed and I did find the humor in it, as did my audience. I noted that John Wayne Bobbitt, recently in the news for having his penis cut off by his angry wife, was making truckloads of money for personal appearances, interviews and movie deals (okay, X-rated ones, but still . . .). "I guess I got cut in the wrong place," I deadpanned. I showed a collage of all the press clippings, noting how The Post shot of me in a hospital bed looked sexier than my headshots. I talked about the stupid things people say after you've been stabbed ("Did it hurt?" or "That was your first mistake, being out that late"). I observed that I may have had better luck had I survived a stabbing by O.J. Simpson, as everyone involved in that trial seemed to be making gobs of money.

My show was reviewed by Backstage Magazine and Roy Sander gave it kind of a middling assessment and didn't really get my "unleashed" concept (I guess what I considered to be bad was still good to a normal person), but he loved my storytelling and patter — so maybe the stand-up had paid off for me after all.

Saturday nights became the most fun night of the week. Clare and I finished our shift at nine and often had dinner together, but returned to watch and hear the night crew do their hilarious routines. There was more talent in that place than you could find on almost any television show or movie, but since New York was full of competition and piano bars were not considered cutting edge enough, the talent went largely undiscovered. Most of the time, I'd spend all the cash I'd made that evening, and stagger off to the Christopher Street bars to drink more, and taxi home before dawn, often with a one-night stand in tow.

The good times were rolling and this, I thought, was all the healing I needed.

Chapter Nineteen

The new year opened with such promise: Maurice had a good job, his boss liked him and gave him responsibility, and I was getting lots of additional work at the bar, as well as my usual heavy teaching load. I was in my last semester as a graduate student and had started a novel. It was about the music business, but I was allowing my own dark side to come out. It featured a main character, a dance diva on the comeback trail, pulling out all the outrageous stops to make it big again. Sex, cursing, gay nightclubs—I needed to surprise people with something unexpected from me. *Off the Charts!* was darkly comic, but there was a lot of anger in that book.

Maurice continued to work at Rose's Turn on the weekends. He told me, "I want to get ahead, use that cash for my spending money and save the money I make at Donnelley." I couldn't have agreed more.

The giddiness of the New Year's promise couldn't possibly last. He paid his portion of the rent and then started buying up clothes and CDs and DVDs. I didn't complain at first because he had been struggling for a long time and, like a kid, wanted to buy "toys" with his first paycheck.

By the end of January, though, his dark side was getting the best of him again. I was nervous every time he got paid on a Friday because I wasn't around when he was cashing the check. If I had been, I would have insisted he hand over the next month's rent and probably would have accompanied him to a bank to open a savings account, with a passbook that I would hold onto. It seems ridiculous that I would insist on such an arrangement with another adult essentially my age, but he needed that kind of supervision and tough love. Then again, my sense was that Maurice was still a young teenager. His child-like behavior was frustrating, but it's also what made him endearing. I suspected something traumatic had happened to him back then from which he never fully recovered. The drugs and sexual problems I suspected were merely his way of self-medicating and finding pleasure to try to erase the pain. The bigger question for myself was this: Why was I comfortable playing this parental role with another adult?

In any case, my fears were well founded. One Friday night at the beginning of February, I grew alarmed as I watched television late and hadn't seen or heard from him all day. He was supposed to work at Rose's Turn that night and he just never showed up. Henry called, concerned, and I don't remember the excuse I used, but I certainly made it sound as if Maurice's no-show was shocking to me as well.

If his own patterns were alarming, so were mine. Why did I continue to cover for him? The truth was, if I told others about his behavior, it would mean telling the truth about myself. That truth—that I was ashamed at having fallen for this charlatan's shenanigans and even more ashamed that I loved him—didn't exactly fit into the role of savior and saint I had adopted and tried to keep propped up. He needed his lies and I needed mine. We were the perfect match of dual dysfunction.

He didn't come home on Saturday either but, thankfully, he returned on Sunday afternoon, in time to take a nap before heading off to Donnelley that night.

I lit into him when he walked through the door. "Maurice, I got you that job at Rose's Turn and now you're just going to party all weekend and not show up? If you want to fuck up your own life, fine, but now you are fucking up my reputation and if you start losing jobs at this point, I'm not going to let you stay here. You can't go down this road now. We've been through too much."

"I'll call Henry," he said.

"Well, that's fine and good but how do I know this isn't going to happen every time you get paid? You need to do the right thing! Do you have any money left?"

"Yes."

"You look like shit. You'd better get some rest so you can get up and go to work."

He collapsed on the couch and I went back to whatever I was doing. I made sure he was up and out the door on time to get to his job.

There were other ominous signs. "I don't like this midnight shift. It's hard to stay up and there's not enough to do. I just sit and watch TV and call cars for the lawyers, answer phones, and order food," he complained. It was Magnolia Bakery and Focus Pointe all over again.

"Are you crazy? You sit in a plush office and watch TV. You have responsibilities and you get to talk to people using your charm. Would you rather be back at TomKats, making your way to Queens at four in the morning and working your ass off for twelve hours straight and never knowing when you're going to get a paycheck?"

"I know. I just wish I could work the day shift."

"Give it time, Maurice. You've only been there six weeks. Get through this for six months, do good work, and I'm sure David will promote you to a better time or position. He loves you."

Thankfully, he was paid every other week, so the following weekend, I knew he wouldn't be going on a bender. He had managed to convince Henry to give him another chance and was back at Rose's Turn the following week.

Oddly enough, Maurice was highly sentimental about Valentine's Day, which was approaching. Conversely, it has always been one of my least favorite days. Unless you have a true love, I've found it a cruel day to foist on the rest of the population.

He astounded me by presenting me with a card that he must have spent some time picking out. It read as follows:

> "I've learned so much from loving you. Loving you has taught
> me a thing or two—that life can be free and easy, tough and
> complicated, a smooth ride, or a long, hard climb . . .
> I've learned that the face I love can smile a mile wide and
> fill my day with sheer delight . . . that the voice I love

> can sweeten the night with one whisper in my ear . . .
> yet that same face, that voice can tell me things that
> are hard to hear about myself—things I'd never thought of,
> even things that put me in my place . . . The real meaning
> of love—the good, the bad, the beautiful, the true—I've
> learned all this and more from loving you."

And then he added his own words:

> "Kevin, thank u 4 loving me, you continue 2 challenge,
> inspire, frustrate, and amaze me. U R my angel on earth.
> Thanks for leading by example. May 2007 be the year
> we've been waiting for . . . Much love, Maurice."

I didn't know what to make of this card, but I was so moved by it. I don't remember what I'd written on his card, but it was a lot safer and more antiseptic than the one I'd received. I was afraid if I said too much, I'd be stuck: If I professed love so openly, he'd either be afraid and take off, as he had the weekend of the move to Bay Ridge, or he would take advantage of my feeling and never take responsibility and I'd never work up the courage to throw him out. I always kept the door slightly ajar—the easier to push him out or run out myself. I was drowning in the shame of my cowardice. Neither one of us could express our love physically—which is how I defined a romantic relationship—but the card told me he was thinking of us as a couple. Still, I couldn't see the overall progress he was making, only the setbacks, and I was running out of patience, despite a magical moment like that card.

What was so heartbreaking was that he couldn't live up to his own ideals and aspirations. He couldn't hold onto a good job, he couldn't resist the lure of a drug or a sexual encounter. Yet in his most lucid moments, he knew what he wanted: family and a home. And there I was, always threatening to take it away from him. Perhaps if I hadn't insisted on being a parent, things might have turned out differently.

The next time he got paid, he disappeared again for the weekend and again didn't show up for his shift at Rose's Turn. Henry was through with him and crossed him off the bartending shift he was to help me with for a show on Saturday. He could have made well over a hundred dollars in cash on that one show.

Again, he got home on Sunday—he still somehow had his wits about him enough to remember the Donnelley job.

"Well, you've been fired from Rose's Turn," I announced, as if he didn't know. "You could have made two hundred dollars this weekend, but you'd rather snort it up your nose."

Like a wounded dog, on occasions like this, he just crawled under the covers wordlessly, hoping his demons and I, his angel, would just go away.

"You need to get yourself into a rehab program. Donnelley is your last hope, you can't lose that job."

It was no use. I don't know what prevented him from getting the help he needed, but it occurred to me he had probably spent his entire life on the precipice and didn't know any other way to live. I had thrown him a number of lifelines but in the end he still preferred to balance on that precarious edge. Why? What had happened to him? Was he afraid or defiant or suffering from a mental disorder? I didn't have the skills to cope with his level of problems.

As for my own problems, I could cope with them and function quite well, I thought. The truth was, I was getting by. I had done many things but I wasn't much closer to an actual career I loved than I was when I'd arrived twenty years before.

I offered Maurice the best love I knew how to give and a roof over his head and it appeared those weren't going to be enough. I didn't want to accept that all my hard work might not be able to fix his brokenness.

We got through the rest of February and he still had the job. March was what was known as a filing month in the printing business and would be busy at Donnelley. David gave him extra shifts, more hours, more responsibilities. With the overtime, I don't know if Maurice had ever made so much money, certainly not since his high-end dining manager and bartending jobs in Washington and Richmond in the '90s. This was a dangerous thing.

Sure enough, around the second week of March, Maurice pulled another disappearing act. This time, he failed to get back home by Sunday and, naturally, did not call in sick at Donnelley.

When he stumbled in on Monday morning, I begged him to call David and beg for his job, for another chance. David had really taken Maurice under his wing, gone out on a limb for him, and now, during busy times, Maurice decided to pull a no-show.

He lost his job.

What now? The time for lectures had passed. Certainly, I said my piece but as critical as I was of him, it was clear that he was hating himself, had blown everything he'd worked for in the last couple of years. He had hit rock bottom. It was like yelling at a mortally wounded man to get up and fight. No amount of yelling was going to do the trick. A mental health crisis was every bit as debilitating as a physical limitation, perhaps more so.

"Get some rest; get yourself help," I told him without emotion. "I need you to work, but I'd rather you be healthy and clean. You have one month either to get yourself a therapist or a program or to get another job you can hold onto. Preferably both. I've given you a million chances. I can't continue to live like this. Do it, or go back on the streets." There was nothing more to say.

Chapter Twenty

Maurice couldn't collect unemployment because he hadn't been employed at one place long enough, but he somehow managed to get himself back on food stamps. He started going to church with me more often. Other than that, because he had no money, he stayed home.

I didn't know if it was stress or what, but he started complaining that he was having trouble swallowing and an oozing cyst developed on his abdomen. Ever the self-healer, Maurice bought bandages and hydrogen peroxide and went to work cleaning and dressing the wound himself. I told him he should see a doctor, but he didn't have insurance so he didn't see it as an option. He may have been right; my own doctor, when I asked, said he couldn't take on anyone without insurance.

We went to the Maundy Thursday service at Middle and he thanked Jacqui for her homily and for reading the Psalms.

Later, Jacqui came up to me. "Are you and Maurice, you know, a couple now?"

"We're not having sex," I answered, as if that were the question.

Without hesitation, she said, "That's probably very healing for Maurice that it's not a sexual relationship." In one sentence, she seemed to understand his problems and their deep roots more than I did and I had lived with him for a year and a half. "He seems to have changed," she went on, seeming to recall his turbulent first year in New York. "He's in a much better place."

While I was seeing his unemployment and this unknown malady, which were adding stress to my life, she was seeing spiritual growth. It gave me a moment's pause.

I mentioned nothing to Jacqui or Heather about Maurice's mysterious illness. I felt it was a breach of his privacy, so precious to him, and I also was reluctant to ask for more help on his behalf.

Two days later, the Saturday before Easter, I insisted Maurice go to the emergency room. I accompanied him to Maimonides Hospital in Brooklyn. The occasion was bleak, but it was another reminder that I simply enjoyed spending time with him.

We waited for hours in the crowded emergency room. I was asked to leave momentarily while a doctor asked him questions. Finally, late in the afternoon, after he had been X-rayed, a female doctor came over to tend to the cyst on his torso. She was very sweet but warned that it would hurt; she had to probe into the wound and remove a growth, then sew it up—all without anaesthesia. Perhaps because they didn't know his medical history, they couldn't offer anything that might provoke an unwelcome reaction. Or because he was uninsured and was not going to be admitted, why not give him a quick emergency room fix without the extra cost?

"I'm right here," I told him. "Just hold my hand and squeeze it when it hurts."

The pain must have been unbearable because he was squeezing hard and his eyes seemed to roll to the back of his head, but he never cried out. When she was finished, she put a bandage over the stitching and another doctor came over with a prescription for acid reflux.

Later, I asked the lead doctor what was wrong, unaware that, no matter how close a friend I might be, he would be prohibited from giving me a diagnosis.

"He needs to see his own doctor to follow up," he told me. I was perhaps looking skeptical, seeking a better answer. "But don't worry, it's not like he's going to die or anything." Whatever the circumstance, it was a callous remark.

We went back to our local Bay Ridge drugstore to fill the prescription. There was a problem with his Medicaid card—it had expired since he'd gotten it after Katrina—so I ended up paying for it using my credit card.

I was beginning to wonder when the caregiving would end for me, and what kind of stress all of this was having on my own health. Plus, a few dollars here, a few dollars there—it was all adding up to growing debt for me. Was I pulling him up or was he pulling me down?

It hadn't been too long before—March 2003, to be exact—that I had been sitting in my accountant's office when he calmly recommended that I declare bankruptcy. I had been $25,000 in debt, which, at that time, was about two-thirds of my annual income. The debt had started with the stabbing and snowballed with the making and promotion of my recordings and, finally, a period of unemployment in 2000 when the company I was working for closed down. I had been denied unemployment because I had my own business—the floundering record company! There wasn't a fancy car or jewel to show for all of my effort and debt, and yet—raised on the New England doctrine of hard work and do-it-yourself—declaring bankruptcy was the most self-shaming decision I had ever made.

Now, here I was heading right back down the same path. I thought I was following God's directive but God wasn't sending any windfall.

Could I give up my responsibilities for Maurice without his feeling that he was once again being abandoned?

I wanted to be the one that stuck with him through thick and thin. We were now in the thick of it.

Chapter Twenty-One

Maurice insisted on roasting a turkey with all the trimmings for Easter the next day. However bad he might have felt, he thought anything could be cured with food and he would force himself to enjoy it, if need be.

As spring blossomed in all its glory, however, the desperation of a winter famine kept its hold on us—the pull of addiction for him, the worry of mounting debt for me. Maurice wasn't working and thus wasn't paying any rent. He hadn't saved up while he was making money, as I had urged him to do. At the same time, I was enmeshed in a novel workshop, one of the final classes in my long, steady march toward the MFA degree, so couldn't work much beyond my teaching and my one or two nights at Rose's Turn. It stuck in my craw that Maurice had burned that bridge, so that easy money was no longer available to him.

The immediate medical crisis of Easter weekend seemed to be taken care of, but Maurice seemed a little more lethargic, had less get-up-and-go.

"Maurice, you need to find some kind of job, even part time, so I don't have to shoulder this responsibility," I said. I had taken out a loan for the final year of school so I could work on my thesis, the novel, and so had incurred more debt. I feared that the school loan was helping us to survive, not allowing me the opportunity to cut down on job-related work so I could focus on art-related work. As his health conditions decreased, my resentments increased.

He started making the rounds of city agencies to get back on food stamps and job programs. The thing is, because he hadn't stayed in the system—largely because I had taken him in—it meant he had to start all over again, with all the red tape that involved. If you know how to work the system, I've learned, there is no better place to be than New York City, but at the time I couldn't be bothered with his problems—I had plenty of my own—and Maurice was drowning in the bureaucracy, not knowing where the life raft was.

All of that was bad enough, but at the beginning of May, he did what he usually did when he was depressed and couldn't handle it: went on another weekend bender, without calling me. I believe he had some tax return money that he used. Either way, I'd had enough.

I went to Heather Juby for advice. Heather, a psychologist, was rather new to Middle Church, having been hired when Jacqui arrived, but she quickly made herself known. Thin and about five feet tall, with long, wavy, strawberry blonde hair, Heather looked as fragile as a porcelain doll. However, porcelain can also be one of the toughest substances around, and that was Heather. She took a loving but firm, no-nonsense position with the church's troubled population.

Heather always had a calming presence. Nothing seemed to surprise her and when I told her of Maurice's recent hospital visit, she didn't react. It probably didn't matter to her; she was looking out for my wellbeing at that moment and knew what had to be done.

"Make sure to tell him he needs to leave on a Wednesday or Thursday because beds in the shelters are hard to come by on the weekends," she said. It seemed like such a cold assessment, but she knew what I did not—the only way he was going to get the full measure of government resources was to go back to being homeless and in a shelter.

I stewed about it the whole week after his return from his lost weekend, avoiding him as much as possible. He was very sensitive and knew when I was angry. He was afraid of my non-talkative moods and hid further under the covers of his bed and his shame.

Finally, on Friday I went into the living room—his room—and said, "We have to talk."

"Okay." He patiently listened while I said nothing for what seemed an eternity. "What is it? You can say." He knew what I was going to say.

I hated myself that I could not just be firm and strong. I started crying yet again. "Maurice, you have to leave. I've given you chance after chance after chance. I can't continue to support you if you are not going to get help for yourself, because otherwise the same problems are going to keep coming back."

He said nothing, just stared at a spot on the floor.

I continued. "Maybe I shouldn't have taken you back when you were in St. Paul's house. You were really cleaning up your act then. I've made it too easy for you, I've enabled you to continue your self-destructive habits." How I hated that word, "enabled." It was psychobabble in my mind and I felt the word laid the blame more on me than him. Further, by telling him such a thing, I was probably sounding like one of his social workers. More than one friend had used that word against me regarding Maurice and it cut too close to the bone.

I resolved myself for the final salvo. "Katrina was not your problem. It may have been the straw that broke the camel's back, but the drugs are your problem. It was a problem before and after Katrina. And if you don't face that and get help, then nothing else is ever going to get fixed."

Finally, he looked up. "When do you want me to leave?" He was avoiding the issue I had just addressed, but I hardly noticed. By his avoidance, we could both escape—or postpone—the messiness of that conversation.

I made it quick and easy. "Now," I said, unleashing a whimper. While I knew I was doing what was necessary, I still felt that I was being heartless, sending him back to the shelters. But I wasn't sure I could go through the weekend with him underfoot, making me second-guess my decision.

He probably sensed that and knew, by then, where my weak spots were. After another minute, he asked, "Can I wait until Monday? It's hard to get a shelter on the weekends." Just as Heather had said.

"Why did it have to come to this? Why do you insist on living so close to the edge? Why do you put me in this awful position after all I've done for you?"

Maurice, usually at no loss for words, was frustratingly silent when it came to discussing his own problems. He couldn't confess and wouldn't articulate them. To do so might mean the beginning of unraveling the lies, and he had built his entire adulthood on a web of lies. I wasn't sure I wanted to untangle them myself. At the time, living with his hidden lies was even easier than shining a light on the uncomfortable truths about myself. As long as the perception was that his problems were bigger than mine, we could maintain our current dynamic — the comfort of the known. Besides, my problems were tame compared to his, so why work on them?

I gave in. "Monday." I would be up early and off to teach and I didn't want him packing up and leaving while I was gone because I wanted to make sure to get the key and make sure he didn't, out of anger, leave with anything of value — not that I had much. I hated myself for such a thought, that such a basic trust of him was still uncertain. "I want you to leave in the morning when I leave for work," I said.

It turns out, I didn't have to wait that long. We went to church as usual on Sunday, subdued but friendship seemingly intact, then returned to Bay Ridge. Finally, he came to me. It was his turn to talk.

"Kevin, I need to tell you something."

For Maurice to start a heart to heart about himself was a rare thing indeed. I braced myself for the next big lie that would get him out of moving out. I sat down in my chair in the living room, opposite the couch where he always sat.

He was surprisingly direct. "I have cancer."

"What?" I didn't know whether to believe him or not, although there had been signs that something was going wrong in his body over the last couple of months. "Who told you that?"

"Remember when I went up to Columbia Presbyterian a couple of months ago to take part in that study?" In another fast-money scheme, Maurice had answered one of those ads to take part in a study for a few hundred dollars. As I recall, a doctor from there had left a message on the machine some weeks ago. "Well, I didn't do the study, but a doctor called me and said they found some things in my blood that caused concern. So I called back and they said it might be cancer."

"Did you get his name?"

"No, I accidentally erased the message and didn't write it down."

"Someone tells you you have cancer and you don't remember the name and forget to write down the number?" It was outrageous and not all together believable. I mean, wouldn't the doctor follow up? "Why didn't you tell the doctors that at Maimonides?"

"I don't know. I wanted to see if they came up with the same diagnosis."

Apparently, they didn't. "Well, then maybe you don't have cancer," I said.

"I want to go back to the emergency room tomorrow and have them check some things again," he said.

Jesus, where would this all end? There clearly was something wrong with him, but he was also able to parlay this into more time. How could I send a sick person to a shelter? I couldn't.

"Okay, you go to the emergency room tomorrow for a follow-up. I don't mind your staying here as long as you're moving forward and taking care of yourself. But if you are really sick, you obviously can't be partying all weekend. That's just plain stupid."

"I know. I can't do that anymore."

I walked over to give him a hug. "This is a new beginning. You need to get better and then we'll move on from there." That was it; I sounded like a fucking Hallmark card. Back in my arms again. I had no fight left in me and he no doubt knew it. Or maybe it was love, however tentative and fragile it might be.

"Thank you, Kevin."

We both breathed a sigh of relief: he, because he had told his secret; I, because at least now I had a reason to keep him in a stable home environment. I dared not think of the long-term consequences.

Chapter Twenty-Two

I've never been very good at dealing with illness; neither was my father. However, unlike him, I'm quick to show my emotion – that, I inherited from my mother, who was often chided by us for tearing up at something as insipid as a Hallmark commercial. Sometimes I think the excessive showing of emotion evades a conversation as much as the emotion that my father stubbornly held in. We avoided broaching difficult topics with my mother, for fear of hurting her. Quite a handy protective device, those tears. But whether showing emotion or not, illness brought discomfort to those of us watching it.

My grandmother, Lois, died in 1946, when my father was twelve. I can't imagine a more painful time to lose a mother. What's more, he was left with a father and three brothers, so there was no strong female presence in the family other than a couple of aunts and, later, a stepmother.

The story is that she was ill for several weeks, closed off in her bedroom day after day while a doctor occasionally came in for a house call. This was rural Maine and her heart condition was considered incurable. The deal back then, I guess, was just to make the patient as comfortable as possible. Mainers are hardy, stubborn folk, anyway, so the thought of going to a hospital to end one's days was not an appealing option for most.

To four boys, dealing with a mother's decline must have been difficult, but at such a time and in such a far-flung place, people were stoic about difficulties. Today, we would say there was a lot of denial involved. Rather than face the impending death, my father chose to ignore the pain. He never went into her room to see her in the final month of her life.

One late night, a team of people came to the house to take Lois to the hospital. She was in severe pain and screamed in agony as they carried her through the rooms and hallway and out the door, while the boys cowered in their rooms. They would never forget those screams.

Some time later, as Lois neared the end, my father was brought to her in the hospital for a last visit. By then, however, delirium set in and she didn't recognize him, didn't know his name. How does a twelve-year-old boy ever get over that?

*   *   *

In 1981, my mother's mother, Ella, was diagnosed with cancer. She too lived in that same small town where Lois had died thirty-five years before.

Times had changed, though, and there was some hope for a cure and a recovery. My grandmother went into the hospital in January, around the time of her sixty-eighth birthday. She would never leave the hospital again, as cancer finally claimed her life in July that year.

I was in my first year of college when Grammie got sick. Occasionally, my family would pick me up on campus, north of Boston, for the weekend visit to Maine.

My grandfather lived about twenty miles from the hospital, down a long, winding road called the Notch. Nevertheless, he visited her without fail every single day for the last six months of her life.

In April of that year, old Mr. Whitney, who had lived across the street from us in Massachusetts, also died. I remember my mother telling me, "You should go to the funeral. You are going to have to go to one some day." At nineteen, I had never been to a funeral. I thought that was such a wise and unusual thing for her to say. Again, my mother's strength rose during a crisis. I didn't go to Mr. Whitney's funeral, though, despite my mother's advice.

At one point, we were visiting my grandmother and she was in intensive care, so was only allowed one visitor at a time. My family sat patiently in the waiting room and my father said, very firmly, "Go visit your grandmother." One at a time, we took the long walk down the gray hallway to her room.

Inside, Grammie was flat on her back with tubes coming out of her arms, legs, and mouth, but she was alert. She talked in her sing-songy voice, as usual, and asked me about school. She made no complaints, perhaps trying not to alarm me anymore than I already was. I stood at the end of the bed and answered her questions, but I never dared to get close enough to touch her, to hold her hand.

I somehow held it together, but when I left the room, I found a corner in the hallway and burst into tears. Eventually, I pulled myself together before rejoining my family.

My mother was in Maine helping her father when the rest of us got the call in Massachusetts that Grammie had died. The waiting had been so long and we weren't surprised. For us kids, the news almost seemed like relief—it had been such an ordeal of waiting, without progress or decline.

My brother and sisters and I didn't know what to do with ourselves. Carleton suggested we go to the cinema to see "Rocky II," which had just been released. He wasn't being callous; we just didn't know how to handle the news—any diversion seemed like a good idea. We all agreed a movie sounded good.

We crowded into the kitchen where my father sat at the breakfast bar quietly sipping bourbon out of a small glass.

"Is it okay if we borrow the car to go to the movies?" Carleton asked him.

My father cocked his head to one side as if he couldn't quite believe what he'd heard. He slowly raised his head and calmly took us all in, in one gaze.

"If you can't stay home out of respect for your grandmother," he began, "then I want you to think about your grandfather. Your grandfather, who drove back and forth for six months to spend every day with her after fifty years of marriage. And think about your mother, who's up there with him, her heart broken." That's all he said. His voice cracked and he cried for the first and only time we had ever seen.

We started to cry, too, but in my family, one cried alone. We all found our own little corners of the house and shed our tears, felt our loss, remembered the love.

*   *   *

Our family moved to Massachusetts when we children were quite young. My father soon befriended Charlie, an older man next door. Charlie had been single his entire life, certainly an unusual occurrence in such a small town. Charlie was well read and up on current events as well as history; he was a World War II veteran and a former town selectman. He had an opinion about everything and wasn't afraid to share it — we could often hear his curse-filled rants from our own house, across the wide expanse of lawn. Yet my father, who lost his own father soon after we had moved, took to Charlie and the old man became something of a father figure to Dad. Charlie was so loud, most polite folks couldn't stand to have him around for more than a few minutes, but my father could spend hours with him in Charlie's pack-rat house full of old treasures. My mother put up with it because she probably enjoyed some quiet herself, as Dad could also be a ranter.

Even when we moved to another part of town, Charlie was a regular visitor and Dad often stopped at his place after work for a drink or two. Or three. That, my mother didn't like so much, but she still invited Charlie over for Christmas dinners and the like, even if other guests were somewhat offended. My parents were always welcoming in the solitary folk. I guess I inherited that trait as well.

I happened to be home for the weekend in 1993 when Charlie was found dead inside his house. He was in his eighties by then, so had lived a long and eventful life, but it was still sudden and I ached for my father's loss.

All weekend long, Dad laughed and told anecdotes about Charlie, often closing his tale with a laugh and an exclamation like, "That goddamn son of a bitch!" or "Jesus, that Charlie was a funny bastard!" We listened along and shared a few of our own memories. On Sunday, as I was packing to head back to New York, I couldn't take the denial any longer. My mother walked into my room to see me sobbing over my suitcase.

"What's wrong?" she asked, her own waterworks starting.

"I wish he'd cry or say he missed him or something. He's in such pain and he refuses to grieve," I grieved.

"I know it. That's just the way he is," Mom weeped.

And so, I did what my father could not do. I cried for Charlie. I cried for my father's loss. I took on losses that were not mine.

*   *   *

When I was about twelve, Audrey began inviting her best friend Paula over to the house after school. Paula was the youngest of five kids, raised by a single mother, Gig — short for Virginia. Paula's father had left when she was two, never to be seen again.

Soon after that, our family adopted Gig and Paula into ours. Gig loved my parents, and would play Scrabble with my mother or sing along as my father played piano. Especially memorable were those Christmas Eves. From the time I was a teenager, Paula and Gig were with us every Christmas Eve until Gig's death in 1996.

Gig also was diagnosed with cancer. She was sixty-seven at the time. Given her history of heavy smoking, it wasn't really surprising, but it was still a shock.

By 1996, one assumed that many cancers were treatable and that, if not, then at least time was on your side — that death would be a long process as it had been for my grandmother. There would be time for visits and goodbyes.

Gig got the news in February that year. Paula was then living in Boston and, of course, went home to be with her as soon as she heard the news.

While the diagnosis was bad news, I think that most of us felt as I did, that she would go through her treatments and either beat it or not — but that it would be a long, drawn-out ordeal like it had been with Grammie. Gig was a fighter, everyone knew.

I had been working two jobs at the time, seven days a week. I had needed to make up for all the debt I had accumulated after the stabbing ordeal in 1994. I sent Gig a card and wrote that I would call her the following weekend. I even wrote a note to myself to call Gig after work on Friday, March 1.

Audrey called me at work on Friday afternoon to tell me that Gig had died. Oddly enough, my mother had been the one who had taken her to her chemo treatment that day and had been with her in the hospital room when Gig had some kind of attack. Doctors and nurses rushed in and my mother was pulled out of the room, but Gig died right there, suffering a massive stroke.

I had waited too long, never calling to tell her I loved her.

If someone I loved became seriously ill in the future, I vowed I would never let that happen again.

Chapter Twenty-Three

Perhaps grateful that I had given him another lifeline, Maurice began making calls to find a doctor and get his Medicaid reinstated. He was assigned a doctor nearby in Brooklyn, but he grew frustrated with the long wait and didn't have anything particularly kind to say about the doctor after he finally saw him.

I went on with my business. Maurice was able to get around, although his energy was lagging a bit. Somebody had to keep paying the bills so I didn't have time to go with him on the rounds to government agencies and doctors. I quickly understood how frustrating it must be for a poor or sick person without means to navigate through the red tape of government programs. When I got home at night, Maurice would horrify me with stories of waiting all day in grungy offices and filling out paperwork again and again.

Maurice, despite his condition, was ready to reach out. He decided he wanted to have a barbecue to kick off the summer season. He even made handwritten invitations for friends at church. On Sunday morning, during the passing of the peace—which is more of a great hug-and-kiss-fest at Middle—he made his way around the congregation handing out the invitations, perhaps twenty of them all together.

The party was scheduled for Saturday afternoon on May 19th. Maurice was in some pain and quite tired, but he got up early and began marinating the ribs, making the potato salad, and preparing the batter for fried chicken. We had enough food for twenty people. He had progressively lost much of his appetite over the previous month and was noticeably thinner. All that food, and he could hardly eat a bite of it.

Our friend Belinda came early. She had promised to help out and she also had her own fried chicken recipe, so had good-naturedly challenged Maurice to a duel on that score. The three of us had fun laughing and talking while they prepared the food and I tried to clean up the living room and dining room.

As the afternoon went on, it became clear that a lot of people were not coming. Sandra had at least called and said she wasn't feeling well so wouldn't be coming. Becket, a sweet, older gentleman, stopped by. The four of us dug in, unwilling to wait for more people. Erin, a bubbly fountain of energy and sparkle—and whom Maurice had a crush on—called to say she would come later.

Early in the evening, Belinda and Becket left. We were both disappointed by the turnout. I was angry because it seemed that people didn't know or care what a big deal this was, that Maurice was finally reaching out to them. I was angry because I could see how tired and aching he was, and yet he put on a brave face and did the work.

"Doesn't anybody in this town ever visit each other, just to hang out?" Maurice asked, revealing, perhaps, what he wanted and needed more than anything else: family.

"New Yorkers' hearts are small," he went on. "They'll hand you a few bucks but they can't be bothered to spend any time with you. I don't know how people live like this, all this running around and no quality time." New York didn't stack up to New Orleans in terms of hospitality, and I had to agree with him on that.

Erin called and said she was on her way, although it was after eight o'clock. Erin was a petite African-American woman, a fashion designer with a lot of style. A year before anyone knew Michelle Obama, Erin had that chic straight hairstyle that curved inwards toward the neck and shoulders, and big, doe-like eyes. Erin was always very expressive with her enthusiasm, which she often displayed.

Maurice adored her, so he was willing to wait even though he was obviously exhausted.

Part of the problem has always been that people who live in Manhattan can't be bothered to go to another borough. Those of us who lived in Brooklyn took it for granted that we'd be going into Manhattan several times a week, but try getting one of them out to see you, well, that was another story. However, any time someone finally was coaxed into coming out to Bay Ridge, they were impressed.

Erin was no exception. When she finally arrived, she oohed and aahed with delight as we showed her our five rooms—palatial by Manhattan standards. "I *love* it!" she exclaimed.

At last, she sat down on the couch next to Maurice and couldn't say enough about how great his food was. He looked so happy sitting next to his secret love.

Finally, she helped us clean up a bit and, because it was raining outside, we walked to the train under my umbrella.

"Maurice is really sick, you know," I told her.

"Oh my God, is it serious?"

"Yes, I think so. It may be cancer," I said, and explained to her that he was trying to get his Medicaid squared away and find the appropriate doctors.

Erin was saddened by the news and wondered what she could do to help.

"I'm not sure at this point. He just needs to get an accurate diagnosis, first, and some treatment options. Thank you so much for coming," I said as we reached the subway entrance. "We were kind of disappointed by the turnout because he worked so hard to try to make some friends today, but thank God for you and Belinda and Becket."

We gave each other a hug and she repeated her offer of help. "Whatever I can do," she chirped as she walked down the steps to the train.

The next morning, Maurice packed up two huge platters of ribs and gave them to the kitchen staff at church to put out for brunch. Needless to say, they were much appreciated and disappeared quickly. He also made up a plate for Sandra, who lived just two blocks from church. We rang her doorbell and she came down and gratefully accepted the platter.

Sandra had known about Maurice's recent ailments. "To be that sick and thinking of me," she said, giving him a hug.

It was an act of kindness that she never forgot.

Chapter Twenty-Four

Maurice's increasingly precarious health couldn't have come at a worse time for me. It reminded me of the old saying, "When you make plans, God laughs," although I don't think God was laughing much about our situation.

Maurice was sick and not working, and I was barely working and about to embark on writing the novel. To that end, I had accepted an invitation from Linsey Abrams, my thesis advisor and head of the Creative Writing program at City College, to spend a week in Archer City, Texas, for a retreat. Archer City is the hometown of Larry McMurtry and the film of his novel, *The Last Picture Show*, had actually been filmed there. That invitation had come a few months before any of these latest developments had transpired. Nevertheless, I would go, with Maurice's blessing.

The trip took place during the last week of May. Maurice was still getting around, but obviously tired and having trouble swallowing, so the weight loss continued. That was the worst possible cosmic punishment to inflict on Maurice. Why not a broken leg or migraine headaches? But the sheer joy of food was what Maurice *lived for* and for him not to be able to eat . . . well, it was too heartbreaking to bear.

I also wondered why nothing much seemed to be happening on the treatment front. If he really had cancer, why wasn't he being admitted to a hospital? He had an appointment or two with a Brooklyn doctor that he didn't like much, but I heard nothing about outpatient chemo treatments. He needed more help than I could give him and he was too weak to help himself. Yet he was insistent that he didn't want to bother Jacqui or Heather at church.

Despite all that, I had one of the most wonderful times of my life in Archer City while at the same time calling Maurice almost daily to check up on him. He was always cheerful on the phone, joking as he always did about the little annoyances of life.

For a few quiet hours every morning I was able to write and really get a good head start on the novel. In the afternoons and evenings, the ten of us at the retreat would take small trips around the Texas frontier land and enjoy meals together. One such meal was a crawfish boil: literally, a box of crawfish that you brought to your table and dumped out in front of yourself and started eating. Unforgettable. As an added bonus, Larry McMurtry was in town and invited us over to his mansion to look around, and even agreed to a sit-down interview with the group.

But the best part of the trip was the quiet moments of story telling and reflection with my fellow writers.

I had an enlightening conversation with Linsey, who had been with her partner for twenty-five years or so.

"I realize now that it's really about the companionship more than anything else," I said.

"Of course," she agreed. "When you're young, you go into a relationship with all these preconditions but as you get older, you go with what's comfortable. And that's not such a bad thing."

It was the first time I was acknowledging to someone else—and perhaps myself—that I was beginning to think of Maurice as a companion. After all, I had seen him through some dark days and still liked having him around. Surely that counted for something. For all the drama, there was a comfort with him. Or perhaps I was comfortable with drama.

*   *   *

After the trip, we all said our tearful goodbyes at LaGuardia Airport. Archer City had been a true paradise, a rare chance to be around like-minded individuals for a short time, get some rest, and only worry about writing. Those opportunities came around in life about as often as Halley's comet.

When I got back to the apartment in Bay Ridge and opened the door, Maurice began a cute little ritual that never ceased to crack us up. He was lying on his bed watching television, and when he heard the door opening, he quickly turned off the TV with the remote and rolled his head to one side, pretending to be asleep. In other words, to avoid having a conversation with me. "You faker, I caught you and so now you're going to listen to me," I said.

He opened his eyes and laughed in that inimitable way he had, a mischievous twinkle in his eyes. I told him all about my trip and he eagerly listened.

His days were not all that exciting at that point, but that's when he got me hooked on *Law and Order* and *Law and Order SVU* and *MadTV* and *King of Queens*, his favorite shows. And that's when he had time to put together gourmet dinners almost daily—delicious, fatty things like southern fried chicken with all the trimmings, jambalaya, pork roast. Saturday mornings became about big breakfasts. He loved the Pillsbury cinnamon rolls, frosted and with gobs of butter melting over them, fresh from the oven. Like a king, I would go to my favorite chair in the living room and ask, "Can you make me an elixir?" That's what I called his coffee concoction, some combination of Café Du Monde coffee, Half 'n' Half, Cremora, sugar, and God knows what else—Starbucks didn't have anything as good.

Food was his way of giving back to me, his way of showing appreciation and love. The food preparation continued, no matter how sick he was.

Around that time, too, we began a ritual that moved us in the direction of a physical intimacy. I don't remember who started it, but we sat catty-cornered from each other when we watched television, he on one end of the couch and I in my easy chair. He wore heavy woolen socks and I had knitted slippers. Wordlessly, one of us would reach out his foot to the other and touch it. We would continue our viewing with our feet touching.

But despite that domestic bliss, there were more serious problems at hand. He was so independent-minded; I hesitated to get too involved. He had fended for himself his entire life and thought healing could be had with lots of food and rest, and he kept trying to get both, despite his pain. I wasn't much more progressive in my thinking; I was not one to take a sick day unless I was immobile.

One stunning June evening, I announced, "You need to get some fresh air and exercise. Let's go down to the water." New York Harbor was about three-quarters of a mile west and the view was not only breathtaking once you got there, but you'd walk past upper-class homes and gardens along the way.

Maurice complained at first, not wanting to leave his nest, but eventually he slowly got up and put on his slip-on black, rubber-soled shoes — a remarkably resilient pair of shoes I had bought him at Payless a year before for his job interview, for a mere fifteen dollars.

It was a long, slow walk to the water and I immediately regretted my insistence on this exercise. He looked absolutely pained with the effort. When we reached the park at the water's edge, he lay down on a bench and dozed for a half-hour or so until I insisted we make our way back before the setting of the sun.

I had a disposable camera with me that day and took a photo of him walking toward me on the sidewalk. As I looked at the photo later, I couldn't help remarking, "What was I thinking?" His cheeks were gaunt, his eyes hollowed out, and there was no spring in his step that spring evening. I had fallen into the healing ways of my father: exercise and fresh air would do the trick.

A few days later, I came home from work and, as I walked in the door, I was hit by a blast of heat. It was a warm day, but this was not normal. I strode into the kitchen and all four burners of the stove were on but nothing was on them. What the hell? I turned off the burners and was about to unleash a tirade on Maurice.

I glanced in at Maurice on his bed in the living room, the next room, and couldn't believe my eyes. Maurice was lying in a fetal position, all wrapped up in blankets and my old red sleeping bag (I'd had it since I was a teenager and it was barely scraps at that point, but he loved it), and shivering from head to foot. I hated to think how long he had been like this.

Immediately, I ran to the closet to fetch a comforter. I threw it over him and then threw myself on top of the pile, covering him with as much of my body as I could. His teeth were chattering so he couldn't even speak.

"Maurice, sweetie, we need to do something. This isn't normal." I tried to remain strong, comforting.

He nodded his head but said nothing. I held him tightly and prayed aloud, and rubbed his arms through the layers of fabric.

I don't know how or why, but after several minutes, the chills subsided. After I unraveled him, I discovered that the bedding and his clothes were soaked with cold perspiration.

"Maurice, we need to get you into a hospital." It was the most sensible thing I had said, and I should have said it two months earlier.

"I'll be all right," he said. It was mind-boggling. As sick as he was, he feared the hospital even more.

"Maurice, I have to work during the day and I can't come home to this scene again. No matter how cold you get, you cannot ever, ever turn on the burners like that again. Do you understand?"

He nodded his head.

"You're not eating, you are getting chills and sweats. You have something more serious than what you or I can fix."

"Where am I going to go? This Medicaid still hasn't come through and I don't like that Maimonides."

I didn't have an answer. But that night I called Jacqui and explained the situation. She agreed that he had to get to a hospital and told me that Middle Church had a good relationship with New York Presbyterian and she could help set him up there.

"He's very stubborn," I told her. "Do you think you could talk to him?"

The next morning she found out exactly what I was talking about. She offered to send an ambulance out to Bay Ridge, but he told her he wanted to put it off another day so that he could pack a suitcase!

In the end, he managed to forestall the inevitable by another couple of days, fielding calls from Jacqui and Heather, who also got involved.

Maurice and I agreed to go to Middle Church one morning before I headed off to work, to meet with Jacqui and Middle's social worker. There, in the parlor, the social worker took down information about Maurice and then the four of us held hands and prayed.

Maurice himself offered up a touching, heartfelt prayer. "Lord, whatever happens, we know you are in control. I thank you for Kevin and Jacqui and this wonderful support system here. Please bring wisdom to the doctors and thank you for keeping those who care for me strong. In Jesus' name, amen." No prayers for himself, I noted.

Jacqui walked us to First Avenue and flagged a cab for us. She gave me cab money and kissed us goodbye and wished us well, tears glistening in her eyes. Then, off we sped to the Upper East Side.

We arrived at the emergency room and I stayed long enough to make sure he had checked in and filled out his paperwork. I found him a comfortable chair in the waiting room and made sure he felt okay before heading off to work.

Maurice seemed relieved. Someone cared about him, someone was giving him help.

I was relieved. I felt he was in good hands and I would have a respite from the daily worries about what to do with him at home.

The next leg of our journey, however, was just beginning.

Chapter Twenty-Five

After working at a temp job that day, I went back to the hospital. Maurice was still in the ER on a cot with his overstuffed duffel bag.

"I am starving. They haven't fed me all day," he reported. I looked around at the crowds of sick people on cots in the hallway and behind curtains. This was one of the finest hospitals in America?

"Who should I ask about dinner?" I wondered aloud.

"Could you go get me a Quarter Pounder?" he asked.

"Am I allowed to bring that in here?" Like my parents, I was timid about breaking the rules, confronting authority. *He doesn't have insurance, shouldn't we just be grateful to be here and not make waves?*

"I don't give a damn," Maurice said, that familiar mischief glinting in his eyes. "I'm hungry and that's what I want."

"Okay," I said. "I'll be back."

There was a McDonald's just a couple blocks away, which he had no doubt scoped out during our cab ride that morning. I got the meal and returned about twenty minutes later. My fears were unfounded; nobody stopped me for contraband McDonald's on the way back into the ER.

Maurice, when he got food he liked, could be as happy as anyone else would be winning a car. He cheered and sat right up, getting salt and ketchup all over everything in his eagerness to eat the food. Food was his healer, and it was as if all pain had disappeared. It was one of my greatest pleasures, watching him eat.

I stayed for a couple of hours and we even got into a conversation with a handsome young intern who told us about his schooling and work in the hospital. Maurice was trying to set me up with him. I had to remind him that I was about twenty years older than the intern.

"That's all right. Have a little fun now, and then he'll be able to take care of you when you is old," he said in his high-pitched ghetto voice.

By the time I left, Maurice still didn't have a room but he was in better spirits. I hugged him and told him I'd be back the next day.

Maurice called me the next afternoon; he had finally been placed in a room. "Doctors, nurses and medical technicians are coming in every five minutes taking blood cultures," he said bitterly. "When am I supposed to sleep?"

"Maurice, you are in a hospital, not a hotel," I reminded him. "They are trying to find out what's wrong."

He went on as if he hadn't heard me. "And what is worse, the food is awful and they put garlic in my lunch, even though I told them I was allergic to it." Given a choice of bad food or no sleep, Maurice would always choose the latter.

"They're doing their best," I said.

"I knew you'd take their side," he snapped.

"I'm not taking a side! I think you just need to be a little patient while they do their work. They are trying to make you better."

"Now I understand what was going on with that study at the Tuskegee Institute," he said, referring to the case when black men were deliberately given syphilis. Maurice had been in the hospital for just over a day and paranoia was setting in.

Obviously, he was scared, probably even terrified. He may have never stayed in a hospital overnight before and here he was, surrounded by people poking and prodding him. He had no sense of home and I was the closest thing he had to family. I began to understand why he had taken so much care packing his favorite things for the hospital stay: his Batman tee shirt, a portable CD player and several CDs, a blanket (thank God, not the raggedy red sleeping bag), a stuffed animal, his portable radio so he could listen to NPR, more clothes than I thought he could possibly need in a hospital, and even silverware.

"Okay, well I'm coming in tonight. What do you need me to bring in?" I asked, dreading the answer.

"Bring a shaker of salt," he said. "And can you get me some chicken wings?"

"Are you on a special diet? Should I really be bringing that stuff in?"

"I'm telling you that's what I want!" he barked. "Shit, I'm telling you a man could starve to death in this place."

"Okay, okay," I said.

When I arrived, I could see that he was still in an agitated state. A phlebotomist came in to take another blood culture and he quickly dispatched her. "No! You people have been sticking needles into me all day and aren't giving me any answers. You ought to have enough blood by now!"

I gave her a look of sympathy as she threw her hands up and exited. I tried to talk sense to him: "Maurice, you need to let them do their work. You're in one of the best hospitals in the world. They know what they are doing."

"Look, if you are my friend, I need you to be on my side! I have all of them against me and I need you to take my side."

"There are no sides," I protested. "We all want you to get better. Believe me, they want you to get better and get out," I said, and then laughed. "And if this is how you've been acting, they *really* want you out of here fast."

"Yeah? Well, I think they're trying to kill me."

I saw a lot of untouched food on his table. "I thought they were starving you. Look at all this food. Why aren't you eating?"

"This stuff is awful." He retrieved the salt-shaker from the bag of goodies I had brought. "That's why I need this. And next time, can you bring in some real butter? Enough of this margarine shit!"

Maurice had also refused to wear the standard yellow hospital gown. He was the only patient in that place wearing black sweats and a black tee shirt. When I asked him about that, I got an earful. "I refuse to wear that girly thing. Refuse!"

Jacqui, God bless her, had a full schedule of travel and other church business, but she tried to check in, at least by phone, once a day during his stay. He complained to her as well about the conditions, as he saw them, and she was soon on the phone to food services, pleading with them not to put garlic in his food. A trained psychologist, I think she understood what was going on with him.

Jacqui also coordinated visits by others. Erin told me, "This is also how we're taking care of you. You need to get rest and do the other things in your life. We'll do the visitation."

They perhaps got more than they bargained for, but rarely complained. Maurice had requested his favorite peanut butter when Sandra went to visit and then when she got there he informed her that it was the wrong kind. "I wanted to ask him if he'd rather have my company or the correct peanut butter," she told me, "But I knew what the answer would be." She left his side to make the long trek to the grocery store to get the peanut butter. Having recently been through her mother's long illness, she understood his needs. "What he eats is the only way he has some control over his life right now."

Maurice was also calling Audrey to complain about the service and that the doctors couldn't figure out what was wrong with him. So far away, she couldn't do a lot to help, but managed to be a voice of calm in his inner storm.

Being sent to New York Presbyterian was a godsend for Maurice — even if he failed to realize it at the time — and for me. Now he was officially "in the system," and this allowed visitation by social workers, psychologists, and medical specialists. Although he was combative with the first psychologist to pay him a visit, eventually a social worker was found who was willing to take him on — a woman with the fitting name of Vicki Sunshine. Maurice just needed to find someone he could trust in order to take the baby steps needed for recovery.

After about a week of what would ultimately be a three-week stay, Maurice finally had a quiet moment when I visited him. He pointed to the chart hanging at the end of the bed.

"So that's what I have," he said, inviting me to take a look.

I picked up the chart. There was a lot of terminology I didn't understand, but I got the gist of it.

He was in an advanced, dangerous stage of the disease. He was never able to say aloud what it was, but he let me read it.

Maurice had AIDS.

Chapter Twenty-Six

After my physical and emotional recovery from the stabbing, in the mid-'90s I went on a creative tear. I continued to do cabaret shows around New York, for a short time did some stand-up (of the open-mike variety, not professional), conducted my singing workshops with growing success, and even started a short-lived monologue performance group.

Most ambitious of all, I went ahead with plans to record a CD. At the time, I had settled down to regular employment at a financial printing firm in Chelsea. The work was not exciting but it paid reasonably well and there was enough down-time that I could address and mail my flyers on the job. There were also a lot of nutty personalities there, but somehow we became one big dysfunctional family. We liked to let off stress by going out for a heavy-duty evening of cocktails after work on Fridays. We complained to each other a lot but, looking back, it was a happy time for me.

Best of all, with that stability and some promise to my singing career at that point, I was gung ho with a business plan to raise money for my CD. My goal was to sell one hundred shares of the CD at $150 each to raise $15,000. I never got quite that far, but I did raise over $11,000, which was enough to send me well on my way. I hooked up with Dave Hall (no relation), a rock singer and producer, and we had a great rapport sifting through songs and practicing for six months before heading into the studio. It was the most creatively satisfying project of my life.

In February 1998, we recorded "New Light Dawning" over the course of a week, and the CD was out in June of that year. A mix of original songs and covers, I got an incredibly positive response to the disk. Unfortunately, I didn't realize at the time that I would need thousands more dollars to properly promote the thing and do shows. It would take some time and considerable debt before I figured that out.

The couple of years following the release of the CD were both exhilarating and frustrating, with every high and low imaginable: on my own, I got airplay on several independent stations across the country and people I didn't even know were buying my CD; on the other hand, I went on costly weekend tours to New England and Philadelphia with my band, often playing to just a handful of people – the depressing side of the business that most musicians live with.

By the turn of the millennium, I was exhausted from the constant promotion and had amassed considerable debt. Nevertheless, I was also in a successful relationship with Ken, someone who had promise of being a lifelong partner, and I had signed on as permanent staff at the financial printer after several years of full-time freelance. I had benefits for the first time in years.

Ken introduced me to his doctor and I decided to get a complete physical and the whole battery of tests while I had the benefits; there were rumors the printer was going to go bankrupt so we weren't sure how long we would have jobs.

About a week after my physical, the doctor called me and told me I needed to come back to the office. It was a day in early March, patches of snow still on the ground. My cabaret class had a show that night.

I waited anxiously in the examination room and then Dr. Glick came in and pulled up a chair. In as gentle a way as possible, he told me that I had AIDS.

I went into such a state of shock that I don't remember if I cried or was even surprised. He explained that the disease had many scenarios. He drew a train on a track on a large piece of paper — I don't know why the paper was there or where he got it — and he told me that sometimes it moves on a fast track and sometimes a slow one. I was on a fast track. I would need to start anti-viral medication right away.

All I could think about were the AIDS survivors who had been taking toxic cocktails, the life sucked out of their wrinkled cheeks, their bellies distended. I couldn't face a future of that.

I also let my mind swim back in time, to try to figure out who gave this to me. I hadn't been sick — which often happens immediately after an infection — so I had no clue. However, I was fairly sure I must have contracted the disease during those who-gives-a-damn days of despair in the year or two after the stabbing. So, in a sense, the asshole had managed to get me after all, I thought bitterly.

My more immediate concern was that I had a show to do; my students were counting on me and I had to be the amiable host.

It was a gray day and I chose to walk back to the west side, through Central Park, which still had snow cover on the trees, benches, and statues.

Somehow, I put the news of the day in the back of my mind and got ready for the show. I don't think anybody could tell anything different about me and I even went out with the cast after the show for a few drinks. Ken had joined us by then and at one point leaned over and asked, "So what happened at the doctor's today?"

"I'll tell you later." I brushed him off and laughed and raised a toast to the students who had given such a great show.

Finally, back in the apartment, when all the layers of clothing and pretend had been peeled off, I revealed the truth.

Although Ken said it didn't matter to him, at last I cried.

Everything I had worked for — my recovery, my career, my relationship, my life — was, in my mind, blown to smithereens once again.

Still, I had been lucky. I had an incredible support system around me. I had found Middle Church a couple years before that, so an associate pastor (who had since left) was able to spend time with me after my diagnosis, and I found great spiritual comfort with the gospel choir and everyone at Middle.

Chapter Twenty-Seven

Maurice had been slowly on his way to becoming a more stable, productive person, as Jacqui had observed in April, but the AIDS diagnosis was clearly a setback—as it would be for anyone.

Although I had told him soon after he moved in that I had the disease, I'm not sure why Maurice was never able to talk specifically about AIDS to me. I suspect the shame was too deep. I could understand that; while I could tell good friends and potential dates about my status, I felt no need to broadcast the news to the world—or even my own family. They were conservative New Englanders and my mother had a weak nervous system. Why burden them with the news so long as I remained healthy? All those years into the crisis, the stigma was still great and people's ignorance was perhaps greater. It would be a long, slow coming-out process—more difficult than the first one—telling people I loved about my HIV status.

No doubt, Maurice was going through the fear that his active, carefree lifestyle was being threatened. It didn't matter how often I told him, "Look at me! It hasn't slowed me down a bit!" He had fended for himself for so long that he probably adamantly believed that he could fend off any disease by eating. That would explain his hoarding of food. He had his own small refrigerator in his hospital room and it was chock-full, and paper bags that he had accumulated from visitors bringing things were being filled up as well.

Maurice rebelled with his food and clothes, the only two things he had control over, as Sandra had observed. In the meantime, as compassionate as I could be, I was worried about how my own lifestyle would change with Maurice's diagnosis. He clearly was not going to be going job-hunting after he got out of the hospital, and the arduous process of applying for disability could take months—someone told me six. I was barely able to support myself with my meager teaching and temp assignments while writing my thesis, let alone support someone else. My friends, more concerned about my welfare, agreed.

Still, here was someone who had never felt a sense of home and was now in fear for his life. I had been asking the same question since about two weeks after he'd moved in with me in 2005: How could I kick him out?

That initial hospital visit lasted nearly three weeks, but Maurice got his wish and was discharged just before his birthday on June 27th. It so happened that I had a seminar to attend that afternoon. Erin was there to pitch in, and she helped him pile all those bags into a cab and took him back to Bay Ridge—most likely a $50 cab ride from the Upper East Side.

She practiced what she called "Auntie Erin's tough love" with Maurice (never mind that she was around the same age); she had been so exasperated by his immaturity about some things and his "give me this, give me that" royal attitude while in the hospital. She also told me, more than once, that I was enabling his childish behavior. Erin was right.

I had grown up around families where the wives often parented their husbands, haranguing them about their childish behavior. I had always been disgusted with it, wondering why the women stayed with their husbands. Now, I had become my mother and these other women, without the benefit of a marriage. Perhaps we copy the kind of love we see.

Around that time, I had befriended a fellow deacon at Middle, a middle-aged guy named Dwayne. Dwayne was a hero in my eyes. He had been homeless for years, in and out of shelters, had been in street fights, had major drug problems, had been in and out of jail, and had contracted HIV. You name it, it had happened to Dwayne. He had even managed to have a couple of kids. He finally woke up from his haze when he was picked up by the police and brought into the precinct. "I thought they were going to arrest me but they just looked at me with disgust and let me go. I realized that I stunk so bad that I couldn't even get arrested," he told me. That was his wake-up call.

I took him out to breakfast one day that summer to explain my situation to him and solicit his advice. Dwayne had managed to turn his life around: he got disability, a small apartment, and a part-time job. And he had become one of the most visible, valuable volunteers at Middle Church.

Without my saying so, Dwayne sized up Maurice right away—as a drug-using player who had learned on the streets how to use people. He insisted that Maurice needed to be pushed out of my apartment to be forced to find his way through the system and, ultimately, responsible independence.

What Dwayne may not have seen was that Maurice did have a caring side and wanted to turn his life around and have stable love in his life. Although incredibly bright, he was still emotionally a thirteen-year-old. A thirteen-year-old was not equipped to handle an AIDS diagnosis.

What I didn't see was that Dwayne had been through everything Maurice had been through and probably more. As an objective outsider, he knew the scoop better than I did. I also didn't see that the AIDS diagnosis, although very serious, gave me another opportunity to excuse his behavior— bad behavior that had exhibited itself long before his hospital stay. Finally, the illness gave me another reason not to throw him out.

But beyond all that, why couldn't I tell any of these people that I loved him? They knew it. Why didn't I?

His birthday was a quiet day at home with good food. He mentioned wanting a PlayStation 2 for his birthday and I argued with him about it.

"If I get you that, you're just going to sit around all day glued to that thing."

"It will be good for me while I'm recovering at home, work my coordination skills and keep me out of trouble." He had a gleam in his eyes like a bratty, expectant child.

The argument went on for days, off and on, and as we were leaving church on that last Sunday in June, he walked me right past one of those electronic game stores and stopped and said, "Pretty please?"

Maurice won that battle—as he seemed to have won most of them—and I went in and pulled out my credit card for the purchase of the PlayStation and a few games. I justified the expense knowing that I'd be working Gay Pride at

Rose's Turn that afternoon, raking in lots of cash, and that he was probably right: it would keep him occupied while at home. Still, my resentment was building with each purchase, although not enough to deny his request. The purchase was easier than the ongoing argument. I needed to find easy whenever I could find it, notwithstanding that "easy" was continuing to elevate my stress level.

I went into my own state of denial. Looking back at my journal entries for that summer, I wrote surprisingly little overall and not much about Maurice. His illness was getting in the way of my own plans. A partial entry from June 29th, when he'd been home for just days, reads: "Maurice has been home but he's sleeping a lot. I think he's slowly coming to terms with how sick he really is. It's basically full-blown AIDS, which means he may never be able to work meaningfully again. That brings up a lot of questions as to what the next step is for us. I'm his friend, but I did not sign up for better or for worse, which is basically taking care of a sick person for the rest of my life."

And then, just a week later, I wrote: "I am growing impatient with Maurice's laziness, lying around on the couch for hours on end. Although he's had a catastrophic illness, he's just been given a clean bill of health so he needs to start picking up the pace. I will tell him to look into housing options next week—not looking forward to that."

I had again taken on my father's attitude about illness: if you can walk, talk and eat, then you are okay! Get to work! Furthermore, being released from a hospital after three weeks of treating a myriad of problems did not equal a "clean bill of health."

I had previously made plans to go to Las Vegas for a long Fourth of July weekend, meeting Wendy, Jim, and a couple of their friends, who would be celebrating her fortieth birthday on 7/7/07. The idea was that it would be her lucky day. My forty-fifth birthday was the day before, so it was a way to celebrate with her, her husband, and their friends.

It was a long trip to JFK Airport from Bay Ridge by train, but at last I boarded the flight. Several hours later, I was looking out over the odd, rust-colored, treeless desert mountains as the plane made its descent toward Sin City. Vegas had been in the midst of an unprecedented heat wave and the captain announced that the afternoon temperature was 116 degrees.

I arrived a day before Wendy's group, so I took the time to explore the surroundings around my hotel, the Excalibur. I was on a strict budget for the week and Vegas is no place to be if you can't spend money. Everything costs money, and I mean everything! Internet for $12 a day? I don't think so. $20 to use the hotel gym? Count me out.

The visuals were unlike any place I'd ever been before, and yet it was all fake: a fake Paris, a fake New York, a fake pyramid, fake personalities. The place was soulless.

I was ready to leave on the second day. Luckily, Wendy and Jim and their friends arrived and we had some good times over dinner and then in a country-and-western bar where we watched people ride the mechanical bull;

one of Wendy's friends even tried it herself. And also available for those thirsty for thrills was riding the rollercoaster at the New York Hotel; or there was the possibility of seeing the comic, Lewis Black, perform — with his mock-angry sarcasm, he really captured the money pit that is Las Vegas.

In short, the city embodied every value I despised: greed, mediocrity, falseness, and lack of intellect. I never wanted to return.

When my four days came to an end, I was slot-machine poor and had about sixty bucks in my pocket. There was a delay at a stopover, so I didn't land in JFK until about two in the morning, which meant I had to take a car service back to Bay Ridge. Both the airport and Bay Ridge were in Brooklyn, so how bad could it be? With tip, exactly sixty bucks — that's how bad.

I was glad to see Maurice — in fact, I had called him while I was in Vegas to see how he was doing and to entertain him with my stories of the city that I loathed.

Yes, Maurice was out of the hospital but he still had a dangerously low T-cell count and was faced with a daunting list of prescriptions to eradicate lingering infections and to begin boosting those T-cell numbers and lessening the viral load numbers.

Basically, when one has AIDS, there are two forces at work: 1) the disease attacks the T-cells (white blood cells), which contribute to a strong immune system and fight off infections; and 2) at the same time, because AIDS is a virus, as it spreads, one's viral load increases. A healthy viral load is zero; a healthy T-cell count is about 1200. When the viral load increases, the patient is becoming sicker, but if the T-cell count is decreasing, there are less white blood cells to fight off the illness.

In Maurice's situation, it didn't occur to me that he was likely putting forth a Herculean effort just to be able to walk, talk, eat, and remain cheerful.

In fact, he went back to eating with gusto. "I am never going to get like that again," he said, referring to his twenty-pound weight loss in the previous couple of months, which had been highly noticeable on a guy who was about five-foot-seven and slender to begin with. To him, food was still the cure-all. He was skeptical about the medications and, when he did take them, claimed they made him nauseous, which interfered with his cherished eating plans.

Many were calling me a saint for what I was doing for Maurice, but I was not. Yes, when he was in the hospital I tried to make the long, inconvenient trip over there three or four times a week. Yes, he stayed in my apartment rent-free during his illness. Yes, we were great friends, enjoying movies and music and walks around the neighborhood. But that summer there was an undercurrent of anger inside me as well, at being put in this position by Maurice, myself, and even God. Maurice had just been pulled from the brink of death and yet he didn't want to take medicine. I had used all my connections to get him into a great hospital and I now faced the prospect of becoming a long-term caregiver. And God? Well, I hadn't had any more clear directives since that first "Take him in." Was He done with me, too?

All this was with no end in sight. I took every opportunity I could to escape.

Another drama that unfolded that summer was the closing of Rose's Turn, a place that had been a second home for so many of us for years. Really, there never was and never will be a piano bar like that again. The staff remained mostly unchanged through the years because we all knew we'd never find jobs like that again. Customers were a mix of regulars and happy tourists, gay and straight, so there were never any problems typical of most bars. There was occasional over-drinking, but never anger or violence.

I had the bittersweet privilege of working the final happy hour on closing day, Sunday, July 22, 2007. The closing had been widely reported in the media and there were even film crews from around the world filming that last week at the bar, which was like a long funeral for all involved. I remember that at the end of my shift, I went to the mike with a small group of singers who had regularly stopped by to perform a song, and we sang "The Glory of Love." I was weeping and I looked over at my pianist, Dan, and his teardrops were spilling down on the keys as well.

When my shift was over at nine o'clock, I looked up toward the front door and there was Maurice, beaming. He was chatting with Henry, the owner, who had fired him six months before. On that day, all was forgiven and Maurice, too, could call this place home.

"Home" was a word and a concept that was so important to him, and yet so elusive.

As a practical matter, it had not yet hit me how much I was going to miss that weekly cash income. In addition, the advertising firm where I was working three days a week that summer was coming to an end in September, and I was having trouble consistently booking my cabaret classes. And Maurice wasn't working and it would take months before the disability payments kicked in.

I decided to take another vacation, this time a week with my parents in Massachusetts and a weekend in Ogunquit, Maine, my annual pilgrimage with old friends. This would be a working vacation as well: I had to finish the novel before school started in September, and I would be able to spend most of the week at my parents' small one-bedroom cottage on a lake in northern Massachusetts, about five miles from their home.

Maurice never once complained about my trips, even though I was leaving him in the Siberia of Bay Ridge. Heather assured me that when I was away, he reached out to others, which was comforting to me. He finally bonded with Liberty. There are psychologists who believe that a good first step in getting a person to learn to love is by getting him a pet—sort of a primitive, practice love on the way to the maturity demanded of a one-on-one human love. This may have been the case for Maurice, and I later found something he'd written on the *reunion.com* site many years before—that if he could have a pet, it would be a cat. Without his ever telling me so, I had granted him that wish.

The best thing about that vacation was that in those long days at the cabin—I told family and friends not to bother me until after three in the afternoon—I wrote about ten pages a day, which was rather phenomenal. I would finish that novel's first draft, after all!

The weekend in Ogunquit was not one of our better ones. There was some squabbling over which restaurants to eat in and the nightlife antics seemed perfunctory, not joy-filled. I wished I had brought along Maurice: the gorgeous scenery, the salty breezes, the delicious seafood—it would have been very healing for him, and he would have added a refreshing mix to the rest of us, who seemed to be in a haze of "been here, done this." I hadn't followed my heart.

When I returned to Brooklyn, Maurice and I were happy to see each other, but he was in a bit of a funk and he still seemed to require long hours of sleep. That meant tiptoeing around the house and having no access to the television while he was asleep. At that time, my freelance work for the summer was winding down so we were both spending a lot of time at home.

"My whole summer is gone," he sighed, depressed that his favorite season was spent bedridden.

Realizing our dire financial situation—no doubt from my daily, worried reminders—Maurice had managed to make some cash here and there, putting ads on Craigslist as a bartender for parties and as a masseur.

"You give massages?" I asked, incredulous, after he asked me to proofread his ad. Was there nothing he couldn't do?

"Oh yeah," he said. "Back in my heyday in Richmond, I had a little side business going." He insisted it was all legit, not x-rated, and he showed me the oils in his bathroom drawer. The price he offered certainly indicated that he *wanted* to offer a purely medicinal massage . . . although the client sometimes asked for more. Maurice had too much pride in his skill to go that undignified route, he assured me.

There was always some kind of tale: the sweet guy who was 300 pounds, the woman in her sixties, the Hassidic family man. "He wanted a happy ending for that sixty bucks! Can you imagine?" he told me, rolling his eyes.

I had to admire his effort, making a couple hundred dollars a week traveling to far reaches of the city for these one-hour sessions. He was able to summon up his strength for those short gigs and get cash enough to contribute to the food and bills.

In the meantime, Maurice took his medications, but sporadically at best. Because his diagnosis had come so late, bringing with it a host of other infections, he had a drawer full of medications, from the beginning. I had just my one nightly pill. He was good about taking the medicine for the throat problem, because that affected his eating, but the other medicines that didn't offer a tangible result he could see or feel, he insisted gave him bad side effects; or perhaps he simply was afraid of the damage from the medications.

"You'll smoke a crack pipe from the street but you won't take a pharmaceutical?" I snapped. "To hell with the side effects, you need to get those T-cells up! Look at me. You can live a healthy, productive life but you need to take the medicines."

I did not have the nurse-like quality to bring him the medicine every night and make sure he took it. I assumed that he would want to get better, would want to live. For someone with his life story, that would be a long process he'd have to talk through with Vicki Sunshine. But he was only seeing her once a month and he seemed reluctant to seek out other professional help. He really liked Vicki but he once said to me, "I'm tired of going to people who are paid to care."

Slowly, he would work through that attitude. But time seemed to be running out.

Chapter Twenty-Eight

Those who have been given a diagnosis of an incurable disease may understand the layers of self-protection you have to work through when faced with an AIDS diagnosis. It may not be the death sentence it once was – although it's surprising how many act as if it were – but it is at least a gray cloud that will forever cast a gloomy shadow over your life.

I was in great physical health at the time of my diagnosis, but I thought, "Okay, I've got ten years." Today, still healthy, I'm still plagued by an insecurity that I'm running out of time. I can't tell you how many young men I've run into who, upon diagnosis, immediately go on disability as if preparing for the end. Years later, they are stuck in that limbo, still relatively healthy, trying to find a purpose in life. Or the men who continue their smoking and drinking habits, unmindful of the fact that those habits may well kill them before the virus does – or, at the very least, exacerbate the illness.

In any case, I worry about an impending catastrophic illness. I wonder, "How long do I have? How many healthy years are left?" This thought never completely goes away; every cold brings on a sudden, panicked feeling of "Is this the one that does me in?" It doesn't matter that drugs have been discovered to manage and prolong life, perhaps even to a normal life span.

Even with the drugs, at the time of diagnosis there was the fear of the side effects: nausea, loss of appetite, nightmares, hair loss, redistribution of fat, weakening of bones. How many long-term AIDS sufferers were walking with canes, fighting diarrhea or diabetes, bloated with toxicity? If I managed to avoid those common opportunistic infections, I wondered if the build-up of toxins from the medications would give me some kind of premature cancer. Sometimes death didn't seem so bad an option, if only to escape the fears.

Then, there was the psychological effect. Suddenly, my entire life would never be the same. I remembered how difficult my coming-out process was (and thought how difficult it must be for those who were hit with the double-whammy of a diagnosis while still closeted) and realized that now I would have to relive that for the rest of my days. Whom do I tell? When do I tell? It is not only facing the stigma of the disease – and people's potential hostilities and fears – but the real consequences that I might be discriminated against at my job or from insurance providers.

And just because I had the disease did not mean I no longer had a sex drive or desire for companionship – perhaps now more than ever, I had that desire. The dating game became a minefield: Should I tell him? When do I tell him – first date, second date, even later? How do I tell him? The fear of rejection and anger often outweighed the fear of the disease itself because, after all, I knew I felt fine. I wondered if I was worthy to have a partner ever again; I was damaged goods and the stigma in the gay community could be as bad as in the greater community. That is why so many gay men lie about their status, or live in the netherworld of "don't ask, don't tell" and just continue to practice safe sex – any questionable behavior no longer a viable option.

When I was diagnosed, my T-cell count was below the 200 threshold that qualifies the diagnosis as AIDS as opposed to HIV-positive; the viral load had spiked to over 90,000. Shocking, because outside of the occasional cold, I hadn't been sick at all.

After I was diagnosed, I got the pills but stared at them on my bathroom shelf for two or three weeks without taking them. At last, I called Dr. Glick and said, "I can't take them." I explained my fear of the side effects.

"They have to put that stuff on the label but more than likely you will not have noticeable side effects," he said. "And besides, if you want to live, you have no choice. You must take the medicine."

I took the pills. I had crazy dreams for a month or so, but nothing after that. Within months, my viral load was back to zero and my T-cell count was over 400.

I immediately became a client of Gay Men's Health Crisis (GMHC) and signed up for a free eight-week therapy group for the newly diagnosed. This experience was valuable just for being around other healthy-looking men of varying ages who were experiencing the same fears and questions. However, I quickly grew frustrated with the inability of many of them to dig deeper than the surface of their issues. Week after week, hour after hour, the conversation would go in circles, with no talk of feelings or displays of emotional breatkthroughs. I had been well trained with seven prior years of one-on-one therapy and was deeply involved with my spirituality through Middle Church. When the option came later to extend our group for an additional eight weeks, I opted out. At the time, I had a feeling of superiority over those men, and yet I couldn't stick around to help them with their breakthroughs, and assumed they couldn't help me reach one. Cut and run, life was too short to sit around in a circle.

In a satisfying relationship, with a great group of friends around me, and with my singing career in full swing, I decided I wanted to live. I joined a gym. I kept busy. My energy was great and my attitude was mostly upbeat. Nobody would have guessed I had the disease. I was in tip-top shape. "Don't ask/don't tell" became an easy option for me.

By the time Maurice's health issues surfaced, I had already dealt with the ramifications of my own illness — or so I thought. I was basically in denial about it and that had served me well on some level. I had lived an active life, working steadily, meeting friends, and participating in volunteer activities. Yet there had been no serious relationship. The secret became the barrier to intimacy.

I had no side effects from the medication. I probably upped the busy-ness factor a notch, as if to prove to the world and myself that I would be unaffected by this diagnosis.

There were signs that the relationship was crumbling with Ken. I was putting career first again and that meant I was home less often. Our sex life was quickly diminishing. In my own mind, I went for the easy answer: I have AIDS; he doesn't want to touch me, and who can blame him? It couldn't possibly be because I was putting up the emotional wall. I didn't realize that talking to him about my insecurities might actually help the relationship, not hinder it, and he didn't ask or push. Put me on a stage, and I'll talk about anything, but put me across from someone at a dinner table or in the same bed and I clam up.

Some fifteen months later, on our annual weekend to Fire Island, we were fully avoiding each other and it was quite ugly. Now, a relationship takes the effort of two and I'm sure Ken would be the first to say he shared in whatever was going down between us.

Nevertheless, within two weeks of that summer weekend, Ken announced he was through. I don't know why I was surprised. Despite the issues of the previous months, there was a comfort in the day to day, seeing him there. Until the end, there were no big, dramatic scenes.

I pleaded with him to stay, to no avail. He was out of my place by August. For me, there had been no boyfriend since. He found another one immediately.

Now, years later with Maurice, I was faced with the ugliness of a real health crisis in someone I loved and I'd have to deal with it.

As I recalled the early reaction to my own diagnosis, I could see why Maurice was in denial. Not having nearly the support system that I had and supposing he had lived a life with even more sorrow than my own, I could see why he was ambivalent about mounting another fight for survival.

Lingering in my mind, I was afraid that his survival — the stress of caring for him as well as my precarious financial situation — could threaten my own survival.

How do you reconcile wanting someone you love to live and at the same time live with the guilt of wanting them to leave?

It is a particular kind of grief I would not wish on anyone.

Chapter Twenty-Nine

By the end of August, Maurice had declined significantly again. Rather than take the medicine offered to him, he sometimes preferred to self-medicate. One night, he didn't come home and then a second night he was gone, too, with no phone call.

I called Heather in a panic. I never told her about the drug problem I suspected. First, I considered it his business to tell someone when he was ready. Second, I was hiding my own shame that I had been foolish enough to take someone in who had such a problem. Dwayne, for one, figured it out right away because he had been there. I'm sure Heather knew as well.

In any case, Heather was always a calming voice in a crisis. "It reminds me of an animal, like a dog," she said to me. "He would rather just go off to be by himself to die." I could see him doing that, but it was not a comforting explanation. I didn't want him to die alone, abandoned. He may have been all right with that, but I was not. I would have been very angry with such uncertainty and lack of closure.

On the third day, as I was getting ready to go to work, Maurice came through the door. Here was a man I had given a home, but he looked like a homeless person from the streets (and maybe that's exactly where he had been): his clothes smelled of urine and body odor, his eyes were cavernous dark craters, his hair matted.

I lost it. "Where the hell have you been?"

Maurice didn't give me an answer, just shuffled past me to the living room, his bedroom.

"Don't you dare fall onto that couch in your condition! You stink like shit!" I shouted. I was angry that I had lost sleep for two nights worrying over him, not caring then that he was immersed in his own self-hatred.

Maurice simply lay down on the living room rug and curled up in a fetal position, wordless. I wasn't finished. "Look, if you want to die, then go jump off the Brooklyn Bridge! But don't you dare come back to die in my living room!" With that, I grabbed my bag and stormed out the door, slamming it behind me.

All day long, in the quiet of a midtown office, I regretted my harsh words. He certainly deserved some kind of reprimand for his behavior, but my reaction seemed cruel and over the top. I had attacked his sense of self-worth, which was already about as low as it could go.

I came straight home after work. When I walked into the apartment, there he was, still sprawled on the floor, just as I'd left him. He didn't look up. I looked closer to ascertain if he was breathing. He was.

I got down on the floor beside him and wrapped my arms around him. "I'm so sorry, Maurice. I said some terrible things this morning."

"It's okay, you were angry and you had every right to be," he said in a small, child-like voice. It was hard to stay angry with someone so pitiful.

Despite his condition, he was able to distinguish between *acting* angry out of righteous indignation, and *being* angry as simply an emotional response that isn't always warranted. It was all the same to me: angry meant bad. In my family, it was the emotion of last resort. If it could be converted to laughter or even tears, all the better.

Who was the adult here? Who was parenting whom? I was in a fog, blinded to any light he was shining my way.

Within a week, he had weakened so much that it was time for another trip to the hospital. Still, despite his labored breathing and lack of appetite, a team of people had to talk him into going. At that point, I think he really wanted to die. I had been talking to him about hospice care and he was not receptive to the idea.

This time, Maurice was not the angry rebel he had been during his June hospital stay. Now, he was simply resolved to an unpleasant fate, one he didn't seem to care to change.

On one visit, I brought him the requested Quarter Pounder and fries, but he didn't take any delight in it. He sat on the edge of the bed, his head bowed, seeming to simmer with regret and sadness. "I've been sick this whole summer. What a waste," he croaked.

I tried to encourage him, but he saw no solutions.

My church team was behind me on the need for hospice care. The feeling was that this illness could go on indefinitely—months and months, if not years—with two steps forward and three steps backward, especially given his track record with medication. We lived in Bay Ridge and I was based in Manhattan—not only because of my jobs, but also for volunteer and social activities that were important to me. He would be alone in the apartment for long days, having to fend for himself.

Heather found a social worker named Carlos who offered to visit Maurice at the hospital and tell him about the hospice in upper Manhattan where he worked. I agreed to meet Carlos at the hospital, but he got there before I did and made the mistake of going in to visit Maurice on his own to give his pitch.

Maurice was in no mood for it. By the time I got there, Carlos was waiting outside the room. We went over to a waiting area to sit down and talk. Carlos had dealt with all kinds of personalities before, so he was used to seeing resistance. "He needs some time to think about it," he explained. He assured me that hospice care was not what it used to be—that is, a place to die—and that Maurice would be given medicine daily until he was strong enough to leave, being fully set up with Medicaid and disability. I'm not sure I believed him—I still thought of hospice as a place to go when all other options were used up—but, either way, it was fine by me. I could visit him a few times a week and I wouldn't have to worry about finding him dead on my couch.

I thanked Carlos and took his card. The urgent consideration was that one had to be discharged from the hospital into hospice care with the doctor's consent; you couldn't just go home to think about it and then call up the facility and say, "Okay, I've decided I'm now ready for hospice care."

I went in to face what I knew would be an angry Maurice. He was, but his tone was more measured now, not the paranoid, frightened, shouting Maurice of June.

"I was sleeping and that guy just comes in and starts talking to me," he said, shaking his head. "No tact whatsoever."

"I'm sorry. He was supposed to wait for me," I said. "But he's not necessarily your case worker, he just came in to explain the hospice where he works."

"We've lived together for two years, and now that I'm sick you want nothing to do with me." Wounded, he aimed for the heart.

"That's not it at all," I said. "I want nothing more than for you to get better. But you see my schedule. I'm gone from morning till night most days. I can't take care of you the way you need to be taken care of. You need to make sure you are taking your medicine at the same time each day. You need to be monitored, just until you get into a routine where you can take care of yourself." I then explained that time was of the essence, that if he was going to go to hospice care, that decision needed to be made while he was in the hospital. I urged him to look at the brochures, to talk to Heather or Jacqui about it.

A pall had been cast over our visit. He now didn't trust me and saw everyone conspiring to get rid of him.

Later, I relayed the course of events to my team at church, because they would often get a different take on events from Maurice himself. However, although they didn't give me specifics, Jacqui and Heather were able to tap into the deeper side of Maurice and have conversations with him about his mortality and spirituality. Their sense was that he was ready to go on to the next world, but that he was more concerned about me.

Over the next couple of days, Jacqui spoke with Maurice's doctor, a woman I didn't particularly like or agree with on many issues. She didn't think he was eligible for hospice care. I'm not sure what her yardstick was—a T-cell count of 2 didn't qualify?—but apparently if you could still walk, talk, and think, you should go home. If that was the yardstick, maybe my father qualified as a country doctor, after all.

In any case, that's exactly what happened. Just as I thought Jacqui was making headway with the doctor, Maurice called one morning to say he'd been discharged. He was on his way home.

"That's great," I told him, but I was furious. That fucking doctor couldn't be bothered with ever talking to or consulting with me, the person Maurice lived with and who had to take on such responsibilities. I immediately called Jacqui to tell her what happened, and she was also angry. The hospice care option was now out the window, at least until the next hospitalization.

Maurice seemed to be thrilled to be home. He had circumvented all of our efforts to send him to hospice care.

However, I had another card up my sleeve. I had been talking with Dwayne, who had been telling me tales of his own addiction, homelessness, and HIV diagnosis. He had convinced me that there were services available to Maurice; that as a person with AIDS, he could be given housing as well as disability, food stamps, and possibly more. Dwayne convinced me that I needed to start getting tough with Maurice and push him to seek out these options; otherwise, I might be stuck with him on my couch for years to come.

My anger was the fuel that would get me to act tough at last.

Chapter Thirty

Jacqui shared my annoyance with the situation at hand. She scheduled a meeting for the three of us in her second floor office at the church, shortly after Labor Day weekend. I don't think Maurice knew what was coming and, cruelly, I hadn't given him a heads-up. My feeling, perhaps justified, was that if I had, he wouldn't have shown up for the meeting.

Jacqui expertly played the psychologist role as well as senior minister to ascertain from each of us our feelings and what we thought should be next on the agenda. She explained that we were each entitled to our feelings and that we each had the right to say what we wanted.

Maurice was in a pleasant mood, perhaps just enjoying the attention he was getting from someone as busy and important as Jacqui. It became clear, though, that the focus of the conversation would be the question of when Maurice felt he could move out of my apartment. We made him understand that his illness was not only taking a toll on him but also on me, and that there might be better ways for him to be taken care of.

When asked by Jacqui when he thought he could move out, Maurice answered, "By December First." He went on to explain that he needed time to get his strength back and that it took time to navigate the various state and city agencies to find housing and get disability payments.

When she asked me the same question, I answered — still stinging from his doctor's early discharge of him the week before — without emotion, "October First."

I probably expected an angry reaction from Maurice but what I got knifed me in the heart. He immediately burst into tears, stammering that he couldn't do it. Jacqui went over and rubbed his shoulders and assured him all would be fine. I had seen him defeated and down many times in the two years I had known him, but I had never once seen him break down and cry.

Somehow, I managed to remain stoic and dry-eyed while Jacqui comforted him. If I gave in, I reasoned, he would win again. It was a superhuman effort on my part.

Maurice had an amazing resilience. Whatever blows came his way, he was able to withstand them and get back on his feet. He held no grudges. I prepared for a bitter few weeks ahead and even imagined he was so angry that he'd steal my things and leave me during the day while I was working, without word or explanation. But he wasn't the same person he had been in 2005 or 2006. The recent struggles had weakened his body but freed his spirit in some way.

By the end of the meeting, he seemed fine and, finally letting go of my stern disciplinarian persona, I took him to Pizzaria Uno on the way to the train station, where he became that excited kid again, bursting with enthusiasm over the deep dish sausage pizza with extra cheese.

In the coming weeks, I had two thoughts about that pivotal meeting. On the one hand, the deadline did get him moving toward finding solutions to his predicament. He immediately started making calls and was assigned caseworkers for housing and the disability process was put into motion. On the other hand, part of me wonders if he gave up emotionally after that meeting, that it was too much of a blow to lose the home he had known for the last two years and to live on his own.

"I've done all that before," he had once told me, long before that meeting. "I want to live with somebody and share memories and grow old with someone." He probably meant me, but I was too caught up in the Maurice I couldn't trust, the Maurice I was struggling to support, to be able to envision that reality.

Another time, soon after that meeting, he repeated to me, "Now that I'm sick, you want to have nothing to do with me."

"That's not true," I told him. "I want you to get better but I don't think that's going to happen with my leaving you by yourself and being in the city for long hours day after day. I just want to find the best way for you to be getting the care you need."

I don't know if he believed me or not—he was perhaps too wounded to think the best of people, even me—but I do know that, although he got busy that fall doing the paperwork and making the rounds to various agencies, he also stopped taking his medications with any kind of consistency.

Chapter Thirty-One

In the middle of September, the Consistory and staff of Middle Church had their annual weekend retreat in upstate New York. It was nice to get away from the troubles at home and spend time talking about the future of the church.

Late that Saturday night, after all the meetings, we had some down time. I was talking to Erin about Maurice and she was coming down hard on me for letting him get away with so much. "There are resources for him, you can't let him drag you into this, back and forth to the hospital."

Jacqui was nearby and overheard the general conversation. "Are we talking about our friend Maurice?"

We nodded and made room for her on the couch. "The thing is, I don't think he's going to make it through the winter," I said.

"I don't either," Jacqui agreed.

"We don't know that!" Erin protested. "We worship a powerful, awesome God!"

"That is true," Jacqui said. "But if he's ready to go on some level, we have to honor that and perhaps God honors that, too." She obviously had had a different kind of conversation with Maurice than Erin and I had.

"In any case, I'd hate to have him move out only to die alone in some apartment in the Bronx," I said. I was already caving on my October deadline.

That was my greatest fear, his dying alone. If the end was coming, I felt it was only just that I be there to see it through. Otherwise, I saw no point in all of this. I wanted that master plan, and prayed for God to show it to me, not leave me in chaotic confusion.

And yet, what if he held on for months and even years, drawing a meager disability check and staying in my living room? Sandra, having seen her mother through a long illness, had told me she worried about the long-term effects of the build-up of stress on my immune system.

"But on a practical level, Erin is right," Jacqui said. "We can't operate on the assumption that he is going to die. We have to act as if he is going to live and treat him like a responsible adult. And maybe, despite his fears, he can live up to our expectations."

The church was about to embark on a capital campaign for extensive renovations. We were growing fast and our current facilities were not adequate. Although it was good, spiritual work with a wonderful team of people, this was another level of stress for those of us on Consistory. Also, I was trying to finish my novel/thesis rewrite by December.

Aside from all that, I was operating on the assumption that Maurice would not live much longer. That wasn't necessarily a bad thing, because there was an urgency not to put off until tomorrow an activity that could be extremely meaningful for him. I did not want to have regrets. I had learned that painful lesson with Gig's death.

Maurice had always wanted to go back to Niagara Falls, one pleasant memory from his childhood. I was low on money, but I didn't think I could wait until spring to fulfill that dream. The following weekend would be our trip to Niagara Falls.

Chapter Thirty-Two

It takes at least eight hours to drive to Niagara Falls from New York City. I couldn't do it alone and I couldn't afford it by myself either. I needed to find a friend who knew Maurice, who also wanted to go to Niagara Falls, and who could split the cost of the car rental and hotel bill. Erin would have been ideal but she was unavailable.

I decided to ask my friend Alisa, whom Maurice had met once the previous winter when the three of us went to a movie. Alisa and I had met many years before in a group therapy setting, so we knew more about each other than most people did. She had a cheerful demeanor and was always taking up new hobbies like guitar playing and biking and volunteering for various charities. She was a few years younger than I, but with her ready smile, expressive voice, and light brown bobbed hair, Alisa had the energy and appearance of someone even younger. Of course, I knew her history and there were turbulent currents roiling below the surface that were often revealed in gallows humor. I also knew she would be up for an adventure.

I had kept her up-to-date on Maurice's illness and she had compassion for his situation. She was willing to help and, like me, had never before been to Niagara Falls.

We picked up a car in midtown Manhattan on a Friday morning in late September. It was a warm, sunny day and we had a spirit of adventure. It took a while just to get through the traffic and before getting on the West Side Highway. I stopped at H&H Bagels, Maurice's favorite, so he could get one for the road.

At last, we were on the open road. Within a few minutes, we made a quick stop on the Palisades Parkway to find a bathroom and take pictures on the cliff overlooking the Hudson. Looking at the weekend's photos later, I looked so big and fat—I had put on weight from stress and Maurice's cooking—next to Maurice, who was small and frail. There was plenty of laughter that first day, but the photos captured a sadness in his eyes.

We had all brought our CDs along for the trip and we took turns playing our favorites and explaining why we loved them. By mid-afternoon, however, I was simply driving with purpose because we were miles and miles from Niagara and had hours to go. Also, Maurice had made a picnic lunch and we were driving for miles along back roads through the mountains and could not find a picnic table anywhere.

Eventually, we found a spot and I parked the car. We enjoyed our sandwiches and snacks and then Alisa volunteered to drive the rest of the way. By this time, Maurice was sleeping in the back seat, exhausted from his illness.

As we got closer to Buffalo, Alisa pulled over to let me drive. "Oh, you're giving me the fun part, huh?" I cracked.

I had made reservations at a hotel on the Canadian side. I'd heard that was the best view of the Falls. Looking at the map, I decided the easiest way to get there was to cross the Peace Bridge and drive up Queen Elizabeth Way on the Canadian side.

It was no easy pass through Customs. We had to park the car and go into a building to show our passports to an officer inside. Maurice didn't have a passport but he brought his birth certificate, license, and social security card. Alisa and I passed our ID screening quickly, without so much as a question. But then . . .

"Maurice, could you step into the other room with me please?" the soft-spoken, Asian inspector asked kindly. Alisa and I shot puzzled looks at each other as Maurice gave us a pitiful, apologetic look and followed the man into a room.

"What is that all about?" Alisa asked.

There could be no more covering for Maurice's sins. "Well, back in the '90s, Maurice had some run-ins with the law. It might have showed up on his background check."

"What kind of run-ins?"

"I think a drug offense," I said.

We waited nervously a few more minutes and then Maurice came back out to the counter. He gave us a sad smile. "They are not going to let me in because there's an outstanding offense on my record, like ten years old," he told us.

We'd already been on the road for ten hours and it was getting dark and I had to find us a new hotel room. I was furious, but he looked so pathetic, it would do no good to get upset.

"Okay, we'll find something on the American side," I said.

"I am so sorry," Maurice said. "I had no idea there would be any kind of problem."

"Alisa, do you mind driving back so I can try to call the hotel on my cell phone and arrange something else?"

"Sure, no problem." I was glad she was taking this all rather calmly.

We turned around and headed back, having to stop at American Customs. This time, the woman allowed us just to pass our ID through the window. She looked at it, looked at her computer, got on the phone. This didn't look good.

Within a minute, three armed agents surrounded the car and one of them barked at us to get out of the car. We complied without protest.

"Hands on the car!"

All of us leaned on the car and we were frisked. Maurice, who was dressed in sweat pants and an Army fatigue shirt and fleece jacket, was handcuffed and escorted to a nearby building. He said nothing, his head bowed in shame.

"Where are you taking him?" Alisa asked, starting to weep.

She wasn't answered, but an agent said, "Come with us," and we were escorted separately to another building.

"What is this all about?" I asked the one with me.

"What's the matter? Haven't you ever been arrested before?" he retorted in a jolly kind of way.

"Arrested? We were just taking our friend up to Niagara Falls for the weekend." I was trying to figure out how we would get out of jail from up here in Buffalo and how we would get back to New York with the costly rented car. Even if only Maurice were arrested, it would be a logistical nightmare. How would I get him out and back to New York?

"Wait in here," the agent said, as he deposited me into another large room with a counter. Alisa and her agent were close behind.

A woman at the counter asked Alisa for her purse. The woman then meticulously poured everything onto the counter and started going through it—a compact, a lipstick, perfume bottle, makeup, you name it: everything was opened and inspected.

Alisa was now crying and her tears probably saved us. I was still stupidly worried about Maurice's privacy but Alisa smartly realized that we were in a desperate situation. "He's very sick. He has AIDS. We just wanted to bring him up here as one of his last wishes," she sobbed.

The agent that had brought me in was still there watching us. "Really? I'm sorry about this, but we need to just check some things out. Wait here," he said, and left the building, I presumed to go tell this news to the men holding Maurice.

Alisa and I exchanged small talk and tried to comfort each other through this unexpected chain of events.

About five minutes later, the agent came back in. "You can go now. We've brought your friend back to the car." As the agent walked us back to the car, he went on, "They didn't want him back in Virginia, but tell your friend he has to take care of that open warrant or he's going to go through this every time he tries to leave the country or gets on a plane."

I suspect what the agent told me was true, that the authorities weren't interested in bringing Maurice back to Richmond for a ten-year-old parole violation or whatever it was, but I also think that Alisa playing the AIDS card moved the hardened authorities to some kind of pity. They realized we weren't there to cause harm and, whatever Maurice had done in his past, his two current companions couldn't be any more straight-laced or law-abiding.

Maurice was hunkered down in the back seat, looking defeated. He didn't need this kind of stress and this suddenly put a big damper on our fun weekend outing.

As we pulled back onto the highway, I said, "Well, that's a story we'll be telling our grandchildren." We all released a much-needed laugh to break the tension. I got on the phone and explained to the hotel manager in Canada why we could not make our reservation. After a lot of back and forth and getting some other numbers, we were able to secure a hotel reservation for two nights at the same hotel chain, in the God-forsaken suburb of Blasdell, a good 45-minute drive south of the Falls but, at that point, beggars couldn't be choosers. On to Blasdell it was.

We finally arrived at about nine o'clock, stressed and exhausted. Blasdell was kind of a strip-mall town and the hotel seemed cavernously empty, with a clerk who seemed to come straight out of that old TV thriller, *Twin Peaks*. Nevertheless, we were grateful for anything at that hour.

We opened the door to our room and were hit with a blast of moldy odor.

"Was someone murdered in here?" Alisa asked.

"Open the windows!" I shouted. By that time, we were rather punch-drunk and laughing at all of the strange turns our trip had taken.

After we washed up and put our bags away, we decided to go back to a nearby Applebee's we had passed.

We were served by an overly friendly young waiter who seemed to want to hang out with us. He offered us some much-needed comic relief. When we told him about our ordeal at Customs, he said, "That's nothing. My brother went over there with some friends and one of them had some grass, so they all had to go to a room and strip down to their underwear and the authorities completely stripped the car, ripped up the carpet, the seats, everything!"

Imagining the three of us going through that scenario, we kept mentioning other absurd possibilities that could have made it so much worse. I'm surprised we were able to finish our meal. We were laughing so hard that we were bent over sideways, tears streaming down our faces.

By the time we got back to the hotel, we were ready for bed. Because we were a good drive from the Falls, we would have to make one all-day trip because we would be driving back to New York on Sunday morning.

Saturday morning, we went downstairs for our awful continental breakfast. There seemed to be some kind of hunting convention in Blasdell, a lot of gruff, middle-aged men in flannel, eating their grub. I'm not exactly flamboyant, but I felt self-conscious enough, imagining a scene out of *Deliverance* to cap off my weekend.

Alisa drove to the American side of the Falls. We were rather quiet on the trip, still shell-shocked from the night before, but we did make some jokes about the so-called Peace Bridge as we passed its exit.

At least the weather cooperated. It was unseasonably warm, in the mid-seventies. Most of the summer crowds had gone so we had no trouble finding a parking space—the entire day for five bucks.

As we crossed the footbridge over the raging river, we stopped to take in the view. It really was awesome to behold, and we started to appreciate the reason we had come so far. We walked through a wooded park area, stopping occasionally just to listen to the rushing water.

At last, we got to a paved area that took us very close to the American Falls. Maurice went over to the black iron railing and mischievously lifted his foot up to the first rung, acting like he was going to jump over. I captured the image in a photo. The view was so magnificent that it was hard not to take photos from every angle. I could see why Maurice wanted to come here and I tried to imagine him as a wide-eyed ten-year-old, coming here with his family. He still carried the wonder of childhood with him that day.

We decided to go to Bridal Veil Falls. We donned yellow ponchos and sandals that were provided for us and took an elevator far down below, emerging on a wooden staging that allowed tourists to wander around at the bottom of the American Falls. We were immediately enveloped in a cooling mist and buffeted by refreshing gusts of wind. As loud as the rush of water was, its whoosh was punctuated by the laughter of all the tourists walking along the wet planks, holding tightly to the rails. A large, floor-like platform was at the end of the walk. There, one could walk across the floor in what seemed like hurricane-force winds and actually stand under a stream of the falls, feeling the heavy brunt of the spray; it was a massive outdoor shower and we then realized why we needed the ponchos. I went for it, drenching myself in the baptismal, healing waters. I turned around. Alisa and Maurice were standing back, watching. At last, Alisa just grabbed Maurice by the elbow and ran with him toward the falling water. We laughed and hugged under the cascading freshness for a good minute. Even with the ponchos, we remained wet for at least another hour. It was what a religious experience should be, I thought. We left Bridal Veil Falls drenched, invigorated, happy.

We wandered around in search of lunch. Not much was open, so we had to settle for an overpriced diner, which Maurice grumbled about. Then we found a spot on a grassy lawn only a few yards from the river. We lay down on the grass and Maurice fell asleep right away, I dozed off, and Alisa walked away to make calls on her cell phone.

Some time later, she returned and said to me, like a naughty child, "I had to tell someone!" Of course, she meant the Customs nightmare. We both laughed but I made her promise not to tell anyone else. Maurice must have slept on that lawn for two hours, soothed by the comforting sound of the water. I wondered if he was recalling happy childhood memories.

It was late afternoon by the time he woke up and we decided to go to the Observation Tower for another photo opportunity, and then down below for a ride on the Maid of the Mist.

The boat, which held perhaps one hundred tourists—now in blue ponchos—made its way over to the bottom of the famous Horseshoe Falls and stopped for a few minutes, churning in the waters as a mist sprayed everyone on the deck. Maurice and Alisa each took out a coin, kissed it for luck, and tossed it overboard.

When we returned to shore, there was a path leading up to the north side of the American Falls and Alisa and I decided to walk up it for another view. Maurice chose to wait down below. From the top of the walk, I looked down to see tiny Maurice patiently waiting on a bench. It was then that I realized just how sick he was. Even after the long nap, he was too tired to make the hike with us.

It had been a long, full day. We returned to Blasdell to order in food and lounge around in our smelly room. The day started to go downhill at that point.

Maurice wanted Chinese food and I wanted pizza. I don't know what Alisa wanted, but she chose to side with me. We argued back and forth for a while until it devolved to the point where I said, "Well, if I am paying for the meal, I want something that I want."

I was victorious with that argument, but there was no thrill in it—I had perhaps won the battle but lost sight of the war. We had all become childish at that point. Why couldn't I just give Maurice what he wanted? It was supposed to be his weekend.

Maurice wouldn't eat any of the pizza and then he complained when Alisa and I started watching *Psycho* on the television. "Haven't we seen this a thousand times?" It was not a great ending to what had been a great day.

To Maurice's credit, he never held a grudge and the next morning as we packed up to leave, there he was, excited about going out for breakfast. He got French toast and loaded thick slabs of butter and gobs of syrup onto it, happy as ever.

Still trying to milk more magic out of the weekend, I insisted on going the scenic route on the way home to try to catch some early fall foliage. Alisa was game, but Maurice mostly slept in the back seat. Alisa did most of the driving while I navigated with the atlas on my lap. After a few hours, even Alisa's patience was wearing thin.

We were again on the lookout for a picnic table and a roadside farm-stand where we could pick up some nice homemade goods like pies and jams and pumpkins. Upstate New York seemed to be devoid of such attractions. Miles and miles and miles we drove, to no avail. Maurice was no longer happy with Alisa's mellow music choices on the CD player, so he began listening to his own CDs on his Walkman. Unfortunately, he got carried away with excitement, as he often did with music, and began drumming on the back of the front seat.

"Maurice! Please stop!" Alisa shouted.

"Hmmmph!" Maurice snorted, then rolled over, putting his back toward us and curling up in a fetal position.

Finally, we saw a sign for a farm-stand, and we followed it up a long, winding mountain road with several detours.

"Jesus, they'd better have pumpkin pie after all this!" I griped.

We arrived at the top and it was a small, crappy, family-run operation. There were a few rows of dry doughnuts and various other items in jars that hadn't been dusted in some time. The best thing about that side trip was that we all got to use the bathroom. We bitched all the way back down the mountain. And like a bratty child in the backseat, Maurice started to demand McDonald's, another place that seemed to be in short supply.

Hours later, as we neared the town of Saugerties, we found a McDonald's and a picnic table in quick succession. That seemed to shut us all up momentarily.

By the time we got back to midtown with the car, Maurice and Alisa gave one another an obligatory hug and off we went in our separate directions.

With incredible highs and incredible lows, it was definitely a weekend to remember. The important thing was that we did it.

Chapter Thirty-Three

The October deadline I had set for Maurice to be out of the apartment was unrealistic. I knew that. But it was meant to be a kick in the ass for him to get moving on pursuing state and federal help that he needed. On that score, I succeeded.

Before long, there was a caseworker calling every other week and Maurice actually went to see a couple of apartments in the Bronx. I wasn't happy about the reality of that. I may have wanted him out of my living room, but having him isolated in the Bronx was not the answer I wanted, although he seemed willing. It was I who told him to wait until he found something in Brooklyn or Manhattan.

Watching Maurice try to navigate his way around the system was an education for both of us. It was an extremely frustrating and inefficient process and I began to question the idea of people relying on the government to help them in time of need. In fact, I became convinced that the government intentionally made the bureaucracy needlessly difficult so that people would give up and receive no aid. There were, indeed, wonderful social workers like Vicki Sunshine but, when it comes to doling out the resources from the government, the person who has paid taxes all his life in hopes that he'll get something back when he needs it is just a number and part of a quota.

The agency that deals with housing for those with AIDS is known as HASA, which stands for HIV/AIDS Services Administration, part of the Human Resources Administration. For some inexplicable reason, HASA assigned Maurice to an office on Coney Island, a long, inconvenient trip even from Bay Ridge. His caseworker there was Boris, an older Russian. Boris left messages all the time, always saying there was nothing for Maurice. Unfortunately, he would not call when Maurice had an appointment. Maurice would go down to Coney Island first thing in the morning on a cold day and wait, sometimes for hours, only to have Boris come out and say, "I don't have anything for you today, Mr. Maurice." He had broken English and always sounded like he was constipated. Maurice eventually perfected Boris's voice and that was the only thing about Boris that gave us a laugh.

I had a day off in early November when Maurice had an appointment with Boris. I wanted to go with him. Maurice was thrilled. "You wait until you see how bad it is!"

We had a pleasant ride on the subway and then a long stroll on the boardwalk. That time of year, early in the morning, Coney Island was almost empty. "This is the only reason I like coming down here," Maurice said, looking out at the ocean. "This gives me peace, no matter what happens in there." I flashed back to that Columbus Day we'd spent out there only a year before, when the future seemed as bright as the October sun and hope sparkled like the glints of light on the waves. It seemed so long ago.

At last, we reached the nondescript building one block from the beach. Maurice gave his name to the receptionist and we began the long wait. Once I went up to the receptionist to ask that Boris be called; once Maurice went. All to no avail. One might expect that with Maurice's prison record and survival skills, he might have a thug-like attitude, but he was as patient and kind as could be. I, known for being a nice guy, was quickly losing my patience.

Finally, Boris came out—not even a sit-down appointment for Maurice's troubles—and delivered the expected news. "Mr. Maurice, I don't have anything for you today."

"Excuse me," I began, standing up and moving toward Boris. "I am Maurice's roommate and legal health care proxy. His health is not good enough for him to be coming all the way out here in the cold only to be told that there is nothing for him. Do you not have our phone number so that you can call in the morning and tell him not to come?" I had rarely confronted anyone in my life, and this felt good.

"I'm sorry, I . . . I . . . I," he stammered.

"Sorry isn't good enough. This system is completely ridiculous. Why don't you just call him when you have *something*. And if you don't have anything, don't bother calling. HASA is completely fucking useless!"

A guard walked in from the outer room. "Sir, I'm going to have to ask you to leave."

I snorted. "Oh, don't worry. We're leaving and as far as I can see there is no reason to come back here. There is no help available."

We had a good laugh on the boardwalk. "Maurice, it was so much worse than you described. I can't believe you've really had to go through that every week."

"Shit, I'm going to bring you with me wherever I go," Maurice said.

The following week, Boris made a house call to visit Maurice, and soon after an additional caseworker from another location was also calling and visiting, although progress was slow.

Most significantly, Maurice never had to go back to the Coney Island office again. I had had many battles back and forth on life's line of scrimmage, but I had scored a touchdown on that one. I had won a victory and I wanted more!

Chapter Thirty-Four

Soon after that visit, I told Maurice he could stay for the winter and that we could revisit the move in the springtime. I was worried about his health as the weather got colder, and the added stress of his fighting bureaucracies could not have helped matters. He was so grateful. I told him, though, to keep pressure on the caseworkers, as it would probably take them until spring to find him a decent apartment anyway.

I still feared Maurice wouldn't make it through the cold winter, given his fragile health. And the truth of the matter was that our friendship at that point was the strongest it had ever been.

In addition, around that time, the monthly Social Security checks had started to come in and he was getting food stamps too, so he was able to contribute to the household expenses.

The grave illness had matured him spiritually. There was a restfulness to his spirit, almost Zen-like, that went beyond his physical exhaustion. He smiled easily and protested only the most serious of offenses. Although tired, he wanted to make the long subway trip to church on Sundays.

I was enjoying coming home in the evenings. Maurice cooked lavish dinners—typically very fatty and delicious, in the southern tradition. We rented movies, listened to favorite CDs, took short walks around the neighborhood. The 2008 primary campaign was ramping up and we were CNN junkies. We talked and laughed easily.

One Friday night, we stayed home and Maurice suggested we play our favorite songs for each other and either sing along or dance to them.

Sail on, sugar, good times never felt so good . . .

There we were, two grown men in our forties, re-enacting something we might have done when we were twelve: listening to and singing along with records. With that old Commodores song, we found harmony. Maurice was a terrific singer, but never felt the need to pursue it as a career, as I did.

But that particular Friday night, I didn't have a career, neither one of us had any money in our pockets, and yet . . . good times never felt so good. Two guys singing together just for the sheer pleasure of it, no audience, no expectation, no gig that was going to come out of it. It was the kind of small moment that Maurice excelled in: simple brotherhood and community, just for the sake of it.

Again, those lessons, like a gentle knocking on my soul.

We weren't lovers in that our relationship was not sexual. But in that moment, it didn't matter to me. If I never had sex again, with him or anyone else, I was feeling that I could live with Maurice for the rest of my life. Our companionship was as strong as between any two people, I think. We had certainly been through the worst of times together and weathered the storms, love intact. Although I had told him I loved him frequently, like a parent to a child, I never said out loud that I wanted him to live with me forever. I was afraid with that kind of verbal commitment on my part, he would backslide into laziness or drugs, feeling that he didn't have to work at it. I was vocally paralyzed; I couldn't even tell him of that fear, which might have opened another door to intimacy.

So I kept him a quarter inch from my heart. Did that make a difference? I often wondered.

At the end of November, Audrey, Paul, and Bethany came to town for Thanksgiving. They stayed in a hotel on Sixth Avenue in Manhattan, wanting to do the whole Macy's parade thing.

I worked on the Wednesday before the holiday and then met them at their hotel and we went to the Upper West Side to see the balloons. Or, we tried to. The crowds were massive and it was more trouble than it was worth. Maurice was back in Bay Ridge preparing for the Thanksgiving meal. We had invited a few people from church, but everyone turned us down. That angered me. By then, he had several friends at the church—on Sunday. Why couldn't people slow down, open their hearts to someone who was now willing to give his own, and had wisdom and compassion to offer? Opportunities are rare; time doesn't wait.

Maurice was such a good cook and loved Thanksgiving and was really trying to make more friends. He was aware of the importance of friendship—especially at that time—and that it was primary over anything else in life.

The guys downstairs had also said they were going elsewhere for Thanksgiving, so when I heard them coming into the building around noontime with their bikes, I made sure to peek my head out my door and over the railing to chirp hello. I wanted them to know that I knew they had turned down our invitation, most likely because they didn't like Maurice.

But Maurice went all out and when the two of us sat down for the meal, I said to him, "You know what? It is so nice to have the day off and not to have to go anywhere. I couldn't be happier than simply eating the best cooking imaginable with just you." And it was the truth.

As it turned out, his prayer partner called that evening and said she'd come over. Kele was a woman from South Africa who had had her own turbulent history before finding her way to the States and Middle Church. She had tremendous kindness and compassion, but her strength was rock-steady. She would not be pushed around.

She came over and enjoyed the food with us, and then she and I walked around the neighborhood and had a talk.

Kele was as incensed as I was about the lack of care at the government agencies. "They give you resources to stay alive, but they don't give you a purpose. People stay in those programs for years and it's so sad," she said. Kele wanted to create programming that motivated people to want to work and to change and to grow.

Friday night, Maurice and I went into the city to visit my family at the hotel. Bethany took a great photo of Maurice and me that seemed to capture a happy moment. Broadway theaters were on strike at the time so, to appease Bethany, Audrey and Paul arranged to take her on a limo ride around the city to see the holiday lights. The two of us were invited, but Maurice declined—he wanted to go see one of his nameless friends, which annoyed me because I was afraid he'd be up to no good. And when would he get a chance to ride in a limo again?

The four of us, without Maurice, rode around in the limo for a few hours. It was really too much of a treat for nine-year-old Bethany, who perhaps didn't appreciate it enough.

Saturday night, my family came out to Brooklyn for a visit. Maurice had made collard greens to show off to Paul, who was really the gourmet cook of his family. Then we went downstairs to have dinner at a Greek restaurant (Paul was of Greek heritage). Audrey and Paul commented to me on the sly that Maurice didn't seem to eat much, just pushing food around on the plate. After dinner, we all took a long walk around Bay Ridge, famous for its Christmas lights. It was a frigid night but Maurice happily went along without complaint.

After they left and we were back in the apartment, I made sure Maurice put on pajamas and wrapped himself up in the ratty red sleeping bag as well as blankets, and I made him a cup of tea. He had been shivering by then.

I remained hopeful because I so wanted everything to work out, but seeing him lying there shivering, I didn't see how he would make it to spring.

Chapter Thirty-Five

December 2007 was especially busy for me. I was finishing up the semester having taught four courses, so there were plenty of papers to correct. In addition, there were many commitments at church and I was still trying to get temp work on the side.

I had already decided I was not going home to Massachusetts for Christmas. Maurice wasn't well enough for the travel and even if he was, he'd probably be sleeping all day long when he got there. Not exactly a fun time. If he couldn't travel, I was not about to abandon him on Christmas day.

Once during the month, I managed to get to Macy's and I got him a new comforter and new pillows. But after that trip, my schedule became too hectic to find him a meaningful gift. I did manage to find a small, fake tree with flashing fiber-optic lights, which overall was rather festive. That, along with my Christmas cards and garland and a few ornaments, gave the apartment some holiday spirit. Maurice wanted a poinsettia, his favorite flower. That, I didn't get.

I worked on the Twenty-fourth. I decided to shop for a few remaining gifts for Maurice after work. The problem was, there wasn't much open. I ran through the cold, empty streets of the West Village, picking up gloves here, a DVD there. No thought went into the gifts; it was just a grab for *something*. Maurice had also wanted an apple pie. The only bakery I found open was a Jewish bakery. They had an apple something, more like a tart. Running out of time and options, I picked it up.

Christmas Eve was a big deal at Middle Church: two services, standing room only. As a deacon, I was expected to help with greeting and seating. I had convinced Maurice to come into church for the 10:00 p.m. service, when the gospel choir would be singing.

He moved slowly but was in a relatively good mood when he walked into the social hall before the service. Sober is how I would describe him. Dwayne gave him a hug and asked how he was doing. I made sure Maurice got there early so I could get him a seat. I took him up to the front row balcony and had him save me a seat, and I left the bags with him. I also had a back-up plan for Sandra to join us.

As the church started to fill up, I was given the task of working the overflow crowd, which would be seated in the social hall. These would be the unhappy people who couldn't get a seat in the main sanctuary and would have to watch the concert on a large screen. Another deacon and Brad, one of the ministers, joined me there. But what was worse than that was that I knew I would not be able to get away to sit with Maurice to watch the celebration. It is the only time I've ever been angry about my service as a deacon.

Before the service started, I kept walking to the door that led to the sanctuary and stealing a peek up to the balcony. Maurice sat there patiently. Sandra hadn't yet arrived. I told Judi, an angelic soul who had also been following Maurice's illness, where he was, and she went up to talk with him. I saw him laughing at what she was saying and engaging her in conversation for a few minutes. At that moment, my heart was so full for him. I saw a man who had suffered so much—by circumstance and by his own failings—who was now wise beyond his years. I felt his life story—even the gaps he'd never revealed to me—could teach others, and so I prayed fervently for his recovery.

I did my job that night, trying to appease grumpy latecomers, but I had essentially missed Christmas Eve with Maurice. Fortunately, Sandra arrived and sat with him. She later told me he was asking about me, when I'd be able to come up and sit with them.

I was also supposed to stay and help count the offering, which would have taken perhaps an hour, but I drew the line. I said to Danita, one of the elders, "Maurice is very ill and he came out in the cold and I need to get him home."

She gave me a big smile and a hug. "Hey, sometimes life comes first. You take him home and enjoy your Christmas."

I don't know why I had been so by-the-books. I probably could have explained the situation and been able to watch the service with Maurice. I had let the most important thing slip away from me.

What other moments, both big and small, had I let slip through my hands over the years? I was so timid about going after what I wanted, and too easily convinced to let go of it when I had it.

One small miracle was my friend Jo Ellen's offering me her poinsettia, which she had purchased as a donation. I gladly accepted it—the one thing he'd wanted that I didn't manage to find on my own. Now he would have his poinsettia, after all.

Maurice and I walked out into the dark, late-night cold to catch the train back to Brooklyn. There were a lot of people on the train but luckily we found two seats together. He slept the whole way home.

Once there, I asked him if he wanted to open any gifts. He could figure out what the big gifts were—the comforter and pillows—in their wrapping. I apologized for what was supposed to pass for an apple pie as I took it out of the bag; he gave a disapproving look.

He opened the gifts. Outside of the bedding, he asked, "Why did you get me these things?" He didn't ask it in a cruel way, but in a wise way, as if he wanted to teach me something. Maurice absolutely knew that I had just grabbed a bunch of stuff and that there was nothing in the gifts that particularly revealed my heart.

I started crying, big, loud sobs. It was the stress of the day, the disappointment of the night, and knowing that I had fucked up on gifts on what might be his last Christmas.

"I'm so sorry," I began. "This really sucks! I didn't know what to do . . ."

"Look, don't cry about it. We can do gifts anytime."

I spread out his new comforter and pillows, making his bed lush, but he didn't give up the ratty red sleeping bag, which was my hope. We laughed about that. The new stuff just became another layer.

"Do you want to sleep out here with me, so we can both see the tree?" he asked.

He had never asked me to sleep with him. It wasn't about anything sexual at all. He just wanted closeness on Christmas. I was so happy he asked for that.

We both got into our pajamas and I turned on the radio station that was playing Christmas music 24/7. We made ourselves comfortable under the layers of old and new covers and I lay behind him and wrapped my arms around him. The colored lights from the tree were flashing and music was playing softly through the night. Nothing more needed to be said. It was Maurice and me against the world.

For me, Maurice had spent the last of his precious monthly check on a huge, expensive roast. It was enough food for ten people, but that was the way he was. As tired as he was, he spent all morning preparing the roast with all the trimmings. I felt sorry for all the people who had not allowed themselves to get to know Maurice, who had perhaps judged him on a first impression, that of someone who seemed to be looking to see what he could get out of others. But that was certainly a mask, one he felt he had to wear his whole life in order to survive. Behind the mask was intelligence, humor and the heart of a child, desperately reaching out for love.

That Christmas was both special and not special. Special, because it was only the two of us, and not special for the same reason. We watched television, listened to music, made small talk. It was the kind of small talk I might have dreaded with family or friends, but with him it felt unforced, easy. Magical.

It was the secret of life. Over the two years, I had discovered love.

And I didn't even recognize it.

Chapter Thirty-Six

I've always had a tug of guilt about completely missing the holidays with my family. This was especially true that year, when my nieces and nephews were still young. So, although I stayed in New York to spend a quiet Christmas with Maurice, I felt I needed to go home to Massachusetts for a few days around New Year's. I hated to leave Maurice alone, but once again Heather promised to check in on him, and the guys downstairs, by then, had offered to be available for any emergencies that might come up.

As it turned out, New Year's was as quiet as Christmas had been. My sister had already pulled down her tree and all gifts had been opened except the ones for and from me, so it was like arriving after the party. Not that I minded the restfulness of it. I also had the opportunity to visit friends outside of the family without the pressure of time, as always happens at Christmas.

I had a long visit with Neal's sister, Joyce. She was now at peace about his passing. "Can you imagine Neal as an old person?" she laughed. "It wouldn't have been pretty." She simply nodded her head with understanding when I told her that Maurice wasn't well and that I would be going back to New York the next day.

It is astonishing to me that when one is preoccupied with the greater issues of life and death, one can pass through festive holidays and barely notice the lights, the music, the smells, the conversations. All I remember is that my mother and I were at Audrey's on New Year's Eve and we watched the ball drop on television. I called Maurice on my cell phone at midnight, but he didn't pick up and we all just shouted "Happy New Year!" to him. That was all.

January was financially trying. I was getting very little temp work. Alisa was offering a seminar on medical editing—not something I was excited about pursuing, but it did offer the promise of better money, so I attended.

I also started Thursday night rehearsals with the gospel choir again, after taking time off during the holiday season. The music provided uplift and it was a chance to share my prayer requests for Maurice with the group at the end of rehearsal. The other big news was that the choir had decided for the first time to go on a mission trip—to the Gulf Coast, specifically New Orleans, in April. Many were skeptical that individually or as a group the necessary funds could be raised, but I was one of the few who stood up and committed to the project when a vote was held in early January.

I came home from choir rehearsal and told Maurice, "You should sign up for the choir trip in April. It's open to anybody who wants to join us!"

He eyed me skeptically. He didn't mention the possible health issues but asked, "Where am I going to get the money for that?"

"You just need to put a $100 deposit down for now. I think we'll raise the rest of the money." I wanted him to come on the trip and I also was hoping that the trip would give him something to yearn for, something to live for.

Maurice smiled mischievously. "I may never come back."

"That's okay. I may stay down there with you!" I replied.

That's as far as the conversation went, but I tried to imagine what it would be like to say goodbye to all I knew in New York—which was a lot of what, exactly?—and relocate to New Orleans with a healthy Maurice. We would have a tastefully decorated little apartment in the French Quarter with a terrace out back, filled with exotic, lush plants that Maurice would water daily. The kitchen would be fragrant with the smells of an experimental dish he was trying out. We'd take in the blues and jazz gigs around town.

I'd be teaching at a university and working on a book and he would be a social worker for troubled teens. My imagination was fertile, but the reality wasn't jibing with it.

The best thing about the first half of that January, while I was on my semester break, was that I was home a lot, so Maurice and I watched movies and ate meals together. The simple things in life brought a measure of comfort and joy, a new feeling for me.

Chapter Thirty-Seven

Both of us were tiring of the long New York winters. "I'm sick of this, I'm ready to move south," I announced one evening over dinner.

"Me too, but I may have to wait until I get to the other side," Maurice said calmly.

"Why are you determined to see this as a death sentence?" I asked, annoyed. "Look at me. There is no reason on earth why you can't take your medicine and get better and resume a normal life."

"What's a normal life?"

That, I couldn't answer for him. If my life was "normal," I'm not sure Maurice would have approved of it. Sure, I had responsibilities and goals and things to do—always, far too many things to do. He probably saw in me what I didn't see in myself: that I was over-committed to too many people and things and under-committed to the things that really were most important. For example, on Christmas Eve, was my duty to the Consistory—seating people—more important than sitting with someone I loved?

Who was I to judge his life? Sure, Maurice had broken many rules, but, when I thought about it, he probably had lived a very full life. All along, I had kept making excuses for his tragic life, trying to turn it around. Was my own existence—a succession of half-measures and timid attempts—so thrilling? Maurice's life had excitement, at the very least: every day an adventure.

What I couldn't face was that in Maurice's mind, it was probably easier for him to die in order that I might live. I know he couldn't stand to see what I was going through and he probably imagined that if he took the medicine, he'd live but I'd be taking care of him for another twenty years. And yet, to get better only to have to go out into lonely New York to live anonymously in his own apartment was not a dream for him but a nightmare. Why go on living?

However, we had to act like "normal" folks and prepare for the "normal" life. We had been gathering up second-hand furniture, a DVD/VCR player and other items for him to take with him when he found his own apartment, and he was faithfully keeping his appointments with caseworkers and such. He played the game for the sake of me and Jacqui and the church.

Truth be told, I was having second thoughts about having him move, too. Yes, the trials of Maurice had been an ongoing stress, but the joy of his friendship on a daily basis was something I hadn't experienced before. We'd been through the worst together and yet our bond remained steadfast, even growing stronger. And my hope was that if he could conquer the illness, the maturity he had gained would make him the great person I knew he could be. Think of what he could teach others, I imagined, turning Maurice into one of my projects. Why couldn't I yet accept him for the great person he already was?

That January, I was hired to be a correspondent for *Edge*, an online news and entertainment magazine, mainly serving a gay audience. It was a small start, but at least I would be getting paid a little to write, and I would be making lots of contacts and having to write articles on a steady basis, which was great discipline.

"I want to live long enough to see you make it big," Maurice told me.

I was encouraged by the comment, as I thought my making it big was a long way off.

"And if you ever get sick," he continued, "I will be there for you, whatever you need."

I completely believed him. "You already are there for me," I said. "You have incredible dinners waiting for me when I get home and you listen to all my gripes about what's going on in my life. I never before realized the value in those simple acts of kindness."

Around the third or fourth week of January—a week before I was to start teaching again—it was obvious that Maurice would have to go to the hospital again. His breathing was labored and he was slow just getting around the apartment. He was no longer fighting going to the hospital. I think we both knew the end was coming. On the morning we were going to the hospital, I read to him Psalm 102, a prayer for the afflicted man. The words were so appropriate, I had a hard time getting them out, but Maurice remained dry-eyed and listened like an attentive child. Some of the key phrases were as follows:

> Hear my prayer, O Lord; let my cry for help come to You.
> Do not hide Your face from me when I am in distress.
> Turn Your ear to me; when I call, answer me quickly.
> For my days vanish like smoke; my bones burn like glowing
>   embers.
> My heart is blighted and withered like grass;
> I forget to eat my food.
> Because of my loud groaning, I am reduced to skin and bones . . .
> My days are like the evening shadow; I wither away like grass
>   . . .
> The Lord looked down from his sanctuary on high,
> From heaven he viewed the earth,
> To hear the groans of the prisoners,
> And release those condemned to death . . .
> In the course of my life he broke my strength;
> He cut short my days . . .
> They will perish, but You will remain . . .

Jacqui arranged to have a car service pick us up in Brooklyn. As sick as he was, he was so appreciative of her act of kindness. Riding in that luxury car, he acted as if he'd won the lottery. It was a nice drive through all the highways and tunnels and bridges finally to arrive, once again, at New York Presbyterian Hospital.

He had a long stay in the emergency room while waiting for a room upstairs to open up. Doctors were coming in and conducting all sorts of tests.

Maurice was coughing up a lot of bloody phlegm and they made him wear a breathing mask, but he still wanted me to go out and get him a Quarter Pounder!

I was prepared, I thought, for his death, and for this hospital stay to be his last. If it was going to happen, I braced for it then. I hadn't started teaching yet and I could spend more time at the hospital. My most adamant prayer was, "God, if You must take Maurice, please let me be there at the end. Don't let him die alone."

Back home, I called Jacqui, Heather and the friends who had been good about visiting him. I felt almost embarrassed at having to take them through this routine again; he might not have been in the hospital if he had taken his medicine with regularity. One of the assistant ministers, Brad, who didn't know Maurice well, suggested the same. He sent me a forceful email saying, "He must be made to understand that in order to get better he has to take the medicine." Well, duh. It's not that Maurice didn't know that on an intellectual level, or that I hadn't urged him to do so. The question remained, did he want to get better? That was a thorny psychological issue that wasn't going to get solved overnight.

Heather, on the other hand, had a different attitude. "This is a good thing. He's getting good care and rest and it also gives you a break. Let Maurice think of it as a stay in a hotel, to get refreshed." This was such a positive way of thinking about it; I had grown up more concerned about the economic cost of it all rather than the overall health benefit, and part of me still worried about that.

In fact, Maurice's attitude about being in the hospital had changed. He was much more pleasant, and was given a private room with private bath. Visitors had to wear yellow smocks and rubber gloves and a mask to visit him—not so much to protect them from his germs, but to protect him from ours.

He had been admitted on a Wednesday. Visiting him in his room on Friday, he was still wearing his own breathing mask and spitting up phlegm. His mood was good but I was sure he was down for the count.

I went home and called Erin and Sandra and others about my view of his prognosis. On Saturday, Erin went to visit him. In the meantime, I had been talking to my mother on the phone—she had found out from a friend back home that it was AIDS, not just cancer—and I was explaining to her that I was protecting his privacy. Somewhere in that conversation, I broke down and started sobbing and had to cut the call short. Why did someone have to suffer so much? Why did I have to lose someone that I had taken so much time to learn to care for and love?

In the midst of all that grief, the irony was not lost on me that I had never told my own family about my diagnosis. That's right, eight years into it, and I was still hiding my own diagnosis. I was a coward: I looked healthy and had not had any health issues; I could get away with it. I rationalized it to myself by saying, "My parents are getting old. Why would I want to worry them with this? They may be gone before I have any issue with it."

My perception was that the family had always taken pity on me: "Kevin is an artist, Kevin is poor, Kevin has a crappy apartment and doesn't own a car, Kevin is gay." Why give them more ammunition to feel sorry for me? Over the years, we had moved to a position of tolerance and respect for each other. I didn't want to upset the applecart. Such was my way, that I preferred to shoulder the burden of that unwieldy cart all by myself, not sharing the good ones or the rotten ones. Thus, nobody was being fed.

Erin called on Saturday night and reported that he looked good and they'd had a spirited talk. He was no longer wearing the breathing mask. How could this be? Surely she was mistaken.

It's an odd thing to try to explain, but I felt cheated. I was emotionally spent preparing for the worst and he was getting better again. I was so angry about the ongoing rollercoaster ride, that I couldn't fully appreciate the good news of his recovery. Heather assured me these were the normal feelings for a caregiver giving aid to someone with a long-term illness. "Grief is never wasted," she told me.

I had given up on the idea of hospice care by then—that was the doctor's decision and she clearly wasn't listening to us—but I was still surprised when Maurice called me on my cell phone on Tuesday and gaily announced, "I'm being discharged today."

"Do they know what's wrong?" I was angry that I was again being left out of the loop. I'd had him on death's door and obviously I was mistaken.

"A touch of pneumonia, I guess, but they took care of that. I can take care of the rest of it at home with medicine."

"Okay." I had my doubts as to whether he'd follow through.

I was there to greet him when he got home and by then my anger had subsided. I was truly thrilled to see him. The little scamp had brought with him all kinds of soaps and lotions and shampoos, which we laughed about. He liked getting his money's worth from those hospital visits.

The rest of that week, he stayed home and rested and ate well and even appeared to be taking his medicine. He was his old self again and I started to have hope that he would rally and would get through the harsh winter and he'd regain a sense of purpose, recover and have a long, meaningful life ahead.

At some point that month, I had my own doctor's appointment. I was shocked when Dr. Glick had me step up on the scale and I learned that I had gained twelve pounds since my physical the year before. That night, I went home to Maurice and said, rather gravely, "You know I love it, but I can't eat like this anymore."

He looked wounded, and I regretted telling him in that way. Preparing dinners was his best way of showing me love. "You'll take it off in the spring," he said softly.

"I love your cooking, but maybe we could just think of some healthier options or smaller portions." It was too late; the damage had been done. I could see that he took it as a rejection of him and the only thing he could give me at that point. He shrugged his shoulders and walked into the kitchen to get a snack.

On Sunday the 27th, I decided not go to church. Classes started the next day and I really needed to gather my materials together and prepare for the week ahead. I was thrilled when Maurice bounded out of bed and put on a nice shirt and tie to go to church. He wanted to go on his own, he no longer needed to have me coaxing him or going with him. He was making his own friends, reaching out on his own. I gave him ten dollars in case he wanted to grab a bite to eat after the service.

Chapter Thirty-Eight

That Sunday, before she began her sermon, Jacqui welcomed back some folks who had been away or ill. Maurice was one of the two or three people she mentioned; I know he appreciated that, being singled out in the congregation, because I know he secretly felt that he was too unimportant to be noticed. He loved and admired Jacqui and was always surprised when she had time for him.

Jacqui preached from Isaiah 9:1-7, providing a personal interpretation of the familiar text. Here are excerpts from her sermon that day:

> Light is shining on the people who are living in darkness . . . in the valley of the shadow of death. I want to do a personal reading of the text: What is the darkness that needs light? . . . Many of us are afraid of the dark . . . the things we think in the dark about ourselves . . . the things around which we have shame or fear or embarrassment . . . we hide them in the shadows . . . addictions or obsessions with our eating or our sexuality and instead of working it out and having it on the table with us, we hide it in the shadow . . . our persona is all about being good and righteous and just looking strong and capable and fabulous, but in fact, we're one step from being depressed because no one knows how frightened we really are, how insecure we really are . . . we can't talk about the things that shame us . . . Many of us spend a lifetime keeping in secret the places we feel that if anyone really knew that about us, they would completely reject us . . . many of us spend a lifetime creating barriers around our real true selves . . . a self that doesn't know how to say "I screwed up and I need forgiveness." We can say the darkness can hide me, but to God darkness is as light.
>
> Before we can work out peace in the world, there's a peace that needs to come inside each of us because God's light shows us what's up . . . we pull our junk out of the closet and look at it and maybe that junk has something that teaches us about ourselves . . . this is the light that chases out the darkness . . . and we must do a process of self-examination so that we can be the whole and holy people of God. Middle Church folks, take a step forward in the darkness. Ask yourselves, "What is it that holds me back? What is it that makes me afraid?"
>
> What's back there in the darkness making me behave in ways about which I feel ashamed? What's back there in the darkness that needs light that the darkness can't overcome? . . . Come into the light, let's go into the light.

There could not have been a sermon more appropriate for Maurice—or for me—that day, but I had missed it. The things keeping him from the good life were his secrets, addictive behaviors that he tried to hide in shame. It was those same addictive behaviors, stemming from insecurities that began far back in childhood, that stood in the way of his own physical recovery. Perhaps he was too beaten down by life at that point, but his despair seemed so deep that he couldn't muster up the will to live, even to take his medicine. Who was I to diagnose Maurice?

What was the junk hidden in *my* closet? I don't look good enough, I don't have enough money, I have no focus, I haven't enough talent, I am gay and have a shameful disease, I don't speak up enough about injustice, I don't know how to act on a date, I need more education, I don't know how to relate to my family. . . . The pile of chastisements grew and grew. Though less immediately destructive than a substance abuse problem and less debilitating than a mental health issue, the pile of self-loathing complaints was weighing down my own potential, significantly.

Maurice called me after the service and went on and on about how wonderful and necessary Jacqui's sermon was; he got something out of it. He told me he would have lunch and then come home.

So why, like the bad child he often reverted to, did he go down the dark road yet again? The only thing I can say to explain it is that, like the main character in *Dante's Inferno*, God needed to take Maurice on one more journey to the underworld, to teach him a lesson one more time. On a psychological level, I believe Jacqui's sermon provoked him in a way that he became tempted to act out.

In any case, by early evening, Maurice hadn't returned home to Brooklyn. He didn't have a cell phone so I had no way of reaching him. I was worried, as he was only a few days out of the hospital and had medicine to take for the pneumonia.

Finally, at about nine o'clock, the phone rang and I picked it up. "Is this the home of Maurice?"

My mind raced: What had happened? Had he collapsed? Was he back in the hospital?

No, it was something truly bizarre. The woman explained to me that she had to verify his address. He had been picked up that afternoon, arrested for trying to swipe Metrocards through turnstiles and taking the cash for it. Because he'd had that arrest for urinating on the street a couple years before, he was taken in. He would spend the night in prison.

"He can't!" I protested. "He just got out of the hospital a few days ago for pneumonia and he has medication to take!" Stupidly, I still couldn't bring myself to tell her about the AIDS even though, I thought later, that might have prompted them to let him go—as Alisa had done so successfully in Niagara Falls. I was still concerned about Maurice's damn privacy, which he guarded so steadfastly—just as Jacqui had said in her sermon. How much of my protection of him was also guarding my own privacy and shame?

"Oh, well, he didn't tell us about that. He should be out tomorrow."

Needless to say, I had a sleepless night just before the first day of the semester. He used his one phone call to call me on Monday night and I begged him to tell the authorities about his condition so they might let him go, but he just said, "I'll be okay, they're not going to hold me for long." His voice was bright and cheery.

My own shame prevented me from calling Jacqui or Heather or anyone else that may have been able to help out in the situation. Maurice had the shame of his deeds, I had the shame of an enabler. Yes, in that moment, it is possible I was more ashamed of myself than his deeds, and that prevented me from calling for help. I was still worried about my image. It was a bad combination in times like these when real, practical help was needed. This was rock bottom for us, but I still couldn't pick up the phone. Calling for help because he was sick was one thing; calling for help because he was in trouble with the law was another.

Maurice stayed in Riker's for three nights. I didn't see him until I returned from my classes late in the day on Wednesday. There he was, on the couch, eating a snack and watching television.

Like Dante, it seemed as if he had seen a great light at the end of his dark journey. His eyes lit up when he saw me and we had a long hug. No good would come of my scolding him.

Maurice could not wait to tell me of his three-day adventure. "I spoke to these guys in their twenties who were so lost and sad. They had no purpose in life and no desire for education. And there was this one guy, he could have been a model—curly blond hair, blue eyes. But he was losing that spark in his eyes."

He barely stopped for a breath. "And I was the only one in there in a shirt and tie, so I got favorable treatment from the authorities. By the time I faced the judge, I realized how much I had, compared to the homeless and hopeless around me. God wanted me to see all that so that I could know the life I could have had. I never, ever want to see the inside of prison walls again. How could I be so stupid? How could I ever take the risk of being sent back there again?"

It was a stunning, revelatory moment for him and, despite my worries about his physical wellbeing, perhaps he was right: He needed to take that journey one last time. Now that he had found his spiritual self, perhaps taking care of his physical self would follow. Or so I wished.

"I want to talk to Dwayne and ask him how he overcame all his demons," Maurice told me.

"That would be a great idea."

Maurice laughed and went into the kitchen. "Oh, and to eat good food again!" With Maurice, it always came back to food.

Chapter Thirty-Nine

The following week, Maurice's health started to go downhill again. Certainly his prison stint hadn't helped matters.

"I think your doctor let you out of the hospital too soon," I said. I was taking a lot of my anger out on her. I thought she should be asking me a few questions and I was still angry that she didn't consider him eligible for hospice care.

"I think so, too," Maurice agreed.

"Maybe it's time to ask around and find a doctor who is more of a specialist at dealing with AIDS." For all I knew, his doctor was such a specialist, but I couldn't believe it.

"I think so, too," he repeated. "This back and forth has got to stop. Maybe I should be in hospice care."

I knew then that Maurice was finally accepting the seriousness of his illness if he was willing to concede such things. And if he were accepting, maybe now he would start taking better care of himself. It was typical of him to skirt as close to the edge as possible before trying to save himself. It was what he knew: the survival, the drama, the rescue. The attention all of that got for him. Perhaps I wasn't the first rescuer.

The following weekend, he felt too tired to go to church, but I went. Early February was a blur, however. I had started teaching again, so I was back into a routine. I had also started singing with the gospel choir after the holidays and I remember after rehearsal during our time of sharing, I would give updates on his condition and ask for prayer. I was preoccupied during all my activities, though.

Maurice was staying home, out of the cold. My mantra continued to be, "If you can just get through the winter." As a native New Englander, I still carried the simplistic notion that weather ruled everything.

On Sunday, February 10th, I went to church again, and then felt I had to go to the show of a former student in the afternoon. The show was good, but the entire time I was there, I was berating myself for choosing this obligation over being back in Brooklyn with Maurice. I still didn't know how to say yes to what was truly important and no to what was not. I was trying to maintain a normal routine while my world at home was crumbling around me.

As tired as Maurice was, though, he was preparing dinner—a skirt steak with a homemade sauce and all the trimmings. When I arrived home, the apartment smelled wonderful and Maurice was bundled up in bed watching television, patiently waiting.

It was a fun-filled evening. Maurice's sense of humor was as evident as ever. The Grammy Awards were on and he offered a running commentary of mostly crude sexual remarks about the presenters and performers. When Beyoncé—one of his favorites—danced with Tina Turner, Maurice offered an accompanying dance from his supine position, jutting his hips up and out while shouting out James Brown-like whoops and grunts. I could hardly breathe, I was laughing so hard.

The next morning he had his monthly appointment at the off-site branch of New York Presbyterian in Chelsea, where he would meet separately with a psychologist, social worker Vicki Sunshine, and his doctor. It was an early appointment, eight o'clock.

After the Grammy Awards show had ended, he said, "Maybe I should cancel the appointment tomorrow." He was so tired and the thought of getting up that early and going into Manhattan held no appeal.

"No way," I said. I didn't teach my first class until 9:30 so I offered to accompany him to his appointment. "If you cancel, it will take a month to get another appointment and I want that doctor to see you tomorrow."

Monday the 11th was easily the coldest day of the winter. I think it was about five degrees outside. I could not afford the $50 car service to Manhattan, so we had to bundle up and take the long train ride in, at the height of rush hour. It was a stupid move on my part, but this was before all the signs were put up on the subways that said, "If you are sick, do not get on the train." But I was determined to get him to his doctors.

I had to help Maurice tie his shoes. His breathing had become so labored that bending over was too difficult. I wrapped him up in layers of scarf, hat and mittens, and offered him my old but reliable black leather coat—which I had inherited from Neal—but Maurice went with his knee-length cloth coat, one of his proud Salvation Army purchases.

As we headed to the door, I noticed that he didn't say goodbye to Liberty, his most frequent companion and now good friend during the previous six months. "Thank you for taking care of me," he said to me.

"I wish I were better at it," was all I could reply. He was being so sweet and I felt that I had failed him on the basic caregiving issues.

We got an early start because of his condition and we had to stop on the landing between the two floors of our building so he could catch his breath. Luckily, the subway stop was just one block away—a long avenue block—but the terrain was flat.

Maurice steeled himself and we headed out the door.

The wind was howling and the frigid air stung my face. Maurice kept up his steady pace toward the subway and I walked alongside him to make sure he was going to be okay. Then, down the long steps we went, through the turnstile and then down to the platform.

It was about seven o'clock, so there were lots of people on the train and we didn't get a seat. Maurice leaned against the door and closed his eyes, taking measured breaths. At last, at 36th Street, enough people got off that we were able to get a seat—I don't know that he could have made it without that seat and I was ready to ask for one if the way hadn't cleared at that express stop. I convinced him to stay on the local R so that he could have the seat, even though it meant we would probably be late for the appointment.

Sure enough, it was 8:15 a.m. when we finally pulled into Union Square. I was ready to take a cab from there rather than wait for another train and have another walk. We went up to the street and Maurice was puffing and panting in the cold as I tried to flag down a cab. After a minute, one stopped and let someone out and I grabbed it and ushered Maurice into the seat.

"I don't know if I could have stood out there much longer," he said. I knew he was really sick to say that because he wasn't one to complain about his ailments.

We got to 24th Street and we crossed the icy street and went into the building. We walked up to the counter and Maurice gave his name. His first appointment was with the psychologist.

"Oh, she's not in today," the receptionist told us. Maurice wordlessly turned around and went to sit in an easy chair.

I lost it. "Don't you people have phones? He is very sick and we just came in from Brooklyn on the coldest day of the year for this appointment!"

"I'm sorry." She said nothing more.

"Well, his doctor and social worker better be here today because he needs to be seen by somebody."

"Yes sir, they are here today and they will see him."

I turned on my heel and went over to Maurice. He was surprisingly calm, perhaps too sick for theatrics. "I almost passed out when she told me that," he said.

"You'll still get seen by Vicki and your doctor," I said. "I'm going to go next door and get you a cup of tea."

I went to the nearby deli and got tea and a *New York Post* for him to read, checking my watch to see if I'd be late to class. It looked like I'd just make it. I returned with the goods and made sure he was settled in. "You don't leave here until someone sees you," I told him. "And I can get back here by four if I have to. Do not get back on the train to Brooklyn by yourself. Wait for me and call me if there is any change." I expected a protest from him, but he seemed content to sit in that chair all day and wait for me to come pick him up.

After my classes, I checked my cell phone. There was a message from an unfamiliar number. "It's Maurice. I'm back at the hospital. The doctor could see that my breathing wasn't good, so she called an ambulance and here I am, back in the ER." He sounded energetic and upbeat, as opposed to that morning. I think Maurice was still shocked that people would take care of him. I was relieved that his damn doctor did something right.

I called him back and told him I was on my way to the hospital. "Can you stop and get me a Quarter Pounder?" he asked.

Once again, there was going to be a long wait for a room, but he did have his own glassed-in area. I stayed for about two hours and he seemed in good spirits. I had other temp work that week on my non-teaching days so I needed to preserve my energy. "Call me as soon as you have a definite room and I'll let everyone at church know."

I was back again on Tuesday night but he was in a temporary room; it was expected that he would be moved again.

"How about on Friday I bring in a Fat Sal's pizza?" I offered. Fat Sal's was his favorite pizza, from our old neighborhood in midtown, and we had it every Tuesday back then.

"Really? Fat Sal's?" Maurice squealed with delight. Nothing could have made him happier.

Maurice also revealed to me a new goal. "You know what? I want to go back to school and become a medical assistant. Because I've been in here enough to see what it takes to make people feel good when you have to come in to draw blood or something even worse." I was beaming; he would be so good at that, using his very best helpful and cheerful qualities.

I had also brought him a Valentine's Day card and he said he was sorry he would be in the hospital that Thursday and wouldn't be able to get me a card. Enclosed in the card was a photo of Liberty and he immediately placed it on his nightstand. I told him I had a couple of busy days ahead and might not get back until Friday — three days later and a day after Valentine's Day. He was fine with that.

I went home and did my usual round of emails to my friends at church, drumming up support. By now, none of us ever knew if this was another temporary setback or the final days.

On Wednesday, he called, absolutely giddy. "Guess what?"

"What?" I was expecting some sort of miraculous news by the sound of his voice.

"My T-cell count is zero! Zero!" he repeated for emphasis.

I was temporarily speechless, but Maurice definitely had a morbid sense of humor so I went with it. "How are you still alive?" It was an honest question. I thought zero T-cells meant you were dead.

"I don't know, but here I am!" He again expressed his eagerness for the pizza on Friday. It wasn't clear to me at the time, but Maurice was happy *because* he sensed the end was near; the long struggle was almost over.

I didn't know how someone could be so sick and sound so happy. Surely, that fine hospital would find a way to turn things around.

"Okay, sweetie. I can't wait to see you on Friday."

The next day, Valentine's Day, I was working in an office where I didn't have a landline and I couldn't get cell phone reception. I called Maurice's number at the hospital from another phone, but he wasn't there and the phone just rang and rang. I called the main number and they said he had been moved but didn't have a number for him just then. I was not able to reach him all day or night and I wondered if he was in Intensive Care . . . or worse.

I went back to work on Friday and around mid-morning Maurice called me on my cell phone. "Where have you been, sucker?" he asked in his ghetto voice.

I explained about the inability to reach him by phone and was relieved that he still sounded fine.

"Are you still coming tonight?" he asked.

"Of course," I said. "Are you still able to eat pizza?"

"Are you kidding me? Nothing is going to stop me from Fat Sal's!"

"Well, all right then. I should be there around six o'clock."

It was a long day at the office; I was looking forward to our visit almost as much as he was.

It was another cold winter evening. After work, I took the subway a few stops to the Upper East Side, where the closest Fat Sal's was. After I ordered the pizza, I went next door to a Duane Reade pharmacy to pick up some sodas and some chocolate for a belated Valentine's Day celebration. I went back and picked up the pizza and took a cab back down to the hospital.

Maurice was sitting up when I arrived, eager and ready to eat. "Has anybody ever loved you like I've loved you," I announced as I carried in the pizza.

To my surprise, he answered the rhetorical question. "Oh, one or two. You're definitely in the top three."

I put the pizza down on the table. "What happened to the other two?"

"I wasn't mature enough to realize what I had," he said.

If I had been smart, I'd have asked for their names and addresses, but I'd been pushed back before when I tried to get information, so I let it go. The previous summer, after his first hospital stay, he noticed his sister's name came up on the Google search, as I had been trying to locate kin. He confronted me with icy contempt that day. Lesson learned.

But that Friday night, he was in great spirits. I cut up the pizza and he dug right in, moaning and squealing with delight at each bite.

One of his favorite shows, *Law and Order: SVU*, was on and we watched it quietly. I wanted to ask him the big questions about life and death, but I couldn't go there. Was I protecting myself or him by not asking such questions? I told myself that I shouldn't stress him with such matters as he was recuperating. Likewise, his silence was probably to protect my feelings. He probably would have been ready to talk about anything. Another opportunity was lost in the silence.

Nevertheless, there was a certain intimacy to the evening, where we just enjoyed each other in the relative quiet. He had another room with a stunning view of the East River, and for long moments we ate quietly and gazed out at the million lights and dark sky.

He ate three slices of that pizza; I had just one. "Nobody makes pizza like Fat Sal's!" he exclaimed. "Why don't you have more?"

"And rob me of the opportunity to watch you eat more?" I laughed.

He just didn't seem that sick, despite the zero T-cell count; it was astonishing how quickly the hospital care could turn him around. "So have they determined what the problem is?"

"No, they took a biopsy and I should get the results back on Tuesday. They're not sure if it's pneumonia or not." He didn't seem concerned, or he was more at peace about it all. As nurses and aides came in to check on him, he was genuinely kind and asking them how *they* were doing. I was so proud of him.

I wanted him in my life forever.

Around nine o'clock, I was already yawning. It had been another long, stressful week and the walk and subway trip back to Bay Ridge sometimes took ninety minutes. "Why don't you go home? I'm doing okay," he told me. "We had a good visit."

"Okay. I'll be back on Sunday, but I think Erin is coming to visit tomorrow."

"Great. Oh, and by the way," he said, "You can take back some of the clothes you brought me on Tuesday. I just need one pair of jeans to get home, I don't need three pair."

We both laughed. We recalled his visit the previous summer when he wanted many changes of clothes, silverware, plates, books, you name it. Now he was content to wear the hospital scrubs provided for him and travel lightly. "You've changed," I said, impressed.

"I'm letting go of some baggage," he said.

I didn't see it in that moment, but he was obviously prepared for whatever was to come.

I was not.

I needed the Saturday just to stay home and rest. Teaching and doing temp jobs and taking care of most of the bills and traveling to the Upper East Side and worrying about a gravely sick friend . . . it was all taking a toll on me. Not only had I gained the paunch around my midsection, but I just looked tired. I was comforted by the fact that Erin and perhaps others would be visiting Maurice that day.

On Sunday, I went to church and then headed up to the hospital. This time, as I went into his room, he had sobered. His breathing was more labored and occasionally he had to pick up a breathing mask to get a few good breaths. The staff was coming in to check on him more frequently.

I tried to lighten the mood. "Did they throw out the rest of the pizza?"

"Are you kidding me? I hid the rest of it in the box under the bed. I finished it yesterday. I wasn't about to let that go."

"So what's going on today with your breathing?"

"They're not sure. They have to wait for the results of the biopsy. I hope this isn't going to affect my sleep."

"I have my doctor's appointment on Tuesday morning in this neighborhood. I'm working tomorrow not too far from here, so I'll come over after work and stay overnight with you. This chair becomes a cot, right?"

"Really? You want to stay over?" Maurice was genuinely touched, thrilled. "That would be great!"

"Yeah, I want to. It will be like our own little slumber party."

"Listen, you might as well, and I got my own private bath," he said, gesturing to his right, as though he had a hotel room with a view.

As tired as I was, it was getting harder and harder to leave him, period. At that late moment, I was recognizing more and more his value to me. It didn't take Maurice's being at the end of his life for him to appreciate the small moments, but that's what it took to get me to appreciate them.

The next day was Monday, Presidents' Day. I had a temp shift starting at noon. A little after eight, I said goodbye to Maurice and headed out.

I didn't have a good feeling about how he had gone downhill since Friday. It was still relatively early. I went to the Web, a nearby bar, to have a drink or two. Part of me felt as if it was the wrong thing to be doing, but on the other hand, I needed to get out of my routine, even for an hour or two, and see some new people.

It was just what I needed. I made small talk with some people on both sides of me at the bar and we were watching *Extreme Makeover: Home Edition*. I shared a few laughs with other patrons. Later, an Asian guy, from Toronto, sat down. He was waiting for a blind date to show up and he was already a bit tipsy. Still, we had a good conversation and for just a little while I was able to forget my grief.

I got home to Bay Ridge at about midnight and collapsed on the bed and fell asleep immediately.

The next morning, just after ten as I was getting ready for work, the phone rang. It was a doctor from the hospital. He informed me that Maurice had been taken down to the ICU and was alert, but was on a respirator. I thanked him and hung up the phone.

I had such a sense of responsibility about not wanting to disappoint employers that I actually thought about going to work, as planned, and then going to the hospital at about nine o'clock that night. Remembering the lesson with Gig back in 1996, I came to my senses. I called my agency and explained the situation. Even though it was last-minute, my boss completely understood and wished me well.

A couple hours later, as I was on the long walk from subway to hospital, I called Sandra and told her the news. I just had a bad feeling.

"You know, he called me on Valentine's Day," she said. "Not even anyone in my family called me on Valentine's Day, and he's so sick and he had the peace of mind to think to call me!" She had been so moved by that gesture. "Well, they'll figure out what's wrong with him, but give him my love and call me back later with the update."

I found my way to the ICU, on a different floor, and went in the room. He was up, but had that mask strapped to his face. "Hey there, Hannibal Lecter," I said. I was trying to make him laugh, but it was a stupid joke. Maurice was fairly vain about his looks—the one thing he usually had control over—and I don't think a joke at the expense of his looks amused him much. He also had needles and tubes in his arms. Still, he was glad to see me.

"They probably won't let you stay in here tonight," he said. It was a small room with a large glass door, and just a chair for a guest. I was flabbergasted that that was the first thing on his mind — whether or not I'd be able to spend the night with him.

"How are you doing?" I asked. I noticed that there was an all-day *Law and Order* marathon playing, so that was one bit of luck for him as the doctors kept coming in and poking and prodding him.

"As best as can be expected, I guess," he said. "They brought me down here at about midnight and I haven't eaten since dinner last night. Do you think you can find out when lunch is coming?"

I went out to the nearest aide at a counter in the hallway and asked. Her answer was non-committal. I went back into the room. "They're not sure," I said.

He rolled his eyes. "They're gonna starve me to death."

A few minutes later, a nurse came in and went over and held his hand. "Look, we can't give you food while you're on the respirator. In case we need to aspirate your lung, we don't want you to be throwing up."

"So I'm never going to eat again?" Maurice complained, sounding like a child who has been told "no."

She patted his arm. "I'm sorry, sweetie, but it's for the best right now. As soon as we find out what's wrong and correct it, you can eat again."

I had been surprised by Maurice's outburst; he seemed to know he was on his way out, but that was not what was being communicated to me by the staff. They updated me whenever they could; they had a great bedside manner and were nothing if not hopeful.

Maurice quickly calmed down and accepted that he wasn't going to get food. "Why don't you go out and get lunch and then come back and tell me what you had," he suggested with a smile.

"Won't that drive you crazy?"

"No, if I can't eat, I'll just live through you."

Because it was lunchtime and I was feeling like a piece of furniture in the way of all the activity, I decided to take a break.

I went out to the hallway near the elevators and immediately called Jacqui on her cell phone. Even in this trying circumstance, I hated to bother her on the holiday. I was surprised that she picked up.

"Hey Jacqui," I said.

She immediately sensed trouble. "What's wrong? Is it Maurice?"

"Yes." I was sniffling. "It doesn't look good. He's on a respirator in the ICU."

"Okay. Do you want me to come up?"

"Would you mind? I think he needs some spiritual guidance. He's having a tough day."

"I'll be up there in about an hour."

I was so grateful for that. I don't know how I would have gotten through the day if she hadn't come up.

In the meantime, I went down to the street and got a sandwich and called Sandra with the update. I was now having a hard time talking to anyone without crying. Just to see him helpless and strapped down, but getting through it all with strength and dignity, was an awe-inspiring sight to see. Sandra continued to be uplifting, sure that the doctors would figure out what was wrong and turn it around. Then I called Paula, and cried on the phone with her as well. Her mature tactic was to remind me of all the great things I had done for Maurice, but she didn't try to give me any false hope. The messages from both friends were things I needed to hear.

I waited in the lounge outside of the ICU so I could see when Jacqui arrived. When she finally walked by, I called her name and she came into the lounge. She gave me a big hug. We sat down, and she offered a brief prayer.

"I'm so sorry I didn't come see him when he was here in January," she said. "But I was so mad at him for not taking the medicine and ending up back in here."

"For someone with HIV/AIDS, taking medicine is a huge psychological step. He wasn't ready for it," I said. I told her of the time when I was diagnosed and how I stared at the bottle of pills for two weeks without taking any of them and that the doctor had to be very stern with me. And I didn't have half the baggage that Maurice had. "But maybe he is ready now, if it's not too late," I told Jacqui.

"Okay, let me go in and see him."

I went in with her and Maurice's whole being lit up at seeing Jacqui. Even then, I'm sure he was thinking, "Wow, she's coming to see *me*?"

"I'm going to let Jacqui talk to you and I'm going to go watch TV in the lounge, okay?" I wanted to let him have a pastoral moment with her, to say whatever was on his mind, and allow her to advise, comfort, pray.

She stayed with him for what seemed like a long time, maybe an hour, but it's hard to say as time was at a crawl that day. At last, she joined me in the lounge.

"How did it go?" I asked her.

"Good, really good," she assured me. "I rubbed his feet and asked him what he needed. I read some Bible verses to him and listened to him. And at the end I asked him if he wanted to live. He said 'Yes,' unequivocally. So I prayed with him for healing."

This was significant, because Jacqui and I had talked before about how he was ambivalent about wanting to live during his previous hospital visits. Now he wanted to live.

"I also asked him if he wanted us to contact any relatives or friends and he said his sister Tracy, so I'll get to work on trying to find her. He wasn't even sure of her last name, just said she had been in the Air Force."

"Yeah, I think he lived with her in Florida in the early '90s, probably the last time he saw her," I said. She was the one I had tried to google over the summer.

"If he comes out of this," Jacqui went on, "I'm going to have a good sit-down with him in my office and ask him why he insists on always taking things right to the edge."

"It's the only way he knows. He has always been in survival mode."

"Well, we've got to get him into a healthier mindset."

"I know. I've been trying."

"You've done some good parenting, Kevin. He has some deep-seated issues, but your loving has done so much for him."

"Thank you, Jacqui. Of course, I can only think about what I could have done better."

We talked some more and then, to our delight, Erin showed up. I don't remember if I'd even called her with the news that day, but she had the day off and she was coming up for another visit. What an angel.

I didn't want Jacqui to go, but she had done so much. I have no doubt that her presence prepared Maurice for what was to come.

Erin and I said goodbye to Jacqui and went back into Maurice's room. He seemed more at peace. He asked us what we'd had for lunch. I tried to pass off my Philly cheese steak as average, which it was, but he wanted the full details about the taste of the meat, the cheese, the onions, and the peppers.

Erin said she wanted to host an Easter dinner and they started planning the menu. "If you get out of here, you can have anything you want," she told him.

His childlike eyes of wonder opened wider. "Anything?"

"Anything," she confirmed.

He was full of energy despite his predicament, and he kept pushing the mask aside so that he could be better understood. At last, a doctor came in and sternly lectured him from his bedside. "Listen, Maurice, you must keep the mask on so that the breathing is effective. The next step after this is really ugly and you don't want to go there, so keep the mask on."

"Yeah, honey, don't worry about it," Erin said. "We can move closer. We can hear you."

Day turned to night outside the window and still we sat with Maurice as he talked. I finally felt I had to do what I dreaded. I walked over to him with a notebook in hand. "Look, Maurice, just in case, can you dictate your wishes to me? I'll write them down and you can sign it and Erin will be the witness."

All through his illness, he had neglected to make out any kind of will—his reasoning, I'm sure, was that he had nothing to leave behind. But that day he didn't argue with me.

"All my possessions I leave to Kevin Hall. Any monies or valuables, I leave half to Kevin Hall and half to Middle Church. I would like to donate my body to science." He spoke calmly and with certainty. The statement really wasn't much longer than that. He and Erin signed it and it was done.

I didn't want to leave, but I was exhausted on my feet and had been there for eight or nine hours.

"You go home and get some rest," Erin said. "I'll be staying longer."

"Okay." I walked over to Maurice and cupped his face in my hands. "You fight this with everything you've got, okay?" He nodded his head and I leaned in to kiss him on the forehead above the mask, and squeezed his hands in mine. "I'll be back tomorrow morning after my appointment."

"Okay," he said, squeezing my hand. I put on my coat, hugged Erin and walked out the door. Outside of the glass, I stopped and looked back in—I needed to see him one last time. He was still talking animatedly to Erin through the mask, a wisp of hair hanging over his forehead.

I could hardly think of a sweeter person to see before going under than Erin. Thank God for her.

Chapter Forty

I got the doctor's call early the next morning before I'd left the house. During the night, Maurice's breathing had gotten worse and he was put on a ventilator. "He's in a deep sleep," the doctor told me. "He won't be able to respond, but he can probably hear you."

"What is the prognosis?"

"We'll know better later today when we get the results of the biopsy and see what is in the lungs that is causing this."

I felt I needed to be there, so I called my own doctor to cancel my appointment, but after the receptionist put me on hold, Dr. Glick came on and said, "You can go see him after your appointment, but we haven't done a full check-up on you in a while and I think we should." That made sense because my doctor wasn't far from New York Presbyterian anyway.

Ever since I was diagnosed, my health is monitored with four annual visits to my doctor: once is a full physical, the other three times are for blood work, a measuring of vital signs, and a quick talk with the doctor. I have never gotten used to the blood work, the prick of the needle as it goes into the soft flesh inside my elbow, nor the seemingly long wait—two or three minutes—as the vials fill up with blood. I always turn my head so as not to see it, but it is small consolation. I've always joked with the phlebotomist about someday being able to spit in a cup to do the necessary testing. But whatever my anxiety was that day about my own prognosis (healthy again, except for the weight gain), I was more anxious about getting to the hospital to see Maurice.

My need to rush was not justified: he was in serious but stable condition. I watched the ventilator pump oxygen into his lungs, his chest rising and falling. I was so used to Maurice talking and laughing that to sit in a room with him in silence was almost too much to bear. And there was no news forthcoming—everything was on a wait-and-see basis. I stayed for an hour or so, talking to him and holding his hand, but I felt useless.

In the meantime, Jacqui had been doing the research. She found a Tracy with the same last name in Minneapolis and emailed her. And she found the same name as his mother's on Maurice's birth certificate—right down to the middle name. He had told me his parents died and I assumed the parents on the birth certificate were his birth parents. Could he have lied about such a thing?

In the following days, I stopped in when I could and I got briefings from the doctors every morning by phone.

On Wednesday: "The biopsy result came back. He has Karposi's Sarcoma on the lungs, which is very unusual. We want to give him a shot of chemo, if that's okay with you." Karposi's Sarcoma, or KS, was a cancerous growth that was very common in AIDS patients in the early 1980s. However, it often manifests itself in black, worm-shaped lesions on the skin so, indeed, the lesions on the lungs were a rare occurrence.

"Whatever you can do at this point, try," I told the doctor.

In all the phone calls that week, the doctors had an optimistic tone and made it sound as if he might pull through.

On Thursday: "His kidneys have taken a hit from the chemo so he's not out of the woods yet, but we're going to try to take him off the ventilator on Friday and see if he can breathe on his own."

I had visited after work about every other day that week, but I never stayed too long. I was exhausted and it was too depressing not to be able to communicate with him.

One night that week, Jacqui called me. "The Tracy in Minneapolis was not his sister, so I've reached a dead end there. But I did speak to his mother, who is in her seventies and living in California."

"What?" I was thunderstruck.

"I know. It's quite a story. It's actually his foster mother. They adopted Maurice when he was about two. There were other siblings, I'm not sure if they were natural or hers or other adoptive siblings. In any case, they started having problems with Maurice when he was about twelve. She told me it was very difficult, but they had to consider the other children." Jacqui paused and let out a sigh. "They abrogated the adoption and put him back into the foster care system. Kevin, she was a very sweet lady, but when I hung up the phone, I just sat at my desk and cried and cried. She didn't say what the problem was, but whatever it was, that is about the worst thing you can do to a child." Jacqui was a trained psychologist, so I took her at her word. No wonder Maurice was sometimes like a bratty teenager: he had literally stopped growing emotionally at thirteen—the same age he told me he "lost" his parents in a car accident, a complete fabrication. He had cut off his adoptive parents so completely, he killed them off in his mind. A tragic car accident was probably easier to handle than the real alternative.

"Anyway," Jacqui continued, "She told us to tell him she loved him if he woke up. I asked her if she was in touch with the siblings and she said yes, but she didn't give me any phone numbers. She said she'd pass on the message."

It was a sad backstory to a tragic life and now his behavior began to make some sense. It was really quite miraculous that he turned out as well as he did.

It was gratifying to get some answers about his early life, but we had struck out in terms of finding family or friends who would come to New York and be by his side. A hoped for reunion did not appear to be in the cards.

To my great regret, I did not get to the hospital on Friday, when Maurice was almost brought out of the coma. I assumed that if they took him off the ventilator, off the ventilator he would stay. Ed Miller, the chaplain at the hospital who had befriended Maurice, later told me that on that Friday his eyes were fluttering as though he were struggling to wake up. At least Ed was there to talk to him and give him words of comfort to hear. By Saturday, he was back on the ventilator and I was just biding my time by his bedside.

On Sunday morning, I was getting ready for church when the phone rang. I was sure it was a doctor with my daily update.

"Hi Kevin, it's Dr. Wheeler." Amber Wheeler was one of the ICU doctors and one of the most compassionate doctors I had ever met. "I think you should come in. Maurice is probably in his last hours."

"Well, I was going to come up after church," I said, stupidly.

"I think you'd better come now. Do you want me to call Ed Miller?"

"Yes. I'm on my way."

"Look, just in case he hangs on and pulls through, I have to tell you: if he survives, he would have to be on dialysis."

As Maurice's health care proxy, this was a no-brainer. As much as I wanted to have him around to just laugh and watch television with, that was no life for Maurice. Imagine him on a dialysis machine and unable to eat fried chicken and pizza. "No, he would not want that," I told her emphatically. Among my regrets I may have harbored, that decision was not one of them.

I finished getting dressed and methodically picked up my backpack and cell phone and Bible and headed out the door. It was a bright day so I put on sunglasses—but the main reason was because I was weeping and didn't want to stand out as grieving kin on the subway.

When I got out at the Lexington Avenue stop, I called Sandra as I swiftly walked the blocks to the hospital.

"I'm on my way to the hospital," I said. "I think this is the end."

Sandra, who is usually such a realist, wasn't really hearing it. "Well, I'm on my way to work but there's so much they can do. Call me later with an update."

Then I called the church. It was about ten o'clock and I managed to get a hold of Brad, the assistant pastor. I told him about the situation and asked him to relay the news to Heather and Jacqui.

Finally, I reached Maurice's room. His appearance had changed dramatically in the last twenty-four hours. A nurse explained that he had stopped urinating since the chemotherapy shut down his kidneys and so his body had become bloated. He didn't even look the same. He was drooling from his open mouth and the nurse showed me how I could use the wand to suck the saliva from his lips to make him more comfortable. It was a simple act of kindness—and who knew if he could even feel anything at that point—but I appreciated the opportunity to do this one last, loving act for Maurice.

I randomly flipped through the Bible and read verses that I thought would be appropriate. I wanted to sing, but couldn't think of anything—and if I thought of a song, lyrics escaped me. Finally, I sang a verse of "Lean on Me." Doctors kept coming in and changing IV drips, giving him comfort until his last minutes. I kept looking at my watch, not wanting time to pass, not wanting this to end, to be final.

I imagined what was going on at Middle Church. The gospel choir was singing a Kirk Franklin song, probably at that very moment, and until just a few hours ago, I thought I'd be onstage singing with them. Now, in my numbness, I could hardly remember the words, only the images: trying to hide tears; asking God why; feeling the rain and wondering where was the sun. And yet, God answers: You are free — to laugh, not cry, live, not die.

Amen. Amen. Amen. But was it true? I felt it was true for Maurice at that moment, finally letting go. For me, I wasn't so sure. The rain was reaching its crescendo, but I didn't see sunshine in the forecast.

At ten minutes after noon, Dr. Wheeler came in and said that Maurice was in his last minutes (it was extraordinary to me how they knew these things with such certainty), and that she would leave me alone with him.

I stood by his side and held his hand and kept saying, "Goodbye Maurice, I love you," as I watched the numbers on the machines descend, descend, descend. There was no great drama; time just ran out.

Dr. Wheeler came in and put her arm around my shoulders. "I'm so sorry."

"He's gone?" I asked. The evidence before me wasn't enough; I needed something bigger.

"Yes, he's gone. I'll let you spend a few minutes more with him."

So Maurice had gone while the choir sang and Jacqui finished her message and would soon be giving the benediction. Gone at age forty-four.

I immediately gave a prayer of thanks to God. God had honored my most fervent prayer: "Please let me be there when the time comes." If I had been at school teaching or if it had been the middle of the night, I might not have gotten to him in time. He may have entered the world as an unwanted child and had many years of loneliness living in different cities, on the streets, or in a prison cell. But he did not leave this world alone.

I stepped outside the room and called the church. The message was relayed to Jacqui in time for her to tell the congregation before the benediction. I went back in Maurice's room. I don't know how long I stayed there, but an aide came in and said she'd like to wash and prepare the body and that I could come back in later.

I went to the lounge. My cell phone rang. It was Heather, and she told me that Jacqui and Judi, the woman who had spent time with Maurice on Christmas Eve and reached out to him many times, were on their way. Thank God, because I was feeling the loneliest I had ever felt at that point.

As soon as I saw them walking toward me down the hallway, I burst into tears and they both held me in a long embrace. I eventually explained to them that they were in the process of preparing his body. They sat with me and Jacqui engaged me in positive conversation about Maurice's life and asked me how I had spent the last hours with him.

By the time we went back to the room, Ed Miller had arrived. Ed told me how much he had enjoyed Maurice's company and Jacqui commented that, seeing him there, she kept expecting him to open his eyes and start talking. Eventually, we joined hands around the bed and Ed said a prayer.

Out at the counter, I showed Dr. Wheeler Maurice's handwritten will. Dr. Wheeler said that because of the condition of the body, it probably would not be good for science — however, it would be very helpful for a "teaching autopsy." However, she gently informed me that, now that he was gone, I had no more legal rights about what to do with the body. Essentially, there was no family — what could be done?

As calm as ever, Jacqui called Maurice's foster mother. I had his birth certificate with her name on it. Because they still shared the same last name, nobody would question it. Jacqui got her to agree to fax over her signature okaying the autopsy and (the next day) the cremation. I swear, Jacqui was a magician.

Jacqui was scheduled to go to an afternoon meeting but offered to stay with me. Judi offered to go out to lunch with me. By then, however, I was ready to make the long trip back to Bay Ridge. Sadly, I pulled Maurice's things out of the closet and jammed them into his bag. The nurse's aide gave me his jewelry that he loved so much. We went down to the sidewalk. Jacqui's cell phone rang; it was Erin, who had been upstate that weekend. We had to tell her the sad news. She asked if she should come back to New York but we told her there was no need at that point. Jacqui gave me cash to take a car service and we said our goodbyes.

From the back of the car, I called Audrey and told her to relay the news to the family. She comforted me by telling me how good I had been to Maurice.

Back home, I plopped his stuff down and just lay on the couch in a state of shock — no more tears, yet.

It was February 24th, the day of the Oscars — something I always enjoyed. For many years, I had gone to Oscar parties with my friend Dave but had pretty much lost touch with him since I'd moved to Bay Ridge. That afternoon, the phone rang and I picked up, thinking it was someone calling about Maurice. It was Dave, who was clueless about the whole situation.

"Hey, it's Dave. I thought I'd call you on Oscar night," he chirped.

"Hi. Oh my God. Um, my roommate just died today."

The moment was almost comic — the poor guy just calling like old times and gets greeted with news like that! Not only that, but I had winced at the use of the word "roommate," a word Maurice disliked. "Friend" didn't seem enough and "lover" or "partner" wasn't entirely accurate, but "roommate" sounded like a financial transaction. I had betrayed his memory in that second.

"Brother" may have been the word I needed.

That is the clearest memory about that day after returning from the hospital. I stayed on the couch and wrapped myself in the comforter I had given Maurice, which still had his scent on it. It would be months before I washed the thing.

However, before the end of the day, I balled up the disgusting, ragged red sleeping bag and stuffed it into a big trash bag and brought it down to the street. I was laughing as I did this, as if I was telling Maurice, "I won this battle!"

I know from his heavenly perch, he was laughing right back. The little one-upmanship, tit for tat, was something he would have totally appreciated. He was gone from this world, but we were still communicating.

Part II

Secrets Revealed and Unexpected Blessings

The wound is the place where the Light enters you.

Rumi

Chapter One

The next day, Monday, I went right back up to City College to teach my three classes. I don't know how I did it, but there was little choice in the matter. Financially, I was barely keeping afloat and, as an adjunct, I had a limited number of sick days. What if some other tragedy was to befall me? I also thought being around the young students would offer some welcome distraction, and it did. Teaching can really pull you outside yourself and toward the greater good; your own problems can take a back seat for a little while.

That week, cards began arriving. I was most touched by a plant from the Consistory at Rutgers Church, accompanied by a card they had all signed.

I also noticed that Liberty now slept mostly on the couch, on the balled-up comforter, as if she too knew Maurice was gone and was trying to hold on to him in some way.

I had decided to have the memorial service the following Sunday, March 2nd, at three o'clock. I didn't want to prolong it any longer than that. Jacqui went ahead with the arrangements to grant me my wish.

I was disappointed that Audrey and her family would not be able to come down for the service; they knew him better than anyone else in the family. However, my mother knew—as mothers know these things—this was extremely important to me and she was determined to come. She would ultimately drag my father with her. He had not been to New York since my first major cabaret show some sixteen years before and had probably hoped never to set foot in Manhattan again. I was thrilled that they would see where I lived, in a safe neighborhood and in a sizeable apartment, and that they would meet so many of my friends, on my turf.

The rest of that week was a blur, just long hours of lying on the couch trying to pay attention to the television. I was merely existing, mirroring Maurice during his times of grief over his losses and illness. I even found myself watching the shows Maurice had turned me onto: *King of Queens, Law and Order: SVU, Family Guy*—even the Food Network.

I tried figuring out whom I could call to invite to the service. Maurice had been so secretive about most of his friends, his "trouble" friends as I called them. There was Kevin, someone I had met and liked, who had hung out with Maurice in some Village bars for most of the time I had known him. Kevin assured me he would be there. Then I called someone else whom Maurice had dated on and off and had mentioned to me several times. Our exchange was awkward, to say the least.

"Hi, my name is Kevin and I'm calling about Maurice. I am his roommate."

"Oh yeah, what's up?"

"Well, Maurice died on Sunday and I'm just trying to let a few of his friends know about the memorial service. It would be nice to have some of them there."

"Oh my God. Thank you for calling. Look, um, I have a meeting to go to in a few minutes but could I call you back and get details?"

I never heard from him again.

I did hear from a few people at the hospital, who wanted to know about the service and who also told me how much Maurice had touched them in his final days. I heard from his social workers at the hospital, and Vicki Sunshine.

On Saturday, I put a chicken in the crockpot and went to midtown to meet my parents at Port Authority. I was strangely comforted seeing them walk through the gate, their small-town eyes scanning the diverse crowd until they finally saw me. New Englanders to the core, they were people of few words anyway, but, in this case, no words needed to be spoken.

Dad's attitude had changed so much since the last time he was in New York, cursing the traffic and fearful of getting lost. He now had a sense of humor about it all and seemed to delight in his surroundings. It was a long train ride back to Bay Ridge, but the only doubtful comment came from my mother: "You do this every day?"

"Yes, I just take a book or my iPod and time passes. But wait until you see what I have out here."

Finally, exiting the subway, in the one long block to my apartment—remembering the same walk I had taken in the freezing temperatures with Maurice a couple weeks before, going the other way—I showed them houses with porches and small lawns, a lively 3rd Avenue with every convenience and, finally, my place on the third floor. Five rooms! They could hardly believe it. I gave them my room for the night. It was a bit noisy because it faced the avenue, but I wasn't ready to put them on Maurice's sleep sofa. I hadn't even changed the sheets. In fact, I hadn't opened the sofa since he had left the house back on February 11th.

My parents were staying for only two nights. I would get them back on the bus early Monday morning before going uptown to teach. The short trip was just long enough for them to get a sense that I was in good hands with Middle Church, and had a decent place to live.

We went to church the next morning. I had them sit with Sandra, since I was singing with the gospel choir that Sunday. I did take a chance and slipped Maurice's tax refund check into the offering plate. In the end, it went through with the other checks; that $1500 essentially paid for the cremation and the funeral. God works in mysterious ways.

After church, I took my parents to brunch and then we went to Washington Square Park to people-watch. It was almost spring-like, sunny and in the fifties, and it was a pleasant time of just enjoying the park and talking with my parents.

Finally, the hour I both anticipated and dreaded had arrived. We went back to the church at about two-thirty so I could meet with Jacqui in her office to talk about the service. Fortunately, I got to the church a bit early and went into the sanctuary. There was a beautiful altar set up with white candles and a bouquet of yellow roses. Standing above it all was a huge blow-up of the photo that Bethany had taken at Thanksgiving: Maurice and I sitting on a couch in their hotel room, heads together, beaming at the camera. Jacqui had the graphic artist inscribe "That's What Friends Are For" along the bottom of the poster. It took my breath away and tears sprang to my eyes. How would I get through this?

In Jacqui's office, we talked through the service with Jonathan, the pianist, Gail, who would also be singing a solo, and Heather. Sadly, although Maurice's foster mother had said she would let the other family members know about Maurice's death, we had heard from no one. There would be no family or old friends attending. I wondered who would be there. The group of us prayed together and I kept wiping away tears. I wasn't ready to say goodbye.

At three o'clock, I went out into the sanctuary. I began greeting people and thanking them for coming. Most of them were there for me, and for that I will forever be grateful: They understood that the memorial service is as much for the survivors as it is for the deceased. There were maybe forty people all together. Besides those taking part in the service, there was my longtime friend Clare from Rose's Turn, whom I had comforted at her mother's funeral a few years before; David, another longtime friend from the bar; Jo Ellen; Kathy and John; Becket; Dwayne; Dennis, an old friend who had never met Maurice but had been an AIDS survivor himself for over two decades; a few people from the gospel choir and Consistory; a dozen people from the church that Maurice had touched in some way; Kevin; and a small handful of people I didn't know. Even Reverend Pyrch and Susan from Rutgers Church came down for the service, which I thought was very commendable.

I sat next to my Dad, my mother on the other side of him, in a pew a few rows from the front. I kept staring at the photo of Maurice smiling, looking right at me. I gathered strength from that, as if he really *were* smiling.

For the processional music, Jacqui—who had always been on the same page with me in terms of pop music—had suggested Chicago's "I've Been Searching So Long." It was the perfect choice:

As my life goes on I believe
Somehow something's changed
Something deep inside
Ooh, a part of me

There's a strange new light in my eyes
Things I've never known
Changin' my life
Changin' me

I've been searching so long
To find an answer
Now I know my life has meaning

Now I see myself as I am
Feeling very free
Life is everything
Ooh, it's meant to be
When my tears have come to an end,
I will understand
What I left behind
Part of me

I've been searching so long
To find an answer
Now I know my life has meaning

Searching
Don't you know I'm searching
For an answer
To the question, oh yeah,
For our minds
Baby, it's true
It's only natural
Good things in life take a long time

(James Pankow)

There was an opening prayer and then Gail got up to sing "I Feel Like a Motherless Child" in her passionate, operatic voice. There couldn't have been a song more appropriate and it was certainly hard to hold it in for that.

Jacqui gave a short homily around the theme of "What's in a life?" She described Maurice as like a butterfly, one who had zigzagged around the country, touching down briefly to bring colorful lightness to so many lives. She spoke of his childlike fears upon first becoming sick, gave a few details of his childhood that she had learned from his foster mother, and told of her final visit with him on Presidents' Day.

"I asked him, 'Do you want to live, Maurice?' And he said yes, unequivocally, for the first time since he had become sick. Before that day, he had always been ambivalent. And so I prayed with him for healing, for life. It seems to me, in his last days, Maurice had learned the secret of life and when he said 'yes' to it, God honored that by, in a sense, granting Maurice that wish: 'You want life? I will give you eternal life now, and you will suffer no more.'"

I assumed Maurice said 'yes' to actual, in-the-flesh life in his final day of wakefulness. Yet the kind of abundant life Maurice may have wished for at that time was beyond what doctors could give him. There was a kind of poetry and beauty in Jacqui's interpretation—that God gave him a greater gift than Maurice had asked for—but I was left wondering if God had taken the easy route. The end of Maurice's life was a majestic, orchestral coda at the end of a long concerto, and yet, if he had truly grown in stature in his final days, couldn't he have brought that light to so many here on Earth if he had lived? Might I have found a complete love, at last?

Others got up to speak. Erin talked about his final days and how he had grown in spirit; Judi spoke of how she didn't know Maurice well, but that she said he was "easy like Sunday morning" (a favorite song of his, unbeknownst to Judi); Heather said that Maurice told her he wanted to be remembered for his "exciting and tragic life" and shared a story of how he sneaked a pot of his homemade Café Du Monde coffee into the sanctuary to share with others at a Wednesday night Soul Care service; Belinda recalled the time they "threw down" for the dinner party in Bay Ridge and how they had just spoken on the phone a few days before his death, planning for another dinner; Alisa tearfully told of the trip to Niagara Falls (leaving out the near-disaster in Customs); Sandra reiterated her surprise at getting a call from him on Valentine's Day and how he closed their conversation with the advice to "share your light"; Kevin simply said, "I wished I had gotten to know him better," perhaps speaking for many that day.

At last, it was my time to speak. I looked at Maurice's smile on the big poster for strength and walked to the podium. "Thank you all for coming," I began. "I'd like to think that a glorious ending makes up for a difficult journey. Maurice's story is an extraordinary story and perhaps a uniquely American story—in both the greatest and worst senses." What I meant was that his was a story of overcoming many obstacles to reach a certain level of success—American in it best sense—but that when simmering issues came to the fore, resulting in criminal behavior and addictions and mental problems, he became stuck in the morass of "the system" and was often judged accordingly by others.

From there, I went on to tell all I had known of his life—so many there had only a few pieces of the puzzle and I wanted to fill in the spaces as best I could. I told of his staying in the Bowery Shelter just down the street from the church and how it came to be that he ended up with me. I told his history as I knew it—growing up in Syracuse, being a gymnast in high school, working for a time at CNN in Atlanta and Disney World in Florida, the fancy restaurants in Washington, D.C. and Richmond where he worked to earn a fancy sports car and a nice apartment—things that gave him the trappings of success but never true fulfillment. Still, I didn't sugarcoat his life, but alluded as well to his drug use and prison stints.

Most of all, I talked about those small moments that gave Maurice such joy: crispy fried chicken, a slab of butter on a cinnamon roll, Fat Sal's pizza, a bargain tie found at the Salvation Army store, ironing a shirt, the couch that became his bed, NPR, the riffing horns of the band Chicago, lights of a Christmas tree, the spray of Niagara, Liberty the cat, and so much more. I stressed that, whether in good times or bad, Maurice never lost his sense of humor.

It was what a eulogy should be—celebrating a life even amidst the sadness. I remained upbeat as I related the events of our life together in those ten minutes. Nearing the end, I tried to draw lessons from the experience:

> In the end, Maurice was incredibly brave. Never once did I hear him complain about his pain, even on that last day with a respirator strapped to his face, needles in his arms, and deprived of food. He talked until he couldn't talk anymore, and he and Erin and I fantasized about the feast we would have when he got out.
>
> Maurice said he had learned so much in the last eight months of his life that he wanted to go back to school to become a medical technician. Barring that, he wanted to donate his body for science. His body was used for a teaching autopsy and Dr. Wheeler assured me that because of his unusual case, in all likelihood, doctors would be writing about him in journals for years to come.
>
> I think he would want us to take a little more time enjoying those small moments in life, talking with each other. Being neighbors, in that southern hang-out-on-the-porch-with-a-lemonade kind of way. And don't wait until tomorrow to do it.
>
> As for me, I want to encourage you to listen for that small voice that might be telling you to take a risk in helping someone beyond your comfort level. I can tell you, his benefit from me may have been great, but I believe my rewards have been greater.
>
> My life was enriched beyond belief by getting to know this magical man for a couple of very special seasons. I love you, Maurice, and will never forget you. I hope you are feasting where you are, like you've never feasted before.

I managed to hold steady until the very end of the speech, breaking down during the last lines as I realized the end was near and he was gone forever. As I finished the speech, I looked out at Dad, and he was crying, tears flowing freely down his cheeks. It was only the second time in my life I had seen him cry.

Perhaps he was finally grieving his own mother. Perhaps he found a kindred spirit in Maurice. Perhaps he couldn't bear seeing his son in such pain. While a later conversation might clarify those issues, I knew it would not come to pass. In his proud silence, he was who he was. What is important is that in that moment, I forgave my father for his shortcomings, as surely as he had forgiven me of mine.

Maurice's death had brought me that, and it was no small thing.

After the service, I greeted and thanked folks again and invited them to Pangea, a nearby restaurant where we would have a bite to eat and toast Maurice's life. As it turned out, only about a dozen people came to that, but it was an intimate group and we had some laughs. Alisa presented me with a photo book from the Niagara Falls trip, an incredible gift. Looking through the photos, I noticed sadness in Maurice's eyes, even when he was smiling. He knew he wasn't long for this world.

Mom and Dad and I went back to Brooklyn before long, making an early night of it. It had been an emotionally exhausting day and we would be getting up early the next morning.

On Monday morning, Dad maintained his sense of humor during the long, rush-hour commute to Port Authority while my mother sweated it out, impatient to get to the destination. At the bus terminal, we had long hugs and there were tears in my mother's eyes — as there had been so many years before, after the stabbing. This time, though, I think my parents had hope for me: They had seen me in a better place, surrounded by friends.

I got through my teaching that day and came home to an empty, quiet apartment. I sat on the couch and put the box of Maurice's ashes on my lap and hugged his pillow to my face. I cried and cried and cried: because he had suffered so much; because he had died so young; because I had loved so deeply.

Chapter Two

I never understood the Parable of the Lost Son (Luke 15:11-32) until I knew Maurice. I was always the good son who worked hard and played by the rules.

When I first welcomed Maurice into my home, we had a brotherly relationship. This made things difficult that first year because I became increasingly frustrated by his disregard for money and squandering what he did have on what I thought was a wanton lifestyle.

As time went on, I found myself taking on a parental role, at times lecturing him and at times pitying him.

When we moved to Brooklyn and, especially, when he became sick, Maurice didn't give up his bad habits immediately. Habits, good or bad, become such because they provide some measure of relief or comfort, and then they become what we know best. It's interesting to me that the word "change" forms the beginning and end of the word "challenge." Even so, Maurice matured in character over time — three steps forward, two steps back — even as his body weakened.

When I was young, I felt that I worked hard for the grades and behaved myself, while my older brother Carleton went to all the parties, got more use of the car, and collected athletic trophies that made my Dad proud. I may have gotten quiet respect, but I didn't get the commendation and I missed out on the good times, I thought.

Living with Maurice, I finally got that parable.

The parable tells the story of a man with two sons. The younger one asks for his portion of the estate so he can use it while he's alive; the second stays and continues to work the land with his father. The younger son goes away and lives a life of debauchery. He is ill prepared when famine strikes and, penniless, finds his way home. Seeing him in the distance, the father runs to him, throws his arms around him and welcomes him back home with a huge feast. The older son is angry and confronts his father, thinking this treatment is unfair. The father responds by telling him, "You will always be with me and all I have is yours . . . but we should celebrate and rejoice, because your brother was dead and has come to life; he was lost and is found."

That was the story with Maurice, and there are three lessons I take from it. First, anybody who really saw Maurice coming in on a morning after a party knew that he was enslaved to his desires; he wasn't free and, ultimately, he wasn't having a good time. Second, he really did waste all of his earthly treasures and when the final difficulty came, it hit him hard. He was not prepared to deal with it until he felt welcoming arms of love around him, and trusted that love. Third, as the "good son," I now have confidence that God "has my back." It takes nothing away from me to rejoice over someone else's redemption.

If it took until the final days of his life to be "found," then so be it. We all have a different finish line to cross before reaching a victory. We can be angry about the timing of it, and I believe God welcomes our questions about it. But in the end, from all accounts from those who witnessed it, Maurice's redemption was complete. That victory deserves a celebration.

Maurice saw truth. When had asked me, "What is a normal life?" he was questioning my values and putting a mirror up to me to examine myself. When he was in prison just weeks before his death and then later told Sandra, "Shine your light," he had come to a profound understanding of life, one that Martin Luther King, Jr. had once observed: "Darkness cannot drive out darkness; only light can do that." Maurice shined his light the best way he knew how in the limited time he had.

And through Maurice, I continue to be found, to find my way, my purpose. I no longer have to hold up the mantle of "good son" and live up to that expectation. I can be more fully human. I, too, have matured and become more like the father in the story. My compassion has deepened and my capacity to love has grown. God has enlarged my territory.

The Parable of the Lost Son is traditionally told on the Third Sunday of Lent. In 2008, that was exactly the Sunday that Maurice died.

Chapter Three

I had never met Vicki Sunshine, Maurice's social worker, but when I emailed her about the memorial service, she ultimately didn't show up. About a week after that, she called to explain. "I've been in this business a long time, but this was one of the most difficult deaths I've ever had to deal with." She, too, had experienced Maurice's magic.

She said, though, that she would be happy to talk to me if I ever wanted to come in and share my grief or try to tie up loose ends. After a couple months, I felt ready to make that call.

I arrived at the center on West 24th Street—the same place I had left Maurice on that cold day in February—and gave my name to the receptionist. Within a few minutes, she came out.

Vicki was a small woman, perhaps in her early fifties, and had the aura of someone who had been a bit of a leftist radical in the early '70s. She immediately pulled me into a comforting embrace—this was welcome, but not at all what I expected from someone who had been in the social work business for twenty-something years. I expected a more clinical, hands-off approach. I immediately understood why Maurice bonded with her; she was not like the rest. She had genuine warmth and caring in her bones, and lived up to her name.

I followed her back to her office and as we sat down, she crossed her legs and pointed to the socks she was wearing. "I was wearing these the last day Maurice was here and he noticed these emblems and said they reminded him of New Orleans, that he had a design like that on the building where he lived," she said with a smile. It was like a coat of arms with a lion and crossed spears. How could that kind of detail possibly have been an elaborate lie, I wondered.

I thanked her for allowing me to come in, but didn't really know where to start. I decided to start with the most uncomfortable topic.

"I find myself really angry with his doctor," I began. "But I know you work with her, so I hesitate to say anything."

"It's okay, say what's on your mind."

"Well, I never understood why she kept sending him home without consulting me as the primary caregiver and why, with his T-cell count of one or two, she never signed him over to hospice care. Even my minister had talked to her about that."

Vicki started slowly. "First of all, Maurice was an adult capable of making his own decisions. She probably operated on the assumption that he would take his medicine. Second, a doctor measures from a different barometer than people like you and me. She has to make a decision based on what she sees with the medical evidence. Until the end, Maurice was still able to get around and do things."

"That's true. But I still think she had him discharged too soon in January. If they had done the biopsy then, they would have seen the KS in the lungs and maybe been able to do something then that could have saved him, or at least let him know what was coming so we could have made our final weeks more meaningful."

"Doctors aren't perfect. When he responded well to the pneumonia medication, she probably saw no reason to probe further. And I suppose in his weakened state, even if it had been found, I'm not sure they could have saved him . . . although knowing would have been good."

My anger could not be dispelled so quickly, but her explanations made sense. I went on to talk about my grief, mainly about the seeming senselessness of his death, just as he was maturing on so many levels.

"I agree," she said, dabbing her eyes with a tissue. "I think he was just starting to turn a corner."

We shared a few more memories and I left her a teddy bear that my niece had given to him, as a memento. She invited me to come back any time to talk some more—perhaps she needed that as well—but I had a feeling that would be my one and only time meeting Vicki Sunshine, the one social worker who brought a ray of hope into Maurice's final months.

*　　*　　*

Another piece of business I needed to clear up was to try to get Middle Church reimbursed for the cost of cremation. Supposedly, because he was a member of HASA (HIV/AIDS Services Administration), that would be covered for someone who was essentially destitute and without family, as Maurice was. Yes, Maurice's final check had passed through the collection plate and essentially paid for the funeral, but if this was a benefit he was owed, I saw no reason not to pursue it, so that Maurice's final check could be a donation to the church that had done so much for him.

The Burial Claims Office was located on a side street in downtown Brooklyn, on the second floor of a nondescript building. I could immediately see that this was not a priority for state money—the walls were bare with crackling paint, folding chairs were strewn about a waiting room, and the receptionist had a computer and a radio, but no real visible comforts around her. Still, she greeted me very warmly and invited me to fill out some paperwork.

Eventually, Mr. Ahmed, a caseworker, was introduced to me. I followed him back to his office, which consisted of a small desk with a computer and an empty card table. He gave me more forms to fill out and I gave him Maurice's ID. Mr. Ahmed, cold to begin with, grew even icier, it seemed, when he saw Maurice's photo. I think he assumed we were a biracial gay couple, and he didn't approve.

He told me I needed a signed, notarized statement from Jacqui, and a signature from Maurice's "mother"—he had noticed her signature on the cremation order.

"She's unreachable and doesn't want to be involved," I said, explaining how difficult it was to contact her regarding the death certificate, autopsy, and cremation. Ahmed allowed for the notarized statement from Jacqui and receipts for recent social security and disability payments to Maurice. That was fine with me, although a bit of a headache. We made an appointment for the following week.

That week, I convinced Jacqui to write a statement, I got it notarized, and I gathered up more materials. When I arrived the following week, Ahmed seemed to find fault with some of the paperwork and wondered aloud if Jacqui's statement was complete enough.

"Mr. Ahmed, I'm doing the best I can here. You know that Maurice was a client of HASA and that this should be covered. It is obvious that he had no real means of support and no way to pay for his own burial expenses and funeral."

"Well, I can't make a decision today. I'll look over this stuff and get back to you."

With that, he showed me the door. My eyes burned with tears. Why was this man, in his position, behaving so contemptibly, without compassion? Why was he making this process so difficult?

As I walked toward the subway, tears were escaping from behind my sunglasses and streaming down my cheeks. I pulled on my iPod Shuffle and clicked it on. The first song that came on was "Easy" by the Commodores, one of Maurice's favorites and the song Judi had referenced at the memorial service. I could almost hear Maurice singing the words about leaving because he couldn't stand the pain, and not wanting chains put on him. He longed for free and easy and gave the impression that's what he was, but I don't know if he ever got that in life.

In that moment, though, I had no doubt he'd found it in his hereafter. Maurice was speaking to me through his favorite medium, music, and letting me know that all was definitely good. The next random selection was "I Will Always Love You," just in case I hadn't gotten the message.

It so happened that I had taken that day to deal with taking care of Maurice's business and that meant another trip uptown to New York Presbyterian to fill out some paperwork there. As I stepped off the train at East 68th Street, I pulled off my headphones and literally stopped in my tracks.

I was hearing something familiar . . . was that possible? On the opposite side of the tracks stood a musician with a guitar and he was singing . . . "Easy" by the Commodores. What were the odds, that I would get off the train at that exact moment and that a musician would be at the station singing that song? The moment was not lost on me. I laughed out loud and stood there listening until the song was over. The rest of *my* day was easy.

About a week later, I received a letter in the mail from Mr. Ahmed. He was requesting an additional *eleven* pieces of documentation before he could process my claim. This included another notarized letter from Jacqui, from the funeral home, from his social workers, something called an Affidavit of

Friendship, Maurice's tax records for the previous three years, and God knows what else. I calculated that the amount of time spent getting all of that together — for no guaranteed approval from Mr. Ahmed — was hardly worth the $900 or so I was seeking on Middle's behalf. Jacqui agreed with me.

But I couldn't quite let it go, my anger needed a release. I composed the following letter to Mr. Ahmed and cc-ed it to his superiors at HASA, the local state representatives, and even Senators Schumer and Clinton:

> Dear Mr. Ahmed:
>
> I am extremely disappointed to receive a copy of the letter sent to Rev. Jacqueline Lewis about additional documentation needed in order to process the application for decedent Maurice _____ regarding the possibility of payment for his funeral expenses. In short, no less than eleven additional documents needed, after I already took time off from work to meet with you twice to bring in documentation, after chasing people down and gathering notarized letters, plus the necessary receipts and notifications.
>
> I am aware that there are certain rules to be followed regarding any kind of reimbursement, but any fool can see from what I have already provided that Mr. _____ was destitute. I don't know if Rev. Lewis is going to pursue the matter — she is much too busy trying to find funding for a growing church with inadequate facilities — but I told her I am done with it. I can't go on with this fight. But thank God for Rev. Lewis: within 24 hours of his death, she was able to track down his former foster mother and negotiate with her to approve the autopsy and cremation.
>
> Your agency should take a lesson from Rev. Lewis. It is very clear to me that the government is woefully inefficient and that perhaps the system is designed to discourage people and make them give up.
>
> For one thing, it is unconscionable that your agency should ask for an Affidavit of Friendship, whatever the hell that is. I'll tell you what friendship is: friendship is letting a man with a troubled past but trying to make good, stay on your couch for over a year while he comes to terms with an AIDS diagnosis. I can't tell you how many times he went out in the cold in his delicate condition to meet with a caseworker from HASA (your umbrella agency, I understand) on Coney Island, only to be told, "We have nothing for you today." Do these people not have phones to call and cancel an appointment? I have no doubt the stresses of red tape and useless travel hastened his demise. In all that time, never did HASA find him an apartment and it took months for him to get any kind of disability to help me out. Essentially, I supported both of us on the meager salary of an adjunct professor. That's what friendship is, and neither I nor Rev. Lewis should have to prove it with documentation.
>
> I do not expect any kind of response to this letter, but I would be remiss if I did not express my anger and utter contempt for these

proceedings. It is clear to me that HASA did nothing for Maurice while he was alive and even less for him in death.

Our taxes support HASA, of course. But go ahead and use the money meant for Maurice for other needy souls. Just don't make them kill themselves to get it.

Yours truly,
Kevin S. Hall

Needless to say, I got a form letter in the mail a few weeks later saying that my request for burial expenses had been denied. At least I got a few minutes of satisfaction writing the letter.

Chapter Four

Whenever tragedy strikes—whether it is an unexpected brush with violent crime, a frightening diagnosis, or the death of a loved one—you go through the what-ifs. "What if I had done such and such, would this still have happened?"

If I hadn't gone out to sing that Thursday night, I would not have encountered Elie Granger.

If I had not stopped to pick up ice cream at the corner of Ninth Avenue, I would have made it home before he rode up to me on his bike.

If I had not been stabbed, maybe I would not have gone into a long depression that involved late-night drinking and hook-ups, which led to the HIV-positive diagnosis.

If I had made a different choice with whomever I met up with that one time, I also might have escaped the disease.

But nothing has haunted me like Maurice's death. For all the good I did, I can't help but ask myself that if I had committed myself to him all the way, maybe he would have rallied to save himself.

Yet because of my own lack of trust in him (rather justified) and a lack of trust in my own judgment, I kept Maurice at just a safe enough distance.

Many years ago, director Woody Allen was caught up in a scandal when he fell in love with Soon-Yi, the twenty-one year old adopted daughter of his longtime lover, Mia Farrow. While the media bore down on him for months on end, he stayed focused on his work and generally did not address the brouhaha, except to say, "The heart wants what the heart wants." He eventually married Soon-Yi and started a family.

All these years later, they are still married and Allen has directed many more films. While Mia may not have forgiven him, the rest of the world largely has. He ignored the judgments being hurled at him, and followed his heart, ending up with a lasting love.

Maurice touched my heart in a profound way, but I listened to the voices inside and outside my head that suggested he "wasn't good enough" for me—or at least not until I "fixed" him. The result was, I kept him a quarter inch from my heart. And maybe that was the difference between life and death for him, joy and grief for me.

In the weeks and months that followed his death, as winter turned to spring, I tried to grab as much temp work as possible, outside of my teaching, in order to catch up on my bills. It also kept me from languishing on the couch, clutching the comforter, and grieving my fate. Fortunately, I was starting to get some medical editing work, which paid a little more.

Gospel choir was difficult. The music is designed to reach our emotional core, and it certainly did with me; I was constantly running out of the room to try to control the tsunami of grief that overwhelmed me. I could barely get through the Sunday performances and we were preparing for the April trip to

New Orleans — the double whammy of concerts and going back to a place Maurice loved. I would be bringing some of his ashes with me, too.

On a Saturday about a month after Maurice's death, I defiantly put all his clothes (outside of the ones I wanted to keep or give to friends) into large Hefty bags and took them to the Salvation Army. There were at least three large bags and I had to cram them onto a shopping cart to roll them down the avenue.

In the meantime, Heather continued to be a godsend. She welcomed me into her office on Sundays after church and listened to me with the utmost patience.

"I'm so sad because people didn't get to know him and see the side of him that I saw," I wailed.

"What did you want people to see?"

"He was so funny, he could just make a comment about something on the news that was so unique, we'd just fall on the floor laughing."

"What else?"

Like that, she let me spill my tears and tell my story. I told of my regret that maybe he wouldn't have died if I had done things differently. "Why did I tell him last fall that he had to move out, right when he was at his most vulnerable?"

"But you kept inviting him back," she said. "Kevin, you did all you could do." She said it with such certainty, that, over time, I allowed myself to believe it.

What if I could let go of the what-ifs?

*   *   *

In 2005, I lost an influential person in my life, Neal. I gained Maurice.

And Jacqui.

Jacqui came aboard early that year to assist the outgoing minister who was retiring in June. He had been beloved and had been largely responsible for the programming that offered the "radical welcome" for which Middle Church became known.

On paper, it all looked good: Jacqui would be a historic first in leading the congregration as a black woman. Her educational credentials were impeccable and she radiated charisma. Additionally, her Colgate smile, laughing eyes, and tall, model-like physique gave her a striking look that focused all eyes on her when she walked into a room.

Still, it became clear that change is not a concept that is easily grasped by many. In theory, the new is exciting, but in practice there's a lot of, "Why can't it be the way it used to be?" Jacqui had her hands full trying to please both the old and new congregants, but it was obvious after a time that the old wineskins would not be able to hold the new wine.

I saw this up close and personal because I was asked to apply for a position on the Consistory in the fall of 2006. At that time, I was in the midst of the drama with Maurice and the monthly meetings and planning for the church's vision would be a way to take me out of all that for a bit and contribute to the good. At times, it turned out, more drama was added to my life.

In her eagerness to please everybody, Jacqui would be the first to admit that she made mistakes. Her vision didn't always jibe with the vision of staffers from the previous administration, including that of assistant ministers—her own hires as well as previous hires. She was finding her way, and it was a rocky road for all of us for a few years. The congregation gained many new members but lost many that had been there for years, and anger and gossip were spilling out in all directions.

How this relates to my story is that, in one painful episode, a previous member made a bit of a bomb-throwing exit by writing and circulating a long, diatribe-filled letter aimed at causing a revolt against Jacqui. This was a terrible time for the congregation, for the Consistory, and for Jacqui. There were a lot of meetings and a lot of prayer.

This isn't the time or place to get into church politics, but I might say that a board of any organization has to follow certain rules of order, and confidentiality of the board is the number rule; otherwise, chaos rules. Suffice it to say that the congregation had a limited understanding of what was going on behind the scenes with personnel issues, programming, and finances. There were certainly disagreements among the Consistory as well.

Anyway, the upshot of this turmoil is that the letter-writer asserted that Jacqui had Consistory members wound around her finger in a psychological manipulation to get us to bend to her will. In my case, it was implied that she had been helping me out so much with Maurice that I couldn't help but give in to her demands.

Hogwash. That kind of reasoning insults my intelligence and doesn't take into account that two people can have a loving relationship that also allows for disagreement.

There were three occasions where I disagreed with Jacqui on important assistant minister positions. Eventually, like a jury, we had to come to an understanding and make decisions. In those three cases, two were hired and, in the end, I ended up being right about one and wrong about the other. The third, whom I liked, was never hired.

However, what such talk did was make me question my own sanity and, in this case, my relationship with Jacqui. That's not a bad thing. Was she simply currying my favor? Was there also love? Why couldn't there be two truths? We seem to find more comfort in one or the other of two truths, we have trouble holding onto two seemingly opposite ideas.

There is no question that she got angry with Maurice. She once kept him waiting for a good long time while she was in a meeting, and then snapped at him with impatience when she finally met with him, according to his version. To his credit, Maurice never held a grudge and he never mentioned the incident again.

When I confronted Jacqui about it later, she said, "What makes you believe he was telling you the truth?" Ah, she shared with him the ability to not directly answer a question if she so chose!

When Maurice was in a coma, Jacqui had confided to me, "Maurice reminds me a lot of my brother." She had had a foster brother who came to live with the family, and he was troubled and hard to manage for a time.

"Oh my God, did you ever tell Maurice that?" I asked. This was a revelation to me and explained so much about her good cop/bad cop treatment of him.

When she told me she hadn't, I felt she had lost an opportunity to really connect with him and possibly help him in an even more meaningful way than she already had.

We are imperfect. Relationships are messy. I am loyal, perhaps to a fault. I don't walk away. I don't expect perfection, but I expect an equal effort. Because I expect a lot, I don't make the plunge into a relationship often. I haven't found my one soulmate, but I've had friendships that have lasted a lifetime.

Jacqui and I will always share Maurice in ways that are hard to describe and nobody else who knew him will share the angle that she and I shared in that triangle. For that, I will forever be indebted to her leadership, friendship, and love.

Chapter Five

I had already signed up for the choir trip to New Orleans months before, but with Maurice's death, the journey became more of a pilgrimage to me. As we gathered at LaGuardia Airport early one morning for that trip, my heart was in turmoil, my mind distracted.

I brought some of his ashes with me that weekend. I had a plan to disperse the first portion there, and the rest at other places he loved—Brooklyn, Niagara Falls, and even Richmond.

The first night, we sang in a shelter, and looking into the eyes of those beautiful, desperate people—so overjoyed to have someone singing for them and praying with them—I saw Maurice and I wept. I wept for the humanity that we often overlook, people that have become overwhelmed by circumstances in this world, and just cry out for recognition, dignity, love . . . hope. The tears of joy for others during the raucous church concerts over the next few days were also tears of grief for me. But somehow, gratitude was oozing its way into the cracks in my soul as well.

On Saturday afternoon, Dean, one of our team leaders, took choir members on a tour of the Ninth Ward, which had been devastated by the storm. I asked him if he'd have time to drive us up to Lake Pontchartrain so I could scatter Maurice's ashes. Dean asked me to speak about Maurice to those gathered around and I did so. Then we got into our vans and he led us up to the lake.

It was a shimmering, summery day, sunlight sparkling on the soft blue waves that lapped up against the stone steps where I would carry out the ritual.

The choir members were respectfully silent as I stepped down to the water's edge and opened the container. I used my bare hand to reach in and take handfuls of the gray-white ash. I flung the ashes over the water and the mass was gently lifted over the waves away from the shore. It was like waving goodbye to an old friend.

When I was finished, I turned and walked up the steps. Several of my friends were silently weeping with me. My friend Russell offered a prayer. We didn't know what to do next, so I just started singing "Amazing Grace." It was the right song: "I once was lost, but now am found, was blind, but now I see."

Nobody who was there that day—whether they knew Maurice or not—will forget that moment on the lake. To be able to share that moment with friends was an incredible gift.

New Orleans: city of sad goodbyes, defiant hopes, creative hearts, new beginnings. To the end, Maurice embodied the spirit of that amazing Crescent City.

I would go on singing, but my goodbye wasn't as final as I had thought it would be.

Chapter Six

As weeks passed, I would find myself at the computer at odd times, googling his name. I was no longer trying to root out family or criminal history, but just trying to piece together the history and mystery of his life. I needed to find a connection to someone who had known him in the past.

I went back to the profile Maurice had put on *reunion.com* some years before. I left a message on the site that Maurice had died and that his memorial had been held at Middle Collegiate Church.

On *classmates.com*, I found his high school graduating class in Syracuse, New York. I clicked on the name of one of his classmates who seemed to be in some kind of
in-charge role and briefly told her that Maurice had died, surrounded by a few friends, in New York City. I told her I would be pleased if someone got back to me with some stories about him as a teenager, something I could hold onto. I never heard from her.

Around the beginning of May, I received a phone call from the secretary at Middle Church. She told me someone from Richmond, Virginia, had called looking for me. He had seen my notice on *reunion.com* and was a friend of Maurice. My heart thudded in my chest: There was an actual friend who had found me and wanted to talk to me. She gave me his number. I thanked her and hung up.

I stared at the number for a long time before I picked up the phone to call the guy, Jeremiah. To my surprise, he answered. I told him who I was, and then he narrated to me his story regarding Maurice.

"Maurice and I dated briefly, but that didn't work out. But he lived with me and my family off and on for fourteen years in Richmond. We took him in and took him back after a couple of spells in prison. Then one day he just disappeared and I never heard from him again." Jeremiah stifled a sob and sniffled.

"That was around the spring of 2005, right?"

"Yeah, around then."

"He went down to New Orleans and lived there until the hurricane, then came up to New York and contacted me."

Jeremiah scoffed. "He didn't go down to New Orleans."

My worst fear had been voiced by this longtime friend, that the whole hurricane victim scenario had been a scam. "Well, I believed him because I had met him there a year or so before and he told me he had gone back and forth there many times and finally went to live there in 2005. He even gave me an address," I added, trying to hold onto the truth as I knew it.

"Well, he may have been there but I don't believe he went down there that summer. That just became a convenient story for him to get pity off other people." Despite what he was telling me, it was clear that, like me, Jeremiah loved Maurice, whatever his faults and crimes may have been. "He had a girlfriend here for a while," he went on. "God, she loved him so much and tried so hard to turn his life around."

I imagined that Jeremiah and that girlfriend had been the two others in his life that Maurice had talked about as being special to him but that he hadn't the maturity to realize it at the time. Listening to Jeremiah, I was mourning the fact that I had been unable to reach him before Maurice's death, which would have allowed for some kind of reunion. Why hadn't I posted information about him on the Internet when he was sick? During those months of illness when I had asked him if there was anyone I could contact, he never mentioned Jeremiah—probably not because he didn't want to reconcile with him but perhaps because he was afraid that Jeremiah, if he met me, would expose Maurice's possible lies. The fact is, I had had so many lingering questions and doubts about his past as it was that nothing I found out during the last year of his life would have upset me. Even if the whole Katrina story had been a fraud, I would have forgiven him as a desperate man in a desperate situation, looking for companionship wherever he could find it.

After I told Jeremiah how Maurice had died, he threw me another surprise. "I'm sure he knew he had AIDS. I don't think he could have been in and out of the prison system over the last ten years without being tested and being told."

If that were true, it would certainly explain his Thelma-and-Louise-like behavior when I knew him, throwing all caution and responsibility to the wind. He knew he didn't have a future and didn't think enough of himself to want to save himself when a premier hospital and proper medication became available to him. Still, if he knew beforehand, he didn't reveal it to me when I told him of my status when he first moved in with me. Then, he seemed genuinely shocked when he got his diagnosis and went through the common stage of denial at the bad news.

Like the survivor and addict that he was, Maurice lived on lies upon lies upon lies in an effort to appear likeable, possibly lovable, to someone. The irony is that, to anyone who cared, like Jeremiah or me, we saw through the carefully crafted façade and saw the sad, lonely person at the core, the lovable person who thought his true self was unlovable.

Jeremiah and I talked and shared stories about Maurice for a good half-hour or so, and we both allowed ourselves to mourn for the loss of such a lost, troubled soul. I assured him that Maurice ended his life well, surrounded by a few friends and a caring pastor and that he had even touched the lives of his health care workers during his final days.

"Thank you," Jeremiah said, his voice cracking. "Thank you for being there for him." My heart ached for Jeremiah, who had cared for him for so many years and never had a reconciliation or final goodbye with Maurice. By comparison, my situation at least had some sense of poetic closure.

I told Jeremiah that I still had some of Maurice's ashes and that I would love to visit Richmond sometime to meet him and his family and give them some ashes to scatter in one of his favorite places there.

"That would be great, but right now this death and grief are all new to me. I need some time to tell my family and grieve over this." I understood that.

In the end, I chose to believe that Maurice really had gone to New Orleans in the summer of 2005. I couldn't find any proof otherwise and, upon looking at my phone bills from the fall of that year, there had been calls to Lafayette, Louisiana, and Atlanta.

Holding onto a few essential facts made seeing the overall goodness in Maurice easier for me, something I needed at that time.

*   *   *

As this book neared completion in 2013, I got another unexpected call. I had left a message on the site *classmates.com*, and someone saw it and contacted me.

Debbie was a friend to Maurice during junior high in Syracuse. She herself had a troubled youth and ran away at age fourteen, and so she never saw Maurice again after that, but she clearly remembered him.

"I was the ugly duckling, and he was so nice to me, always trying to cheer me up," Debbie told me. "He was so sweet and so proper, and had the best smile in the world."

Debbie recalled that he had a girlfriend at that time but that her father disapproved of the interracial relationship, so the two had to sneak around. She also remembered that, shortly after that, Maurice was being perceived as gay. "He tried so hard to be accepted, but kids began to shun him."

Even back then, she knew nothing about his family and nobody knew where he lived. I suspect that was the time shortly after the only family he had ever known had released him back into the foster care system.

Sadly, no family was evident for his biggest triumph. "Oh, he could shine up a room," Debbie said. "There was a talent show in the eighth grade and the entire auditorium was full, probably six hundred people. Maurice sang 'Always and Forever.' I still remember it; it was so beautiful. The entire audience gave him a standing ovation."

*   *   *

After talking with Debbie, I found myself curious about Maurice's family once again. My fantasy was that, when this book was published, I would seek out his foster mother, the only mother he ever knew, and present her with the book, so she would know how his life turned out, and how he blossomed in his final weeks.

His mother died after a long illness in 2010. In the obituary, she was described as a loving mother and an influential, noteworthy person.

His mother had been an opera singer and voice teacher.

Chapter Seven

As the months went on, I began to reconnect with friends and family. At one point, I was looking for a roommate again so I could more quickly pay off my debts.

My friend Amy, with whom I had been out of touch for several years and had missed the entire Maurice chapter of my life, came out to look at the apartment. She fell in love with Bay Ridge but ultimately decided to find her own place in the neighborhood. It was great finding Amy again and to have another friend in far-flung Bay Ridge. Over several trips to the local bars and restaurants, I told her all about the saga of my two and a half years with Maurice.

When I got to the part about how his foster family abrogated the adoption when Maurice was twelve, her eyes widened and she said, "He was being sexually abused."

A light bulb flashed on in my head. Of course! Having been so close to Maurice and knowing his mischievousness, I had automatically assumed *he* was the cause of whatever problem arose in the family. But what could a twelve-year-old be doing? It was more likely something was being done to him. And a past involving sexual abuse clearly lined up with his issues as an adult: drug abuse, sexual addiction and compulsiveness, and both an ease with making sexual jokes and an unease with actual intimacy, and, finally, a deep shame and secretiveness about his own sex life, including his homosexual desires and his AIDS diagnosis (to me, he never said the word out loud).

I may never know the truth about what happened to Maurice and the family of his childhood, but as an outsider hearing the symptoms, I thought Amy might have found another piece of the jigsaw puzzle.

*　　*　　*

Ultimately, my friend Russell, the friend from church who had been so supportive of me in New Orleans, moved in with me for a time.

One day, Russell came out into the living room with a bottle of pills in his hand. "Why do you still have a bottle of Maurice's pills in the cabinet?"

"Oh, they were his sleeping pills and he told me if I ever needed to knock myself out for twelve hours, to take one. I tried one twice, and believe me, I slept all day the next day!"

"These aren't sleeping pills!" Russell said. "This is Zyprexa! This is for people who are schizophrenic and bipolar! No wonder it knocked you out!"

Just like that, another light bulb flashed. Maurice certainly wasn't schizophrenic, but a little research confirmed that he was, indeed, bipolar; the disappearing acts for a couple of days, the manic energy, and the lethargic lows had an explanation. Oftentimes, the disorder is initially sparked by a tragic event that has never been fully resolved—certainly the abandonment by his family would qualify. And certainly self-medication (for example, with an upper like cocaine), which would seem to help pull one out of the doldrums in the short run, would only exacerbate the manic-depressive condition in the long run.

Maurice was bipolar. Another secret revealed.

*   *   *

As I finished a second or third draft of this book and it became clear that I would be trying to get it published, I knew I finally had to do the inevitable.

It seems that my life has been a steady stream of "coming out" processes. We often think of the word in terms of gay issues, but that is not always the case. I had to come out as an artist, come out as financially challenged, come out as gay, come out in a biracial relationship, and, eventually, come out as a leader. Perhaps the best-lived life is the life that is continually coming out, unfolding, blossoming.

The final challenge was coming out as HIV-positive. Some things are easier to tell friends than family, and in my New York life, the people that needed to know were told. It was, after all, a medical issue that should concern only a potential partner and myself.

It is more than that, however. We are a country that has run rampant with obesity, diabetes, heart disease, stroke, and myriad forms of cancer. Most of those conditions are negatively influenced by our behaviors and are often preventable, and yet none of them carries the stigma of HIV/AIDS.

Our culture's shaming of sexual behavior has probably created more problems than it has solved. Rather than discuss issues in a responsible and loving way, we have created an atmosphere where many of us, straight and gay, pretend we are "normal" (whatever that is) while we hide our true "dirty" desires from our partners and friends and family. So the hidden, secretive things become the most sexually charged for us . . . and usually lead us into the most trouble.

In any case, after all the years of living a compartmentalized life with my secret kept from so many, I knew it was time to tell my family.

The script followed the same lines as the "coming out" one did several years before. My father kept on the move, so it was hard to pin him down for a serious talk when I wanted to have it. So, it fell to my mother again.

She, too, never pried or tried to open up difficult conversations, but when I said, "I need to talk to you," she dropped everything and sat down.

"You know I've been writing this book about Maurice and you know he died of AIDS," I began. She was silent, so I continued. "Well, I have it, too."

There was still no visible reaction from her, so I went on to explain. "I didn't get it from him—we never had that kind of relationship—but I've had it for many years," I said. "I should have told you sooner, but I thought I'd be fine until you and Dad died, and you'd never need to know. But with the book . . ."

"Oh no, you did the right thing," Mom assured me. "If you told me back when you first got it, I probably wouldn't have been able to handle it."

That was it. She then asked me about my health and medications in an adult, almost clinical way. She only became emotional at the end of the conversation. "I'm just sorry that you had to go through all that bullying when you were a kid," she cried. "I didn't know, and I wouldn't have known what to do anyway." She got out of her chair and came over to hug me.

I gave her a draft of the manuscript. "I want you to read the book," I said. "If you don't want me to publish it, I won't. But this will tell you a lot about my life."

I went away for a weekend to visit friends. When I returned, both she and my father had read the book.

"I cried through the whole thing," my mother said. Knowing her, I took that as a blessing on the book. "And your father said you were a good writer."

In the months that followed, the book or its contents were never again mentioned by them, but we went on with our card games and Scrabble and meals together and watching Red Sox games and family outings.

We would never be like one of those families on television that openly discuss their problems and resolve them in an hour and then say "I love you" so freely. But the acceptance is there, as well as the unconditional love. They have my back.

And that is enough.

Chapter Eight

At the end of June, a major turning point in my life was about to come full circle, at a time when I never would have expected it.

On Tuesday night, June 24th – four months to the day of Maurice's death – I was with another one of my cabaret classes for a show at Don't Tell Mama, the group's final performance. As usual, I turned off my cell phone for the performance. After the show, several of us went out to eat at a nearby restaurant to celebrate the end of another workshop experience. I hadn't bothered to turn my phone back on.

It was after ten by the time I got home to Brooklyn that night. I walked into my office and saw that my answering machine was blinking – twelve messages! This was unheard of; since the cell phone era, I considered it a big day if I got three messages on my home phone. Immediately, I assumed there was a family emergency.

I nervously hit "Play" on the machine. I was bombarded with similar messages from different people, one after the other.

"Hello, Kevin, this is Allison from the New York Daily News . . ."

"Hello, Mr. Hall, this is Ron from Channel 4 News in New York . . ."

"Hello, Kevin, this is Barbara from the New York Post . . ."

"Hello, Mr. Hall, this is Fox News New York . . ."

What the hell? The guy at the deli downstairs later told me a few reporters had come to my door, microphones in hand.

The news cycle travels very quickly, and more so in New York than anywhere else. It turns out that these calls were a few hours old and I had trouble reaching many of the reporters when I called back. I did, however, reach Allison at the Daily News, *who explained the situation to me.*

Elie Granger, the man who had stabbed me back in 1994, had been arrested. He had been released from prison in 2005 or so and was living in another part of Brooklyn. (This was news to me – nobody from the District Attorney's office had notified me . . . and yet the press could easily find me, even with an unlisted number.) On Sunday, June 22nd, he had allegedly stabbed a woman who had been walking with her teenage daughter.

Now, the press wanted my reaction. After all that had happened in the intervening fourteen years, I honestly hadn't given Elie Granger much of a thought. However, this news brought me right back to that night and the confusion that followed.

While I was able to talk calmly with Allison, who was about as kind a reporter as I'd ever encountered, my nerve endings were at a heightened state. There would be no sleep for me that night. It's not that I was scared or anything, but my mind was on overdrive, replaying that night and its aftermath all those years before. Maybe there was some unfinished business there.

The story was in the newspapers and on the local news the next day and many friends who were still around and had known me were emailing and calling. Just as before, I was being given the kind of celebrity moment that I hadn't asked for or wanted. It was déjà vu.

I don't know why, but I felt the need to tell the story again and, foolishly, I caved in to the press, which was happy to use me for a headline. Channel 2 News *called and wanted to interview me on Wednesday afternoon. I had a job in midtown that day, but they were happy to accommodate me, sending a camera crew to Bryant Park for a ten-minute interview. What would the victim look and sound like fourteen years later? Find out on the six o'clock news!*

I was perhaps not giving them the copy they wanted. I spoke in a measured, optimistic tone, telling the reporter how much my life had changed, all that I had accomplished and that, although I wanted Granger back behind bars, that incident was not something that I thought about a lot.

"Take us back to that night. Describe what happened for us," the unflappable correspondent persevered.

Later that night, I turned on the news. Of course, I had told my family and friends they could watch too—even my Internet friends, hundreds of miles away. What I saw infuriated me. My ten-minute interview had been cut to about fifteen seconds where I was describing the blood all over my shirt. It was decidedly not the image I wanted to project to the world, that of a victim still living with the horror of one night, fourteen years before. What was especially infuriating was that the reporter who had interviewed me knew that. The interview was edited down to one bloody moment— nothing about my spiritual recovery.

This was that Newsday *reporter all over again and I wasn't about to let the moment go by this time. I would not be portrayed as a helpless victim again, to be used to sell product for a corporation. I would tell my own story this time.*

After another sleepless night, I woke up in a fury early on Thursday morning. I sat down at my computer and in about a half an hour, wrote an essay about how I felt and what I wanted to say. Then, with determination, I began sending it to New York's daily newspapers.

There was nothing else I could do that day but await the arrival of my friend Mark-Alan, who was coming up from Florida to visit for the weekend. The last time Mark-Alan had visited was during that memorable Thanksgiving weekend in 2006, when Maurice made most of the dinner in our upstairs/downstairs celebration. Mark-Alan and Maurice had gotten along so well.

That evening, Mark-Alan, Wayne and I had a few drinks and dinner, and reminisced about old times. After dinner, I coaxed them into walking down to the river near the Verrazano Bridge, a place where Maurice had loved to walk; I wanted to scatter more of his ashes there. At midnight, it would be June 27th, Maurice's 45th birthday. It was another emotional goodbye and it was wonderful to have such great, understanding friends with me.

On Friday morning, I was contacted by the Daily News. *They had agreed to buy my piece! I was overjoyed and it was no coincidence to me that this break was coming on Maurice's birthday. He had so often told me he wanted to see me "make it big." While I had no illusions that an Op-Ed piece was "making it big" in any real sense, it was big in the sense that I was getting a professional writing credit and, more importantly, I was putting a rest to a nightmare that had been with me for fourteen years—on my terms. I felt Maurice, my guardian angel, looking down and smiling.*

My essay appeared in the paper as follows:

A crime victim's road back

BY KEVIN SCOTT HALL

Sunday, June 29th 2008, 5:40 PM

I was recently thrust into the news by one of those freak things in life that you can't predict, let alone plan for.

I arrived home from a fulfilling New York evening of watching my students perform for an enthusiastic crowd to discover that I had several messages on my home answering machine and cell phone. (Contrary to popular belief, there are some of us who do turn off their cell phones when celebratory things in life are happening.)

News organizations from all over the city were calling to get my comment on the arrest of Elie Granger, the bicycle-riding terror who had just stabbed a Queens woman, Eduarda Oliva.

Why me? Well, I happened to be the last one Granger had attacked before he was arrested the last time. On Oct. 7, 1994, he stabbed me in the chest and in the arm. I lost a lot of blood; miraculously, the knife missed my heart and lung - by less than a quarter of an inch on each side.

Surely, the media assumed, I had something of note to say.

Without a doubt: I wanted to speak about the unfairness of Granger getting a nine-year sentence for three attempted murders, before being paroled in 2004. I wanted to speak of my outrage about an absentee district attorney who never informed me of Granger's release - and allowed him to live in the same city as his widely publicized victim.

Most of all, though, I wanted to speak about how New York is a great city, and that the energy and resources available here can help you to move on and create a fulfilling life, even after being shaken to the core by violent crime.

In so doing, you can actually begin to forget about the awful thing someone did to you many years before.

I had the opportunity to say all these things, most notably in an interview with a local TV station. But it soon became clear that the media were not interested in that story. My five minutes on camera were edited down to the bloody 15-second sound bite.

That's not the real story. And that's not the story that Eduarda Oliva, who struggles to recover after being terrorized, needs to hear right now.

The real story - my story - is of a young man who arrived in New York fresh out of college, like so many others, to pursue his life on the city's great stages. The real story is of fifth floor walkups, cockroaches, scrambling to pay the rent and trying hard to find community among the chaos.

The real story is of an unexpected horror that threatened to derail whatever meager progress he was making. Followed by anger, heartbreak, questioning . . . and finally, waking up and emerging from the grief.

A waking up to new possibilities. To a profound sense of thanks for being alive.

This young man started to sing again, and even did a comedy routine about the dumb things people say when you've been viciously attacked. He began to teach others. He worked at an agency helping others find work. Many of his clients still keep in touch.

He found a multicultural, spiritual church that represents the best New York has to offer. He went back to school and got his Master's degree and started teaching at City College. He wrote.

There have been no recording contracts and no publishing deals - no triumphs that make the headlines - but he lives every day surrounded by wonderful friends and the knowledge that his message of hope, which he tries to instill in his everyday actions, will make some small difference to those who need to hear it.

This slow road back is precisely what thousands of other victims of crime travel upon in this city. There were some 50,000 victims of violent crime in New York City last year—and the vast majority of them are, without fanfare, reclaiming their lives. As are their families.

This is the story that Eduarda Oliva and her daughter need to hear. This is just one of the 8 million stories in our wonderful New York.

The response I got from friends all over the country, from my church, from places I had worked, from school and from my family, was overwhelming.

Did it lead to a bigger break? It did not. But it was the beginning of the process of writing this book, of reliving all of the old wounds and taking a look at where my journey has led me.

* * *

Many months after that, I was called by the Queens district attorney. She asked if I would meet with her and tell her my story; because my case never went to trial, she was looking at the possibility of having me testify in the trial of Granger in Eduarda Oliva's case. I met with her and we went over some of my previous testimony for the grand jury back in late 1994. I was surprised by how much I remembered . . . and how much I did not. The idea of testifying all these years later seemed far-fetched.

The DA kept in touch with me via email through the inevitable delays. At last, Elie Granger went to trial in late June of 2011. I was called to testify exactly three years to the day that the Daily News *piece was going down and . . . on Maurice's birthday.*

Before my testimony, I met briefly that morning in the DA's office so she could brief me on the types of questions she might ask. Then she threw me a very unexpected curveball.

"The cross-examination could be a challenge," she told me. "He is representing himself."

"He doesn't have a lawyer?"

"I'm sorry, I should have told you." I suspected she didn't because she figured she'd lose me as a witness. "He has counsel sitting with him, but he will ask the questions."

"Is he going to go nuts?"

"No. He must remain seated during his questions. To be fair, I must remain seated as well." She paused for a moment. "Do you think you might recognize him if you saw him?"

"I don't know, it's been seventeen years and our encounter was memorable but very brief."

"Okay, well, nobody is going to tell you where he is sitting and I may ask you. If you can, do so, but if you can't, don't worry about it."

Soon after, we walked over to the courthouse with two other male witnesses. I would be the third to testify. The waiting was the hardest part. I had to go twice to the bathroom as my stomach was in knots, imagining the confrontation.

One of the other witnesses, a short, middle-aged man, was sitting next to me. "Do you testify in these things very often?"

I smiled. "No, never. I was attacked by this guy seventeen years ago."

"Oh my God, I'm so sorry."

"Why are you here?"

"I worked with him at my job. When this happened, I was in shock. I still am."

I nodded my head. In that moment, I was reminded of the extremely conflicted nature a man may have. The other guy was there to testify on Granger's behalf; I was there to put him behind bars.

We both decided to say no more. Later, as he left the courtroom and went onto the elevator, he waved at me and offered a sad smile.

I was up next. An officer escorted me into the small courtroom — with wooden chairs and benches, it looked like it hadn't been updated since the nineteenth century.

As soon as I sat down, my eyes scanned the courtroom. The jury was to my left. There were spectators loosely filling up the rows of benches. And there he was, at a table to my right, with an older gentleman.

My doubts vanished. I knew immediately who he was. True, I had some idea where he would be as an "attorney" representing himself, but although he was older, in a suit, and had grown his hair curly around the ears and back of his head (but still bald on top), there was no mistaking him. I could have identified him walking down 42nd Street.

The DA asked me a few background questions about my job and then took me through the events of October 7, 1994. I demonstrated how Granger had approached me, asked a question, and then plunged the knife into my chest. I was poised and spoke clearly and loudly.

"Do you think you could identify him if you saw him?" she asked me.

"Yes," I answered without equivocation. I was then asked to point to him and I did so.

Then it was Granger's turn. He was a crafty son of a bitch, I'll give him that. He opened a case file. "Didn't you tell a police officer that it was dark that night and that you couldn't remember clearly who had done this to you?"

"No, I don't remember that," I said, which was true.

"Wouldn't it have been too dark to remember what he looked like?"

"You were standing two feet from me," I said, looking right at him. "Close enough to get a look I would never forget."

He asked me about my description of the man wearing a small knit cap over a bald head. "How could you tell he was bald if he was wearing a cap?"

"Because there was no hair anywhere below the hat, around the ears . . . it's a reasonable assumption."

"Couldn't he have had hair under the cap?"

"I suppose you could have had a tuft of hair on the top of your head that the cap covered," I said, glaring at him. I wasn't the least bit afraid of him. I wanted his grilling to go on and on; I was just getting warmed up. The judge told him to move on from that line of questioning.

"How is it that you think you recognize me after all these years?"

"Your eyes," I looked at the jury. "You never forget the eyes."

"How would you describe my eyes? Come on, you're a writer," he taunted. I couldn't be sure, but for a split second, I thought he winked at me, along with his smirk.

"Objection!" said the DA. The last comment was stricken.

Granger went on. He looked down at the floor. "What color are my eyes?"

"Dark brown." Absolutely right.

"There are a lot of men with dark brown eyes. How are mine different?"

I paused to think about it. "There's a sincerity in your eyes, a fake sincerity. Like you really wanted the answer to the question. And then when I'm at my most vulnerable, you thrust a knife into my chest. That's not a face you forget."

I didn't know it at the time, but I had bolstered Oliva's testimony, when she had shouted at him about never being able to forget his evil eyes.

After another round of questions by the DA, Granger tried another tactic. "How many nights were you in the hospital?"

"Three."

"What was the extent of your injuries?"

I told the jury of the deep wound and about how close the knife had gotten to my heart and lung, although it had missed.

"*Why did you spend three nights in a hospital for a flesh wound and a cut on your arm?*" *He seemed disappointed.*

I rolled my eyes. "*I don't know. I'm not a doctor. When I breathed, I could feel a pain because it was close to my lung. I had also lost a lot of blood and I'm sure they wanted to monitor the situation.*"

In those moments, I hated that man. I had always thought that everyone, deep down, was able to be reformed — even Elie Granger. Now, I could see firsthand that even after all the years, nine of which he had spent in prison, he was not sorry and was still playing his sick games. He was only sorry he hadn't succeeded in killing one of us.

Later that night, when the DA emailed me to thank me for my testimony, I told her my thoughts and closed with, "*I hope he dies in jail.*" *I slept like a baby.*

About a week later, the newspapers reported that Granger had been convicted of aggravated assault but had come up somewhat a winner representing himself — the jury did not convict him of attempted murder. It's hard to see how someone who stabbed a woman in the chest without provocation is not guilty of attempted murder, and the readers' outraged comments reflected that. This went down about the same time Casey Anthony walked free in the death of her daughter.

Nevertheless, all hoped the judge would give him the maximum sentence, which could still give him a sentence of up to twenty-five years. For me, it was finally the end of a very long chapter in my life. The last words I said to the DA were, "*Please don't call me in seventeen years.*"

Chapter Nine

It took a couple of years, but I did make the trek to Richmond. I contacted Jeremiah but he said he'd be out of town that weekend. He did, however, tell me about his first date with Maurice some twenty years before.

"We had our first date at Brown's Island in downtown Richmond. He loved jazz, so we saw an outdoor jazz concert at the bandshell, and then went out to dinner. Then we came back and sat on the pier overlooking the river and talked until the sun came up. That would be a great place to scatter his ashes."

Indeed, I found the exact spot during a leisurely stroll along the canal and island in that lovely, sleepy town. As I opened the jar and spilled the ashes over the rail, a breeze lifted the gray-white cloud over the wide river with its foamy rapids and multi-shaped rocks as far as the eye could see. Just as they reached the water, a long-legged heron landed on a nearby rock. It looked up at me with one eye and blinked before spreading its wings and flying off to the sky.

I took that as a thank you.

*   *   *

It took many years before I made the return trip to Niagara Falls and Syracuse to dispose of the last of Maurice's ashes. The practical reason was because it's such a long trip and I couldn't seem to find a three-day weekend to get up there. The psychological reason was simple avoidance: I knew it would be the final goodbye, and one more dip into the emotional trough for me.

Nevertheless, I made the plan for the final weekend of June 2013, on what would have been Maurice's 50th birthday. This time, I wanted to go by myself, so I rented the car and reserved hotel rooms for a night in Buffalo and Syracuse. The first night was spent with a former roommate I hadn't seen in many years, who was now living in the Catskills.

That June had been one of the wettest on record in the northeast and, as if the heavens were complying with my emotional state, that first night I was caught driving in a cataclysmic thunderstorm. The Friday evening traffic on Route 87 crept along at about twenty-five miles per hour for a good twenty minutes. It took all of my concentration to focus on the red rear lights of the car in front of me through the gushing torrents that swept over my windshield.

A similar scene — powerful rainstorms on the highway — greeted me on the next day's trip to Buffalo, and the third day's leg to Syracuse. Nature, God, and Maurice were conspiring to make this goodbye worth fighting for.

The weather and traffic in Buffalo made for an eight-hour journey on the second day. I had never been to Buffalo proper (just passed by it on our trip in 2007); for a small city, it has a confounding street plan, with no rhyme or reason to its one-way and two-way streets — and more of a problem when arriving at five o'clock on a Friday afternoon. I was very happy to check into my room in a downtown hotel.

The rain continued unabated that day, but I needed dinner and decided to set out on foot, clutching a small umbrella. At one point, I stopped under an awning to call Elli, a friend of Amy's, whom I had met a few times, but I hadn't seen her in several years. Elli was to be my guide to Niagara Falls, to help me find a spot to scatter the ashes.

She picked up right away and was glad to hear from me. "I'm on a street in Buffalo waiting for the rain to let up," I said. "You wouldn't know of a decent place to eat downtown, would you?"

"I'm actually not that familiar with the city of Buffalo," Elli said. She lived north of the city, closer to Niagara Falls.

"Well, I have pamphlet of tourist attractions. Maybe I can find something," I said.

"That pamphlet can't be more than a page long," Elli deadpanned. We laughed and made plans to meet in a hotel parking lot in Niagara the next morning.

After we hung up, I ventured back out into the rain. I decided to try a restaurant called Mother's that didn't look too far away on my map. Home cooking, comfort food. Good enough.

Indeed, the restaurant was full, with a waiting list. I found a corner seat at the bar and decided to order a drink while I waited for a table.

There seemed to be groups of friends and families, not unusual for a Friday night in a popular restaurant. And yet, next to me around the corner sat a tall, African-American gentleman, about forty years old, by himself. Eventually I said something innocuous, like, "Pretty crowded in here tonight."

Slowly, the conversation took hold, as he told me about Buffalo and we shared our background information. It turned out that he had just finished seminary and was a minister. Jimmy had had a previous career in the military, some kind of diplomat. When he got around to asking why I was in Buffalo, I took a deep breath and gave him the bare-bones version of the Maurice saga.

"Maurice eventually got sick and I did my best to take care of him during those last six months," I said, in closing. "I've known all along that I wanted to scatter his ashes over Niagara Falls, and now I'm finally here to do so."

Jimmy's eyes bore into mine. "He had the virus, huh?"

"Um, yes," I stammered. There had been nothing in my summary to suggest anything about Maurice's particular ailments or background.

The conversation took another turn. Jimmy expressed his thoughts about homosexuality and the church, saying that the church was behind the times on the issue. Finally, he said, "You know, I could come with you to Niagara Falls tomorrow and perform a little service, if you want me to."

I was flabbergasted. I had known Jimmy for less than an hour (although, by that point, we had decided to eat together and had been given a table) and he was willing to do such a thing for a mere stranger. "That would be amazing," I said. "I don't know what to say. That's really generous of you."

"This is the kind of moment that doesn't come along very often, and I feel I need to minister whenever the opportunity comes up."

With that, I told him about the plan with Elli and that I would call him in the morning.

The next day, I checked out of the hotel, packed my bags, and called Jimmy. The idea was that I would go directly to Niagara and not come back to the hotel. Go directly to Syracuse.

When I called Jimmy, he explained that he was at the gym. "I thought you'd call earlier and I hadn't heard from you," he said. "Can we make it later, maybe early afternoon?"

"I can't, actually," I said. "I already made plans with Elli, who is getting off her midnight shift, and I'm checked out, so can't go back to the hotel," I said. "But it's okay. Having dinner with you was great and you really connected with my situation in a meaningful way."

Jimmy apologized sheepishly and we said our goodbyes. I got into the car and started on the half-hour drive to Niagara. About ten minutes later the phone rang. I looked down and smiled when I saw the number. I answered.

"I'll be there," Jimmy said. "This is really important and God is nudging me. I'm leaving the gym and I'll be there by eleven." The news had not surprised me; it was exactly what I expected.

I drove into the parking lot a little before eleven and recognized Elli in the SUV she had described right away. We got out of our cars and gave each other a hug.

"What's with the Virginia license plates?" she asked.

"I don't know, that's what Avis gave me," I said.

I went on to tell her about the minor miracle of meeting Jimmy and that he would be on his way. Her interest was piqued and she was game for whatever was to happen.

At precisely eleven, Jimmy pulled into the parking lot. He got out of his car and was wearing a long, burlap-type robe over his clothes and carrying a Bible the size of a laptop.

"Well, I don't think anybody will be messing with us today," Elli cracked as he strode over to meet us.

The three of us exchanged greetings and got into Elli's car. Conversation was easy, as though we had all been friends for years, not virtual strangers who were meeting under this unusual circumstance.

That particular weekend was a holiday weekend, Canada Day, with the Fourth of July coming up the following weekend, and yet Elli managed to drive us to exactly the right spot within minutes, including free parking. We were just across the footbridge from Three Sisters Island.

We got out of the car and walked over the bridge. A uniformed park ranger was on the other side, serenely taking in the view and perhaps waiting for something to happen. There were a few tourists milling around, but it was generally quiet.

"Why not just do it on the bridge?" Jimmy suggested.

I had a momentary cautionary reaction, my fear of authority versus my fear of embarrassment. I mentally brushed them away. "Why not?"

We went back to the middle of the bridge and formed a close triangle of intimacy. We were quiet as Jimmy thumbed through the big Bible. "I think the 23rd Psalm would be most appropriate," he said. Elli and I shook our heads in agreement.

Reading the 23rd Psalm was something I could have done on my own, but Jimmy's clear, stately reading of it lent an aura of authority around the proceedings. When he finished, we said "amen" and I reached down to the box of ashes. I gave a quick look to the park ranger, who was looking elsewhere, and then poured them over the bridge. A breeze pulled some of them back onto the bridge itself and Elli was kind enough to sweep them over with her hands.

My eyes were moist, but I was calm. This time, there was a feeling of peace and comfort.

"You know, it was fitting that you two were here with me for this today," I began to explain as we stood there on the bridge. "At Maurice's memorial service, one of the speakers said that he was like a butterfly, touching down and bringing beauty to people's lives, then moving on to someone else. So it's right that strangers who didn't know him should have a part in his goodbye. He was an Everyman of sorts."

Elli and Jimmy nodded in agreement. I continued. "The last time I did this, I was in Richmond, also overlooking a great river."

"That explains the Virginia plates," Elli said with a wink.

We turned as one and slowly began walking across the footbridge toward the car. At that moment, a large yellow butterfly swooped down and flew in front of us, guiding us to the end of the bridge, before arcing to the left and into the sky.

"And there's the butterfly," Elli concluded.

*   *   *

After treating Elli and Jimmy to breakfast, we said our goodbyes and I was on my way to the last leg of the trip, Syracuse. Maurice had lived there from early childhood through high school.

After his death, I looked up his high school and eventually found his graduation yearbook online. It had been emotionally satisfying to see just a glimpse of his life back then. Other than his senior portrait, the only other photo I saw of him was a group shot of the gymnastics team. There he was, the only one not in uniform among his teammates. He still had that wide, hopeful grin on his face despite the sadness behind the eyes.

Finally, we were coming full circle. I had the last boxful of ashes to leave in his childhood town.

I checked into a motel and pulled out a map of the city I had found online. The rental car did not have a GPS, so I would have to navigate the old-fashioned way.

Before long, I set out on my journey, with directions to the high school. (I was never able to ascertain the address of his childhood home.) It had been a cloudy day, but it was one of the few days that weekend without actual rain.

I was really proud of myself as I took a left here, a right there, another right, and so on, and was finding my way around Syracuse with nary a problem. As I neared the school, I saw a reservoir on the right. I got out and explored. It was fenced in and there was no way to get to the water's edge. Should I disperse the ashes on the grass? No doubt he had walked around this pond many times. I decided to wait.

Within minutes, I found the high school. Because it was a Saturday evening during the summer, there was nobody around. I drove around the building and through the parking lots. Finally, I spotted a duck pond next to a parking lot. Perfect.

I got out with the box and walked over to the pond. I said a little prayer and sifted the ashes into the pond. "Welcome home again," I whispered.

At that moment, I noticed a car had pulled into the parking lot up on the hill to my right. I woman got out with a camera and started taking pictures of the sky behind me. I turned to see what it was and —

A magnificent rainbow streaked across the horizon. I had seen so few in my lifetime, and yet there one was, at that moment. I nearly fell to my knees, I was so overcome with the presence of the miraculous. I remembered that the rainbow was a sign of God's covenant with man after the flood: "I will never destroy you again." I had had enough self-torture and second-guessing at that point. That answer was fine by me.

Within just a few minutes, the clouds passed over and the rainbow disappeared. I couldn't help but think that had I not stopped at the reservoir or had I made a wrong turn or had I started out from the hotel five minutes earlier or later, I would have missed the rainbow at that spot, in that moment.

It is in rare moments like that that my faith is restored and is strongest. Many will insist that I was seeing natural coincidences and that I interpreted them in my own way, to make myself feel better. They can say and believe what they wish; I prefer seeing through the eyes of faith. Once you have done so, you can't see life any other way.

The next morning, I packed my things into the car for the final, long drive back to New York City. It had been a wondrous weekend, far beyond what I could have imagined. At times, I had been tempted to put off the weekend again, or perhaps invite a friend along. In the end, it was exactly as it was meant to be.

As I drove onto the exit to take me to Route 84 southbound, I turned on the radio. There was Cyndi Lauper's voice, singing that song — you know, the one about our true colors shining through . . . like a rainbow?

A broad smile grew across my face. Yeah, I got it, God. Thanks for one more, very unsubtle reminder.

Chapter Ten

That summer of 2008, I finally got around to doing what I had avoided for five months: I opened up the sleep sofa that I had closed on the day that Maurice went to the hospital for the last time. There before me were the wrinkled sheets that he had sweated and slept on in his final days. I looked at the bed like it was something sacred, an uncovered, empty tomb.

I chose to sleep in his bed that night, to envelop myself in his scent, his memory, one last time, and awaken to the sounds of birds chirping and the double-width window with the green ivy zig-zagging across it that he loved so much.

I lay down and pulled the top sheet over me and hugged one of his two pillows close to me. I watched late night television for a bit but it seemed sacrilegious, so I turned it off and took in the silence that he always had at the back of the building. I drifted off to sleep.

At some point in the middle of the night, I had a dream of Maurice. We were at my parents' cottage on the lake (he'd never been there in real life) on a beautiful summer day and he was, of course, at the barbecue grill. Neal was there as well and we were all laughing. Other people drifted in and out of the dream, people who were alive as well as those who had passed . . . like a Facebook reunion of people from all walks of life.

I woke up in complete and utter blackness and silence. I wanted to go back to the dream but I could not. I started crying and soon I was wailing, bawling. "Why did you take him away from me?" I screamed into the night, angry at God. It was all about me, and my suffering.

Just as suddenly as I had started, I stopped. I rolled onto my back and looked at the ceiling. I had *heard* an answer to my question, as clearly as if it had been broadcast over a loudspeaker: "Because that is what he wanted."

My own grief over my missing friend would go on and a piece of my heart would always be mourning his loss, but that answer gave me great comfort. *That is what Maurice wanted.* Clearly, that was the case and the reason he never seriously came to terms with his illness or made a valiant attempt to defeat it. He was tired of the struggle. He was ready.

Many of my friends have told me how much I did for Maurice. It wasn't until he was gone that I fully realized how much he had given me. He helped me to see the joy in the small things—a song, a cheesy slice of pizza, a warm blanket, a hug—that many of us take for granted every day. Those things he never took for granted, they were all a blessing and a gift to him.

He loved me unconditionally; he didn't care about my past or my future success or how much money I made or how many friends I had—he simply cherished the moments when I could forget about all my busy activities and just spend time with him. The most important word to him was "friend," and even if it sometimes seemed as if he was not treating me like a friend ought to be treated, that behavior came from his own fear of not being loved, or of being abandoned again. He played out his worst fears and very few had the stamina to stay with him and continue loving him. Most importantly, Maurice taught me that love grows and deepens through seeing each other through the hard times; love does not need sex to flourish.

In short, I saw him inside and out, as he really was. And he saw the full spectrum of who I was as well. And we didn't run away.

Although there will always be a nagging at my soul that maybe I could have done more, offered more of a commitment, in the end I think Maurice saw what his illness was doing *to me*. I was going further into debt, my diet was going downhill, my stress level was increasing . . . when I look at photos of me at that time, I can't believe the pasty, bloated, careworn-looking person I had become. He knew that, and he knew a long, protracted illness with me serving as caregiver was ultimately not going to help either one of us. Of course, had he talked to me about it, I certainly would have told him that his dying was not an answer to the problems—his or mine. But I think that not only was he tired of fighting, but that he loved me so much that he sacrificed his own life so that I might live more abundantly. Yes, that is what I believe, grandiose as the comparison may be.

Maurice may have come in like a thief in the night, through the back gate, his voice not trustworthy. In the end, he had become the Good Shepherd, at least for my sake. The Good Shepherd lays down his life on his own accord, by God's authority. Maurice did not want me to live to take care of him; in his mind, that was not abundance for either of us. Maurice found a way for us both to have abundance, but his way was not my way. God's way is not often our way, and we are fortunate if we can find our way through the grief and anger toward understanding. My many earthly sacrifices for Maurice were miniscule compared to his ultimate sacrifice. If only I could tell him—Maurice, God, both—how much I lost when I lost him. Because make no mistake, I lost more than just Maurice that day. For a time, I lost my faith.

*   *   *

What explains the power Maurice had over me?

I had been completely taken in and bowled over by a drifter, ex-con and pathological liar. He had drug issues, sexuality and intimacy issues, financial issues, and actual mental health issues.

I had rationalized my continued involvement as doing the work of God, what I felt I had been directed to do at a particular moment in time. How crazy was that?

What were my own issues? Intimacy issues, financial issues, an inability to consider my own needs first—you know, put the air mask over your own face before you help your own child? What else? Lack of discernment, an ability to lie to cover my own shame, lack of focus.

What I did have was faith. I have made that faith sound easy and miraculous in these pages: the signs, the songs, the heard voices of the divine.

That has almost never been the case except in regards to the experience of Maurice. For long stretches of my life and through all kinds of pain, I have cried out to God for some kind of sign, and never felt I was given anything specific to hang my faith on.

And yet, I have lived on. I have been blessed despite a number of tribulations: childhood bullying, an angry parent, ugly duckling syndrome, the struggles of coming to terms with my sexuality and the poor relationship choices over the years, the humiliation of rejections of my art, the financial disaster that arose from mishandled business ventures and questionable work choices, two muggings, a stabbing, being diagnosed with an incurable disease. Nobody gets through life scot-free from problems.

I have been inconsistent in my readings of spiritual passages, inconsistent in my prayer and meditation life. I have not always kept my eyes on the prize, the greater triumphs.

Faith is an endurance test, not a magic act. Faith in oneself is a big part of that equation, and I am all for processes that help an individual discover that and recover his or her self-esteem.

For me, it is not the entire equation. I can't function in chaos, without a master plan. I believe in a higher power, and I believe each of us has a purpose, to touch one life or many lives depending on the gifts we are given.

I have grown up with the Christian faith; it works for me. However, my understanding of it has changed over the years and I suspect it will continue to change and evolve. If we are truly made in the image of God, then we continue to change. After all—if you follow the Christian doctrine—didn't God change between the Old and New Testaments? That is the beauty of God and of life itself: change.

Many people of faith will reject this book because they can't embrace people who are not like themselves, or who live a lifestyle they can't accept. They will not see the greater truth, won't see the forest for their focus on the trees. It remains sad to me.

The fact that this experience with Maurice did have so many signs and voices tells me that, finally, my spirit was in alignment with what I was supposed to be doing. I was rewarded with affirmations because I was doing God's will.

But back to the original question: What explains the power Maurice had over me?

It wasn't sex. It wasn't money. It wasn't power. Interestingly, these are the three things most of us strive for again and again.

It was his undeniable life force. It was the smile, the child-like appreciation of small things, the mischief, the laughter, the hugs, the food, the music, the wrestling with trust, the built-in clashes of race and class and sexuality and love's ultimate triumph over them—the human challenges that made me feel fully alive.

The easy path is not always the most rewarding path.

In retrospect, it was simply divine. I may have had regrets in the day to day, but looking at the bigger picture that comes with time and distance, I accept what was, and it was good.

*   *   *

I now have some understanding why Maurice came into my life, and I into his. Love comes from unexpected places.

So do angels. Angels come without warning. Angels are messengers, ministering spirits, but we have to be open to seeing them and, more so, receiving them. While I can find solace in the knowledge that I ministered to him in his final years, Maurice's many messages to me still grow and resonate, like the circles and fading ripples from a splash in the baptismal water.

I wish I had a few more days with him, even minutes. With death, even when we see it coming, there is always something we feel was left unsaid, undone.

I hope I did enough. I hope he knew that.

God willing, if there is a next time, my heart is full. Between my heart and another's, there will be no space for doubt. Not even a quarter inch.

CPSIA information can be obtained
at www.ICGtesting.com
Printed in the USA
FFOW01n1555230414
4958FF

9 781938 459245